The New Testament Story

The New Testament Story

Ben Witherington III

WILLIAM B. EERDMANS PUBLISHING COMPANY
GRAND RAPIDS, MICHIGAN / CAMBRIDGE, U.K.

Wm. B. Eerdmans Publishing Co.
255 Jefferson Ave. S.E., Grand Rapids, Michigan 49503 /
P.O. Box 163, Cambridge CB3 9PU U.K.

Printed in the United States of America

09 08 07 06 05 04   7 6 5 4 3 2 1

Library of Congress Cataloging-in-Publication Data

Witherington, Ben, 1951-
   The New Testament story / Ben Witherington III.
     p.   cm.
   Includes bibliographical references.
   ISBN 0-8028-2765-9 (pbk.: alk. paper)
   1. Bible. N.T. — Introductions.   I. Title.

   BS2330.3.W58   2004
   225.6′1 — dc22
                    2004044123

www.eerdmans.com

To Peter Giancola and Darlene Hyatt, notable storytellers in their own right. I am thankful that we share the New Testament story between us, and feel blessed to have our stories intertwined by the Almighty. Thanks for enriching and helping me salvage various parts of my story.

To Rick Danielson for his wonderful hand-drawn illustrations which add so much to this book.

Contents

Preface

The title of this book is deliberately enigmatic. It could of course refer to the stories within, or at least the major storyline of, the New Testament. On the other hand, it could refer to the story of the New Testament — how it came into existence, who wrote it, how the books were selected and canonized, and the like. I have decided that for this book to be a proper Introduction to the New Testament, it really needs to speak of both these matters. Too often, an introduction simply deals with the historical and literary nuts and bolts of authorship, date, structure, and audience of the various New Testament books without ever really getting down to the matter of the substance of the New Testament, its major story and stories. Thus, though this is an introduction in miniature, my aim is to try to do both less and more than a standard introduction offers.[1]

In the recent canonical theology movement, while the focus is decidedly on content, especially theological and ethical content, the presuppositions behind the approach involve certain assumptions about the New Testament as canon, as Scripture, as Word. For example, treating the New Testament as Scripture is sometimes assumed to mean that we need not get really bogged down with the prehistory or historical substance and particulars of the text; we can just treat it as a resonant and inspiring literary artifact. This in turn leads to a certain sort of synthetic way of handling the text that all too often denudes it of its historical particularity in the

---

1. Precisely because it is intended to be a miniature guide, I am keeping notes to a bare minimum in this study.

hunt for the main theme or the major foci or the overarching story or the relevant and resonant residue.

Then too in the canonical theology movement we have the further problem that the New Testament is not allowed to speak for itself. It is read so strongly on the basis of its Old Testament backdrop and foundations that the newness of the New Testament is sublimated or missed. The only remedy I know for this is to do both a diachronic treatment of the formation of the New Testament and a synchronic treatment of its content. Accordingly, we will first tell the story of how the New Testament books came into being, and how they were collected and assembled and came to be known as the New Testament. This will be followed in the second half of the book by a treatment of the major stories in the New Testament and their similarities and differences, in search of what might be called the New Testament story. Of course it goes almost without saying that *the* story in the New Testament is the story of Jesus, as it was told and retold, cast, and recast. The tellings led to later reflections and certain theological and ethical and social conclusions based on the central story.

And so we must turn first to the story of the assembling of the Story, for the New Testament did not drop from the sky written on golden tablets but rather was carefully and prayerfully produced over about a fifty-year span by a variety of contributors and authors in the second half of the first century A.D. The collection and assembling of the pieces however was not complete until well after the New Testament era. While it is true enough to say "in the beginning was the Word," our first concern is to deny that "in the beginning was the Book," for paradoxically enough there was no New Testament during the New Testament era. The Bible of the earliest Christians was what we now call the Old Testament. But we get ahead of ourselves. Let us turn to the tale of the New Testament itself.

Easter 2004

PART I | The Story of the New Testament

1 | The Tools and the Text

It is hard for moderns like us to imagine the world before the printing press. Indeed it is hard for some of us to imagine the world before computers, the Internet, TV, or before modern libraries, newspapers, or news magazines. The New Testament, however, was not only written before all such inventions, it was also written before an age of widespread literacy. Furthermore, it was written well before there was any such thing as making an audio recording of something someone said. Ancients seldom expected a verbatim transcript of anything except occasionally when one was dealing with legal or royal proceedings. Even then, it was a new thing during the time of Julius Caesar to have speeches produced verbatim from a trial. Cicero's famous secretary and companion Tiro was lauded because of his adaptation of a "recent" invention — "speed writing" (a sort of shorthand) which allowed him to take down speeches in the courts of Rome verbatim in the first century B.C.

The world of the New Testament was a world where the spoken word was supreme. In fact, the New Testament was written in a largely oral culture where the written word did not have the first or last word. Consider, for example, from before New Testament times the words of Plato, who has Socrates warn against substituting the written word for oral traditions because people will stop using their memories (*Phaedr.* 274c-75)! The same sentiments are also expressed by authors who wrote closer to the time of the New Testament era such as Xenophon (*Symp.* 3.5) and Diogenes Laertius (7.54-56). Papias, an Early Church Father who lived at the end of the first century A.D. and into the second century, is famous for his remark on how he preferred the living word and the living witnesses to anything written.

We need to heed the warning of H. Gamble that "a strong distinction between the oral and the written modes is anachronistic to the extent that it presupposes both the modern notion of fixity of a text and modern habits of reading. Texts reproduced by hand, as all texts were before the invention of the printing press, were far less stable than modern printed texts because they were subject to accidental or deliberate modification in every new transcription. Moreover, in antiquity virtually all reading, public or private, was reading aloud: texts were routinely converted into the oral mode. Knowing this ancient authors wrote their texts as much for the ear as for the eye."[1]

These attitudes about and dimensions of orality prevailed throughout the New Testament era, and they simply underscore how remarkable it is that we have these twenty-seven documents called the New Testament at all. So how did we come to have these twenty-seven documents generated in an age before mass production of texts or mass literacy? The story is a remarkable one, and unfortunately we know too little of it. But what we do know is worth telling and, hopefully, telling well.

Those of us who are used to reading the Bible like to use the phrase "in the beginning was the Word." How very true that phrase is will soon become apparent. Before there were any written words that made up New Testament books there were spoken words — thousands of them. The New Testament in all likelihood is barely the tip of the iceberg of verbiage about Jesus that was communicated in the first century A.D. You can almost hear the frustration of the author of the Gospel of John when he says, "Jesus did many other miraculous signs in the presence of his disciples which are not recorded in this book" (John 20:30). Why were they not recorded? Because a papyrus scroll was only so long, and papyrus was expensive and handwriting and hand copying was a very tedious task. These are limitations we rarely experience in most places in the world today.

Consider the matter from another angle. The Gospels are basically about the period in history when Jesus had a ministry in the Holy Land, roughly A.D. 27-30 or thereabouts. Nowhere in the Gospels are we told about either Jesus or any of the disciples writing anything down while those events transpired. The telling of the story in written form likely came later. Or simi-

1. H. Gamble, *Books and Readers in the Early Church* (New Haven: Yale University Press, 1995), p. 30.

larly, all of Paul's letters are written to congregations that had already been founded, who had received the Word orally well before there was any written communication with them. In fact, Paul's letters serve as a sort of surrogate for the oral conversations Paul would have liked to have had with them could he have been present. So much are Paul's letters surrogates for oral communication that they bear the earmarks of such communication — they reflect the techniques of forms of ancient Greco-Roman rhetoric — the oral art of persuasion. In the case of either the Gospels or the Epistles the Word was oral well before it was written. We reverse the process today when we read the text of the New Testament out loud and then proclaim and declaim on the basis of it. Thus, it is fair to say that when we tell the story of the New Testament, we are telling the story of a second-order phenomenon, the story of the literary residue of a largely oral movement which grew on the basis of preaching and teaching, praying and praising, and other forms of oral communication. It was not mainly, in the earliest period of Christian history, the texts that spread the Word, but rather the oral proclamation. The exception to this is the use of the Hebrew Scriptures, or more frequently the Greek translation of them (the Septuagint [LXX]), which are referred to in 2 Timothy 3:16.[2] We must bear these things in mind as we turn now to the New Testament texts, as wonderful and challenging as they are.

The Tools of the Trade and Their Users

Despite the reassurances of innumerable introductions to the New Testament, we do not know very much about who actually wrote some of the books of the New Testament. When I say "wrote," I mean who actually wrote them down. And even when we are very certain who the source was of a particular document, for example, that the letter to the Romans comes from the mind of Paul, we still learn that the actual person who penned the document was an otherwise unknown person named Tertius (Rom. 16:22).[3]

We know then that it required something of a team effort to get some

2. It is so often forgotten in the Church that there was no New Testament in the so-called New Testament era. 2 Timothy 3:16 is about the inspiration and usefulness of the Old Testament for Christians!

3. On Tertius and on Romans 16 being an original part of the letter to the Romans see my *The Epistle to the Romans* (Grand Rapids: Eerdmans, 2003).

of the New Testament documents written, and we will need to discuss the relationship between authors and scribes, and between passers on of traditions and editors, before we are done. Some documents, such as the first three Gospels, are formally anonymous, by which I mean that the author's name is nowhere mentioned in the actual text of the book itself. Nor for that matter are any scribes mentioned by name in the Gospels. The superscripts of these Gospels reflect later Church traditions about the authorship or primary source of the material.

Then of course we have a document like Hebrews, which is clearly anonymous though there have been many guesses as to who wrote the book. Only when we have the name of an author mentioned in the document itself (such as in most of the letters in the New Testament) do we have a concrete starting point for thinking about who produced a particular book of the New Testament. But what we *do* know is that whoever produced the actual first copy of each of these documents could read and write in Greek, which is of course the language of the whole New Testament just as it was the lingua franca of the Greco-Roman world.[4] So let us consider the skill and trade of writing Greek in antiquity first.

Since the literacy rate was never above about 10 percent during the time when the New Testament documents were written,[5] it stands to rea-

---

4. Of course this immediately raises issues because Jesus and his first followers all spoke in Aramaic, as is clear enough from the Aramaic fragments and phrases in the Synoptic Gospels. The question then becomes, Who rendered Jesus' Aramaic teaching into Greek? Could someone like Peter have done this? To what degree were the earliest disciples of Jesus bilingual? The answer seems to be that while their main spoken language was Aramaic (see now the story of the James ossuary and its Aramaic inscription in H. Shanks and B. Witherington, *The Brother of Jesus: The Dramatic Story and Meaning of the First Archaeological Link to Jesus and His Family* [San Francisco: HarperCollins, 2003]), they needed to be able to do some speaking in Greek for business purposes in Galilee, and in order to deal with Romans and others who did not speak Aramaic. This however does not necessarily mean they could read and write in Greek, or at least not very well. Acts 4:13 says of Peter and John that they were *agrammatoi* and *idiōtai*. The root meaning of the former word is "illiterate" (one who could not read and write). But both the context and John 7:15 suggest that the meaning is "unlettered," not formally schooled or trained. See my *The Acts of the Apostles: A Socio-Rhetorical Commentary* (Grand Rapids: Eerdmans, 1998), p. 195. It is thus not impossible that someone like Peter may have at first at least orally translated some of Jesus' sayings into Greek.

5. See H. Gamble, "Literacy and Book Culture," in *The Dictionary of New Testament Background* (Downers Grove, Ill.: InterVarsity, 2000), p. 645.

son that most people, when they wanted something written down, made use of a scribe, a professional writer. Normally such skills would be required for very practical documents — contracts, wills, business letters, marriage documents, and the like. The books of the New Testament are none of these. But in a largely oral culture with much illiteracy it is not surprising that scribes, called amanuenses, were available most anywhere and could take down almost any kind of document for a fee. Yet we must not leap to the conclusion that all the New Testament documents were written by scribes. Why not?

The varying levels of skill in the rendering of Greek in the New Testament shows that it was certainly not always the case that a true professional, skilled in Greek, was used to write a particular New Testament document, but certainly sometimes this was the case, as with the letter to Romans. It is also interesting that the very content of the New Testament documents would have placed them in the category of a sort of literature normally only read by the literate elite. These are not the sort of practical or business documents your average Greco-Roman person had written down or kept copies of.

Beyond the scribal class, literacy was also found among non-elites such as some soldiers, doctors, tradesmen, craftsmen, and engineers. A reasonable case can be made that at least two of the longest New Testament documents, Luke and Acts, were written by someone who was not a scribe and yet was literate because of his trade (i.e., he was a doctor). An equally reasonable case can be made that a document like Revelation was written by someone who had as his primary language Aramaic, and as his secondary language Greek, and so he writes in Greek with some degree of difficulty.[6] The New Testament as a whole is not likely a product of scribal activity, and since most or all of the documents were meant to be read aloud, they were not produced to be pure literature in the modern sense. They were texts with largely nonliterary functions.[7]

How did the process begin then? After a period in which Gospel stories were shared in various settings and ways, and exhortations of various kinds were given orally in the Early Church, there came a time due to fac-

---

6. See now my commentary *Revelation* (Cambridge: Cambridge University Press, 2003).

7. Which is one of the reasons it is so unhelpful and unfruitful to simply treat these documents as if they were like pieces of modern literature.

tors of distance in both time and space that produced some urgency to write various things down. In the case of the Gospels, the urgency was presumably that the original eyewitnesses and earwitnesses were dying off by at least the second half of the first century A.D., and there was a felt need to preserve the traditions they had originally conveyed orally.

It is certainly not impossible that in some quarters this felt need came much earlier and may have produced things like: (1) an Aramaic collection of Jesus' sayings made by the Jerusalem church; (2) a collection of miracle stories involving Jesus; (3) an attempt in Aramaic to tell a larger portion of the gospel story;[8] (4) a written-out narrative about the last week of Jesus' earthly life; and (5) a document largely of Jesus' teachings which was available to both the First and the Third Evangelist and which today we call Q.[9] These earlier precursors to our Gospels are not today extant, and most scholars do not think that any Greek Gospels were produced or available in written form before A.D. 60. This in turn means that letters, and in particular Pauline letters, are our earliest New Testament documents, chronologically speaking,[10] and letters are the documents in the New Testament most clearly connected to scribes.

It is important to stress at this juncture that in all likelihood we must not think of "books" in the modern sense when we are talking about the New Testament documents. In the first place, they were not manufactured in codex or book form originally; rather, they were written on papyrus rolls. In the second place, they were certainly not mass-produced. Initially only a few copies were likely made due to the time and expense involved, and in some cases, such as with letters, there may have been only one copy originally made.

If we are to speak of ancient book culture at all, we are talking about the small circles of the literate elite in the Greco-Roman world, who had the money to have documents reproduced and the time to read them or have them read, and copy them for their friends. Book culture in the modern sense of publications for the masses did not really exist. Authors in antiquity relied usually on wealthy patrons to meet the costs of writing down

---

8. See now M. Casey, *Aramaic Sources of Mark's Gospel* (Cambridge: Cambridge University Press, 1998) on the possible Aramaic original underlying significant portions of Mark's Gospel, which he dates to the 40s A.D.

9. It may have looked somewhat like the Gospel of Thomas, which is a document from the early second century in all probability.

10. See my *New Testament History* (Grand Rapids: Baker, 2001).

their works and having them circulated. It is my conviction that Theophilus, mentioned at the beginning of Luke and Acts, was likely the patron of Luke, and Luke wrote for him and his circle.

But how was the writing done, and on what sort of materials? The standard way to produce a document in antiquity was to write on papyrus. Normally a roll would have been 8 to 10 inches high and up to 35 feet long. Usually, it would be inscribed only on the inside, as papyrus is not a very dense material. There would be two columns 2 to 4 inches wide with about twenty-five to forty-five lines per column. In addition, because of the cost and the space needed, normally there would be no punctuation and no division of words or sentences or paragraphs; it would all be written in capital letters, and so a line would read something like the following: JESUSISNOWHERE. This of course could be read "Jesus is now here" or "Jesus is nowhere." Issues of interpretation already arise just from the lack of separation of letters and the absence of punctuation. Furthermore there were no chapters and verses in these original New Testament manuscripts before the early middle ages!

"Reading in antiquity was customarily done aloud, even if privately. The reason is that texts were written in continuous script . . . without divisions between words, phrases, clauses, paragraphs, and without punctuation, so that the syllables needed to be sounded and heard in order to be organized into recognizable semantic patterns. Correspondingly, almost all ancient texts were composed in consideration of how they would sound when read aloud."[11] It was only near the end of the first century A.D. that the codex or notebook form of texts came into vogue, and it appears that early Christians were some of the first to recognize its usefulness and employ it.[12]

In an age before copyright was an issue, what happened once a patron received a manuscript was as follows: "Publication . . . consisted in giving such a copy to a patron or friend, who then made it available to be copied at the initiative of other interested parties. In this way copies were multiplied seriatim, one at a time. Once a text was in circulation and available for copying, anyone who had an interest in and access to it could have a copy made. Thus books were produced and acquired through an informal and unregulated process."[13]

---

11. Gamble, "Literacy and Book Culture," p. 647.
12. See pp. 73-90 below.
13. Gamble, "Literacy and Book Culture," p. 646.

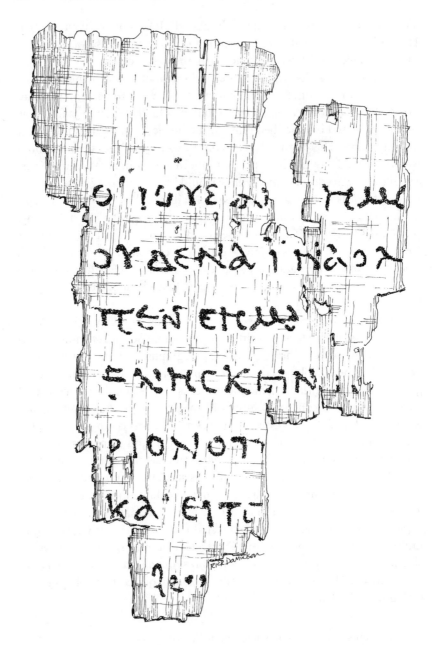

A papyrus fragment of the New Testament. Often this is as much of a piece of a very early copy (second-third century) of a New Testament document as we have.

Most compositions in antiquity were done with pen and ink on papyrus, though sometimes the skins of sheep were used to produce parchment or vellum, a high-quality, highly refined animal skin. The quality of the writing surface, the ink, and the pens all varied. Cicero, writing about A.D. 54, sums up the situation aptly: "For this letter I shall use a good pen, a well-mixed ink, and ivory polished paper too, for you write that you could hardly read my last letter . . . [because] it is always my practice to use whatever pen I find in my hand as if it were a good one" (*Letter to Quintus* 2.15.1). The reed was the pen of choice in antiquity, which was superseded by birds' feathers (quills) in about the seventh century A.D. Carbon or soot was put into a water solution to produce the ink.

Even when one had purchased the necessary pieces of papyri, one was still not ready to take dictation or to write. The papyrus had to be prepared for such writing, not least because there was no such thing in antiquity as lined paper. The scribe or writer would take a ruler and a lead disk to lightly line the paper. Once he began writing he would also need his reed sharpener, which was an abrasive stone, and his knife so that he could create new points in the course of writing. Neither the papyrus, nor the reeds, nor the ink, nor the tools for lining and sharpening came cheaply.

Why was the papyrus so expensive? First, because it was almost all produced in one place, Egypt, near the Nile so that the proper sort of reeds could be harvested for production. Then, consider the process required to produce it. Pliny the Elder says that the papyrus reed which was triangular in shape had to be split with a needle (!) into very thin, wide strips. The very center of the stalk or reed was the "meatiest" portion and so the most useful part for making paper. The green outer layer would likely need to be stripped away.

Once the strips were produced, almost immediately they would be placed on a wooden board moistened with Nile water. Occasionally a mild sort of flour glue was added to aid the process, but normally the sap from the reed was enough to bind the strips together into a piece of papyrus. Once a piece of papyrus was laid out, its edges were trimmed so as to be even. The strips were laid out horizontally and vertically in a criss-cross pattern and in essence woven together. The newly produced piece of papyrus would then be hung out or laid out in the sun to dry. Then finally, up to twenty pieces of papyrus would be sown together to produce a roll (see Pliny *Natural History* 13.74-77). When the roll or piece of papyrus came into the hands of the scribe, he would still need to smooth it out with a shell or a piece of ivory.

Care had to be taken so that the paper did not become too glossy and thereby become a surface that would not take the ink very readily.

In light of all the above it is understandable why ordinary persons would go to a scribe to have something written or, if he or she could afford it, would have their own personal secretary, as, for example, the relationship of Cicero and Tiro shows. In general, the longer the document, the more one would have need of a professional scribe, and by ancient standards many of the New Testament documents are long indeed. All the Gospels, Acts, the longer of Paul's letters, and Revelation qualify as very long documents by ancient standards. Even some of the letters we consider shorter in nature (e.g., Philippians, James, 1 Peter) were by ancient standards certainly quite long for letters. Various New Testament authors were very long-winded (see, e.g., Acts 20:7-11), and since many of the New Testament documents are just substitutes for an oral conversation or proclamation, they too are long. The early Christians who produced these documents obviously had a lot to say!

We have said nothing thus far about handwriting, but in antiquity as today different persons had different styles and ways of shaping letters. The crucial thing would be for the scribe to be someone who had a fair and clear hand, and the ability not to smudge the page while writing. Practically speaking this meant that one would prefer to have a right-handed person write in Latin or Greek, and a left-handed person to write in Aramaic or Hebrew, because the former languages were written from left to write, and the latter from right to left. Notice how Paul would from time to time add his own handwritten note at the end of the document, in a large printed hand. Galatians 6:11 reads, "See what large letters I use when I am writing in my own hand."[14] Since space was at a premium, he would have wanted a smaller, crisper hand to write most of the document so as not to waste too much space.

Ideally, a scribe needed to know both his author and his audience. Ancient peoples believed that letters should portray or display the personality of the author and to some degree take into account that of the audience as well.[15] A secretary might or might not have obtained the skills in

---

14. See Colossians 4:18: "I Paul write this greeting with my own hand," which implies that he had not written the rest of the document up to that point.

15. See S. Stowers, *Letter Writing in Greco-Roman Antiquity* (Philadelphia: Westminster/John Knox, 1986), pp. 32-33.

taking shorthand, and if not the composition process could be very slow. It has often been suggested that in the places in the New Testament, especially in Paul's letters, where we have an incomplete sentence, it is perhaps because the scribe did not know shorthand and could not keep up with the dictation. And of course if there was a pressing matter, there might not be time or papyrus on hand to take something down in shorthand and then write it out in longhand. What we can say for sure is that normally it was not the practice in the first century A.D. for secretaries to compose documents for their authors, except perhaps when it was a pro forma matter of acknowledging that something had been received.[16] When a secretary did write something on behalf of another, it was customary to acknowledge it in the document (see Cicero *Letter to Friends*, 8.1.1).

When someone other than the author was mentioned at the beginning of a document, it was because that person normally had something to do with the document. For example, in 1 Corinthians 1:1 Sosthenes, a Christian, is likely the scribe who wrote this document for Paul.[17] Or again in 1 and 2 Thessalonians, we should take seriously the notion of co-authorship involving Paul, Timothy, and Silvanus in light of how the documents begin. It was not customary to say "we" in such a document unless "we" was meant. Likewise, in the Gospel of John (21:24) "we" means at the least someone speaking for the community of which the Beloved Disciple was a part.

The normal procedure when it came to writing letters was for two copies to be made, one which would be kept by the sender, and the other which would be sent (Cicero *Letter to Friends* 9.26.1). There was no normal postal service for ordinary people to use, and not even an official governmental postal service in the Roman world before Augustus, and so private persons had to make their own arrangements, having friends, relatives, and business associates carry documents to their destinations because they happened to be traveling in that direction. In the case of Christians, this task seems to have been entrusted to other Christians, and in the case of Paul, apparently it was entrusted to one or another of his co-workers. Romans 16:1-2 and Colossians 4:7-9 do not suggest that Paul would entrust his documents to just anyone traveling in the right direction. The issue of

16. See E. Richards, *The Secretary in the Letters of Paul* (Tübingen: Mohr, 1991), p. 39.

17. Alternatively he might be Paul's host.

early Christian social networks needs to be considered when we think of the spread of the Good News in various written forms. Naturally, how swiftly a document reached an audience or individual depended upon the mode and speed of transportation, as well as other factors. All too often, ancient written communications did not reach their intended destination, sometimes with disastrous results. Remember the famous saying: "For want of a nail the shoe was lost. For want of a shoe the horse was lost. For want of a horse the messenger was lost. For want of the messenger the message was lost. For want of the message the battle was lost. For want of the battle the war was lost, and all for the want of a nail." It appears clear that some important Christian documents from the New Testament period are indeed lost to us. For example, Paul in 1 Corinthians 5:9 mentions that he had previously written to this audience not to associate with immoral people. That means there was a letter to the Corinthians written prior to our 1 Corinthians. But that letter is in all likelihood lost in the sands of time. What we have in the New Testament is only a representative sampling of early Christian discourse and communication. We may yet find some of these lost documents of the New Testament period.

The Traditions and the Texts

Early Christians already had a sacred text when the Christian movement began to flourish. We call it the Old Testament. They were then, to some degree, a text-formed community, but it is difficult to discern how much this would have been the case in the largely Gentile congregations that Paul and others had founded. Yet Paul frequently cites or alludes to various Old Testament texts in his letters, and so we must assume that some of the audience, perhaps especially the Jews and God-fearers, had access to the Old Testament or were familiar with its various teachings.

There seem to have been collections of Scriptures made by early Christians, called catenae, to demonstrate or lend authority to some teaching or narrative or point of preaching (cf., e.g., Rom. 9:25-29; 10:18-21; Heb. 1:5-13). Because of the number of citations in the New Testament we know for a fact that some Old Testament books were more popular resources for quotations or allusions than others — in particular the Psalms and Isaiah. The use of the Old Testament, not just in catenae but in a more expository manner by Christians, especially for Christological purposes, is a subject that scholars have frequently addressed.[18] We see this use in a variety of places, but here we will focus on some of the primitive material found in the first half of Acts. It is easy enough to point to midrashic or Jewish contemporizing treatments of the Old Testament — for instance, we find that sort of use of Psalm 2 in Acts 4:25-26 and 13:33, and Amos 9:11 in Acts 15:16. Notice the use of *pais theou*, literally "child of God," of which scholars have repeatedly debated the meaning. Is it to be taken as another form of calling Jesus Son of God, or is *pais* a reference to Jesus as Servant of God? In any case the notion of the decree of God found in Psalm 2 is echoed in various places in the speech material in Acts alluding to Christ as a royal figure. For example, at Acts 10:42 Jesus is called the one "decreed by God as judge of the living and the dead." Or again we see the free use of the verb "to raise up" in Acts 3:22-23, 26, and 4:2 alludes to texts like Hosea 6:2 which are used in the Targums of resurrection.

It seems clear that there were certain key terms or catchwords that triggered the use of particular texts in application to Jesus. For instance, Scriptures that contained the word "stone" were used together to make a point about the rejection and acceptance of Jesus by God's people and God, respectively, a combination of Psalm 118:22 and Isaiah 28:16 in Acts 4:11. The "this is that" or pesher (the interpretation or realization of a biblical text) sort of use of the Old Testament we find in a variety of places in Acts — for example, in Acts 2 where Peter indicates that what Joel spoke of was happening on Pentecost. Or notice the technique of transference where Joel 2:32 (Masoretic Text) is cited in Acts 2:21 as referring to "calling on the name of the Lord." Of course, in Joel the Lord refers to Yahweh, but in Acts the text is used of Christ (cf. Rom. 10:13), and it spawns other allusions — for example, in Acts 3:16, where we find the peculiar phrase "his name, through faith in his name" where Jesus' name is meant as in other early Jewish Christian literature (see James 2:7).

What we see over and over again when we examine some of the primitive Christological material in Acts, is that the Psalms and after that the prophetic material are drawn on again and again to make points about Jesus (cf., e.g., Ps. 2:7 used in Acts 13:33; Ps. 16:10 used in Acts 2:25-28 and

---

18. See, e.g., M. Black, "The Christological Use of the Old Testament in the New Testament," *New Testament Studies* 18 (1971-72): 1-14. What follows in the next few paragraphs is found in a fuller form in my *The Many Faces of Christ* (New York: Continuum, 1998), pp. 11-102.

13:35; Ps. 110:1 used in Acts 2:34-35; Ps. 132:11 used in Acts 2:30; Isa. 53:7-8 used in Acts 8:32-33; Isa. 55:3 used in Acts 13:34; Amos 9:11-12 used in Acts 15:15-17; Joel 2:28-32 used in Acts 2:17-21). More to the point, the *way* the texts are used reflects techniques found repeatedly in early Jewish material especially at Qumran and in some of the material in 1 Enoch. We may distinguish a good deal of this data from *Luke's* preferred use of Scriptures because, as is widely known, "one of his major concerns is to show that Jesus is truly the fulfillment of the Scriptures, as is seen in numerous of his summary statements (Lk. 24.25-26, 45-47; Acts 3.18, 24; 17.2-3; 18.28; 24.14-15; 26.22-23; 28.23)."[19] There is no evidence that Luke knew Aramaic or for that matter the finer points about Jewish exegetical and homiletical techniques,[20] and so we may be sure that a good deal of the data I have pointed to above goes back to the earliest Jewish Christians' handling of Old Testament material as a way to interpret the Christ event. Both M. Black and C. A. Evans have shown again and again that a knowledge of how these texts were handled in the Qumran literature or in the Targums illuminates the use we find of these Scriptures in the early portions of Acts.

We may also check our conclusions on these matters by way of cross-reference. For instance, two of the pet texts used for Christological purposes in Peter's speech in Acts 2, Joel 2:28-32 and Psalm 110:1, are also found not only elsewhere in Acts (Acts 8:16; 9:10-17; 15:26; 22:13-16) but also in the Pauline corpus in the hymn at Philippians 2:9-11. It is correspondences like these that reassure us that here we have yet another window on the Christological reflections of the earliest Jewish Christians.

Finally, there are certain Christological titles that crop up in the earlier speeches in Acts that seem to have a scriptural background but do not reflect Lukan tendencies or predilections (sticking with the tried and true formulae *christos* as a name and *kyrios*)[21] and so may also tell us about the Christological reflections of the earliest Jewish Christians. I am thinking for instance of the proper use of *christos* as a title (e.g., Acts 3:18, 20; 5:42), the use of *pais* probably to refer to Christ as God's child (3:26, cf. above), and the reference to Christ as our Leader *(archēgos)* and Savior (Acts 5:31).

19. C. A. Evans and J. A. Sanders, *Luke and Scripture* (Minneapolis: Fortress, 1993), p. 211.

20. On Luke see pp. 80-82 below.

21. See my discussion of Lukan Christology in Acts in my book *The Acts of the Apostles* (Grand Rapids: Eerdmans, 1998), pp. 147-55.

The title "Savior" is uncommon in Luke-Acts, and "Leader" we find in another early Jewish Christian document, at Hebrews 12:2. Another interesting early title found in the early speech material in Acts is the Righteous One (7:52). This sort of data encourages us to think that the Christological reflections we find in various places in Acts 1–15, including the use of the Old Testament, often reveal the views of Luke's sources and not merely Luke's views of the Christ. In any event it is clear from this evidence that the earliest Christians quite readily used the Old Testament in a variety of ways to interpret the story of Jesus and the meaning of the Christ event. The Old Testament was indeed their sacred text and source book, but it was read most frequently through a Christological and eschatological lens.

There also seem to have been creeds, hymns, confessions, prayers, and other things written down or memorized and used in the period before Christianity actually formally had its own sacred texts. It will be well to look briefly at the evidence that demonstrates these facts as we try to assess the story behind and before the creating of the New Testament texts.

In 1 Corinthians 15:3, in a text written just after the middle of the first century A.D., Paul reminds his audience about some traditions which he had received and had passed along to his Corinthian converts — "that Christ died for our sins in accordance with the Scriptures, and that he was buried, and that he was raised in accordance with the Scriptures, and that he appeared to . . ." Paul has used here the Jewish language about the careful passing along of sacred traditions. Notice that these traditions have to do with the end of the story of Jesus' life on earth. Immediately we are confronted with the fact that Paul is not the originator of the Good News he proclaimed. He would deny being an innovator. He was rather passing along what he had received. In addition, he is telling his audience that he stands in a line of those who pass along traditions.

There were those who came before him who had formulated certain Christian traditions, in this case in the form of a story of Jesus, and he had been told these things. Because Paul was probably converted not very long after the death of Jesus (at most four or five years after Jesus' death in A.D. 35), we may be reasonably certain that Paul is talking about traditions he received from the earliest Jewish followers of Jesus, namely, the Jewish Christians in Jerusalem. In Galatians 1–2, in Paul's earliest letter written in A.D. 49-50, Paul had already admitted as much. He went up to Jerusalem and spoke with James, Peter, and John. We may be sure that they did not merely speak about the weather! This in turn means that the earliest Jewish Christians treated the story of Jesus and other relevant information as they had previously treated sacred Jewish traditions. They had learned them by rote memory. They had repeated them regularly. They had passed them on to others in a rather fixed form. Paul is also telling us that he had continued this trend by passing them along to his largely Gentile converts in Corinth. But it was not just the story of Jesus that Paul had passed along. There was a whole battery of traditions he conveyed.

For example, many scholars have noticed the echoes of the sayings of Jesus found in places as diverse as Romans 13–15, Galatians 5–6, and 1 Thessalonians 4–5. Paul seems to know a range of Jesus' teachings that include ethics, eschatology, and a variety of other subjects (such as whether one ought to pay taxes to Caesar). In other words, it was not just the story of Jesus' life that was being passed along but also some of Jesus' teachings on various subjects. And it is not just Paul who echoes the teachings of Jesus on love, money, and various other matters. Jesus' brother James does the very same thing. In the Epistle of James we find some twenty echoes, allusions to, or partial quotations of ethical teachings of Jesus.[22] Thus it is both the words and the deeds that are being passed along by early Christian teachers in the period before the writing of the New Testament documents.

There is however more — there were also prayers, creedal fragments, and hymns, presumably primarily in the context of worship. For example, right at the end of 1 Corinthians 16 we find the following words at verse 22: "Let anyone be accursed who has no love of the Lord, *marana tha.*" The shorter form of this may have been *anathema marana tha.* In any case, the oath curse is followed by a prayer for the Lord to come, and in this case we can be reasonably sure that the reference is to what we call the second coming of Jesus. One does not pray to a deceased rabbi to return. Jesus is being prayed to as a divine person who will come to his people again. There was already a Christological reformulation of monotheism in the very earliest days of the Church, such that Aramaic-speaking Jewish Christians were praying to Jesus to return. They knew that part of the story was that he would come back to earth again. There was in all likelihood never a form

---

22. On Paul see my *Jesus, Paul and the End of the World* (Downers Grove, Ill.: InterVarsity, 1992), pp. 23-242, and on James see Shanks and Witherington, *The Brother of Jesus,* pp. 146-52.

of earliest Christianity that did not include in its creed the eschatological elements about the death, resurrection, and return of Christ.

In Romans 1:3-4 we have what most scholars think is a Pauline citation of a portion of an early Jewish Christian creedal statement. Since Paul does not really speak of Jesus as the Son of David, nor does he refer elsewhere to the "Spirit of holiness," and since the grammar here is somewhat incongruous with its context, it seems likely Paul is using a source here. What do we learn from this source material? Again we learn that the earliest Christians kept the story of Jesus readily in view, and wished to emphasize what we would call both the human and the divine side of the story. Jesus, according to the flesh, was a descendant of David and thus a possible candidate to be the Messianic One. Jesus however was vindicated to be Son of God in power by means of the resurrection that happened to him through the agency of the Holy Spirit. We are talking about what Jesus was through birth, and through the rebirth of resurrection, and so the implicit story encompasses the whole of Jesus' earthly career. There is however an even more expanded form of the story, retold in a hymn found at Philippians 2:5-11.

It will be useful to lay out in full what this text says before we comment:

Your attitude should be the same as that of Christ Jesus:

who being in very nature God,
did not consider the being equal to God
something to be taken advantage of.
Instead he stripped himself,
taking the very nature of a servant,
being made in human likeness,
and being found in appearance as a human being
he humbled himself,
and became obedient to death,
even death on a cross!

Therefore God has highly exalted him,
and given him the name which is above every name,
that at the name of Jesus every knee should bow
in heaven and on earth and under the earth
and every tongue confess that Jesus Christ is Lord
to the glory of God the Father.

We have demonstrated elsewhere at length that this is likely a pre-Pauline hymn fragment,[23] and so what remains here is to note some important features of this hymn. First it can be pointed out that this hymn fragment is found in a letter from Paul's hand that dates to no later than A.D. 62, and probably earlier. In other words, this material, even with this latest possible date, antedates the earliest Gospel by some years, and in all probability antedates Mark's Gospel by at least half a decade. This in turn means that a very full form of the trajectory of Jesus' career was being told, and occasionally put into writing, well before there were written Gospels. In short, the Gospel story in oral form and written synopsis predates the fuller written Gospels, and probably in at least oral form even predates at least some of Paul's letters. It needs to be recognized that when one considers the confessional formulae, prayers, hymn fragments, and the like together, they all reflect a very high Christology indeed, bearing witness to a faith that Jesus was both human and divine. Thus the Christ hymn in Philippians 2 should not be seen as some anomaly, but rather just a fuller expression of the way the story of Jesus had been told for some time. It needs to also be seen that the suggestion that the story of Adam lies behind this material in Philippians 2 simply is not a cogent suggestion. Adam did not make a pretemporal choice to give up divine prerogatives and become a human being as we are told the Son of God did here. Nor did Adam choose to die; rather, it was forced upon him as a punishment for his sins. It is the unique story of the divine and yet human Son of God that is being told here, not a revisionist story of the tale of Adam.

It is sometimes suggested by scholars that the stories about Jesus' birth found in Matthew 1–2, Luke 1–2, and also John 1 reflect late-first-century notions about the birth of a divine Son of God, notions that were not present in the earliest period of Christian reflection about Jesus. Yet if the Christ hymn in Philippians 2 reflects not only Paul's thought but pre-Pauline thought, it is correct to say that we already had within the first generation of Jesus' followers not only a very high Christology reflecting Jesus' divinity and so his preexistence, but also already a concept of the incarnation, which is simply more fully developed in John 1. What Matthew 1–2 and Luke 1–2 add to this story is the miraculous nature of the conception in Mary's womb, telling us *how* the Son of God came into the world.

23. See my *Jesus the Sage: The Pilgrimage of Wisdom* (Minneapolis: Augsburg/Fortress, 1994), pp. 249-66.

This tradition is hardly more developed or "advanced" than the notion of preexistence and incarnation found in Philippians 2. It would appear then that we need to drop the assumption of some sort of evolutionary model of development of the Jesus story and of reflection about Jesus. Indeed, to judge from later apocryphal Gospels such as the Gospel of Thomas or of Philip we might well want to speak of the degeneration of the story rather than its enhancement in the later period.[24]

Returning to Philippians 2, what then are we told in this text? First, that there is an attitude that Christ reflected in stripping himself, humbling himself, and becoming not only a human but a servant among humans that can and should be imitated by followers of Christ. In other words, to some degree Christ's story provides a blueprint for the Christian's story, though of course Christians are not said to preexist in heaven before they take on human form, nor will they become the exalted Lord of the universe after death. Second, the text makes clear that Christ had the very nature and prerogatives of God, but decided not to take advantage of them. Instead he stripped himself of his divine prerogatives and became not merely human but a slave among humans, and was even to die a rebellious slave's death — on the cross. The main verbs in the first half of the hymn all emphasize what Christ chose to do. Particularly important is the fact that he was "obedient even unto death on a cross." This hints at God's pretemporal plan for the redemption of humankind, to which Christ chose to conform his actions in order that salvation might be accom-

---

24. This is where a study such as that by B. Ehrman, *The New Testament* (Oxford: Oxford University Press, 1997), pp. 1-10, goes nearly entirely wrong. He attempts to predicate the later wider diversity of thought back into the earliest Christian period, even though the New Testament documents do not endorse or suggest things like Gnostic or Marcionite Christianity, which are indeed found in second-century and later documents. He ignores the concern exhibited in early texts like Galatians 1 to make sure to get the story straight, because dueling Gospels was not an acceptable alternative. He also must ignore the care of a historian like Luke in Luke 1:1-4 who represents the major figures of Peter, James, and Paul in essential agreement about the Gospel, though differing some on praxis. Ebionite Christians of the second century may well have been a development of the Pharisaic Jewish Christians of Jerusalem mentioned in Acts 15, but their voice was never considered to be the norm in early Christianity. Indeed, their ideas that all Christians must follow the Mosaic Law were not only rejected by Paul, but also by Peter and James as well. It is a fundamental historical mistake to assume there were no unifying Gospel or doctrinal norms in the Early Church prior to the formation of the New Testament canon.

plished. God required of his Son an atoning sacrifice to accomplish redemption.

The second half of the hymn focuses on what God did for Christ as a result, namely, exalt him to a high position in heaven and give him various of God's divine or throne names. Christ did not exalt himself in a world full of self-promotion; rather he stepped down and served others, which most, especially the elite, in the Greco-Roman world would have seen as despicable, not admirable. The message to Paul's converts is clear enough — humble yourself and serve others and be faithful even unto death and leave the exalting and establishing of your name to God, just as Jesus did. The story of Jesus is not merely a pleasing and saving tale to be told, it is a template for a particular form of Christian living, and this is well before the Gospels were likely ever written.

Thus far we have been talking about Christians speaking largely to Christians in the context of their own homes and worship services. What about the spreading of the story and the Word outside such contexts before there were any written documents? B. D. Ehrman sums up well what may be said about the early preaching and evangelizing using the story of Jesus:

> What did Christians tell people in order to convert them? Our evidence here is frustratingly sparse: examples of missionary sermons in the book of Acts and some intimations of Paul's preaching in his own letters (e.g. 1 Thess. 1.9-10). We cannot tell how representative these are. Moreover, there are some good reasons for thinking that most of the Christian mission was conducted not through public preaching, say on a crowded street corner, but privately as individuals who had come to believe that Jesus was the Son of God told others about their newfound faith and tried to convince them to adopt it as well.
>
> Since we know that in the Greco-Roman world religion was a way of securing the favor of the gods, we are probably not too far afield to think that if faith in Jesus were known to produce beneficial, or even miraculous results, then people might be persuaded to convert. If a Christian testified, for example, that praying to Jesus or through Jesus to God, had healed her daughter, or that a representative of Jesus had cast out an evil spirit, or that the God of Jesus had miraculously provided food for a starving family, this might spark interest in her neighbor or co-worker. Those with an interest in Jesus would want to learn

more about him. Who was he? When did he live? What did he do? How did he die? The Christian, in turn, would be both compelled and gratified to tell stories about Jesus to anyone interested.

Such opportunities to tell stories about Jesus must have presented themselves throughout the major urban areas of the Mediterranean for decades prior to the writing of the Gospels. Otherwise there is no way to account for the spread of the religion in an age that did not enjoy the benefits of telecommunication.[25]

I would demur from Ehrman's deemphasis on the importance of preaching, but nonetheless I agree that private conversations were also crucial to spreading the story. As we begin to bring this part of the discussion of the story before and behind the written Story of Jesus to a close, it will be well if we consider a few samples from Acts of Luke's summaries of the early preaching to both non-Christians and Christians. I use the term summaries advisedly, as most of what Luke presents us within Acts, with the possible exception of the Stephen speech, could not be anything but brief summaries, for they take only a few moments to read out loud today.

In order to appreciate what we find in Acts three things need to be kept in mind: (1) Luke consulted eyewitnesses and the early proclaimers of the Word, as Luke 1:1-4 makes clear. We may reasonably assume then that he was in touch with the basic themes and forms of the early Christian telling and retelling of the story of Jesus. (2) Luke deliberately chooses to selectively present different kinds of speeches to differing audiences. (3) The eschatological perspective of the earliest Christians is evident throughout. By this latter point I mean to stress that the earliest Christians saw themselves as living in the age of the fulfillment of the prophecies and various other Old Testament texts, and they believed these prophecies were fulfilled not only in the life and ministry of Jesus, but also in their own lives and times. They were living in the times when the Old Testament stories were all coming true.

Acts 2:14-41 provides us with a good illustration of exactly what I am talking about. Peter uses a text from Joel 2:28-32 to explain what was happening on Pentecost to the Christians in Jerusalem. The Holy Spirit of God was falling upon them and affecting their behavior. There follows in Acts 2:23-24 a brief summary of the life, death, and ministry of Jesus, a sum-

---

25. Ehrman, *The New Testament*, pp. 41-42.

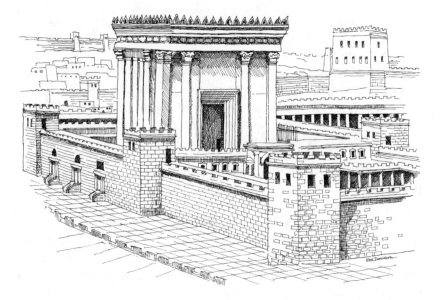

The Herodian Temple where Peter preached his Pentecost message.

mary about the same length as we found in the creedal statements and hymn fragments already discussed. After this in Acts 2:25-28 there is a quotation from Psalm 16:8-11 used to explain the career of Christ. Another text is appended at verses 34-35. The emphasis in the sermon is clearly placed on the resurrection and exaltation of Jesus beyond his crucifixion, which events are seen as a vindication of Jesus — "God has made this Jesus, whom you crucified, both Lord and Christ." Christology is done here in a narratological form, just as was the case in the prayers, creedal statements, and hymns, as we have seen. The story is intact, and can be variously expanded and contracted to meet the situation. In this case the audience is Jews and God-fearers, and so there is a special emphasis on quotation and showing the fulfillment of Scripture.

There is a somewhat similar sermon, equally laced with Old Testament quotations, found in Acts 13 on the lips of Paul, and addressed to the same sort of audience — Jews and God-fearers. Paul, however, like Stephen in Acts 7, first does something of a review of the history of Israel, and the Davidic origins of the Messiah are stressed. In verses 26-36 there is again a brief review of the end of Jesus' career — his condemnation, death, and resurrection, with again a stress on his vindication by God, interlaced with quotations from Psalms 2 and 16, and from Isaiah 55:3. There follows the interesting conclusion: "Through him everyone who believes is justified from everything you could not be justified from by the Law of Moses." The theme of superseding of the Law of Moses by and in Christ was of course to be a significant theme in Paul's earliest letter to these same Galatians (see Galatians 3–4).[26] The speech concludes with a warning to the audience from Habakkuk 1:5 lest they fulfill the Scripture's statements about scoffers. Again the impression left is that the Old Testament prophecies and stories were coming true and could be applied not only to Jesus (though he is the special focus of the language of fulfillment and the quoting of texts), but to Jews, and to followers of Jesus in various ways.

The speech of James in Acts 15 also focuses on the fulfillment of prophecy, and in this case it is a prophecy about Jews and Gentiles being united as the people of God (largely quoting Amos 9:11-12). The quotation is used as a basis for the conclusion that since this eschatological action of God is in progress and Gentiles are being saved apart from obedience to the Law, they should not be troubled with the observance of Mosaic strictures. The so-called Decree then is not a statement telling Gentiles to observe certain Mosaic food and ethical laws per se, but rather a demand that they shun pagan temples and the sort of activities that go on in such temples.[27] In this way they would in fact be keeping the heart of the Ten Commandments by shunning idolatry and immorality. This sermon, unlike the others considered from Acts so far, is not Christological in focus so much as it is ecclesiological in focus. James is concerned with the shape and praxis of God's people as Jew and Gentile united in Christ. He assumes Gentiles have been grafted into the story of God's people and must be accepted.

The speech of Paul before the Areopagus in Acts 17 is yet a different form of proclamation that strikes a balance between flattery and telling off the pagan audience. Instead of quoting Old Testament texts, it involves brief quotations from Greek poets and philosophers, and attempts to convince the audience of Areopagite officials that the unknown god mentioned on some of their altars is in fact now known to be the One who raised Jesus from the dead, namely, the creator God who is also the God of

26. See pp. 52-54 below.
27. See my discussion of this in *The Acts of the Apostles,* pp. 456-70.

Israel. There is indeed a story line here as well, but the story is carried forward from the point of Jesus' death and resurrection to the day when he would judge the world. The resurrection of Jesus is here taken to be the proof that he would one day fulfill that role, just as the resurrection was earlier taken in Acts as the proof that God had vindicated Jesus' ministry and messianic claims.

Lastly, we should take note of the farewell speech of Paul to the Christians from Ephesus in Acts 20. This is the only major speech addressed to Christians, and it is not a surprise that it is the only one that has numerous echoes from Christian writings, specifically Paul's own letters.[28] Here Paul recounts his own stories and exhorts his audience to remain faithful despite trials and tribulations. The speech concludes with a saying of Jesus (20:35) not found in any other source, a fact that demonstrates that the sayings of Jesus were important in some settings (particularly in Christian settings) in early preaching.

In all of these summaries of speeches stories are being told of Christ, of God's people, of a specific Christian life, and these stories are related to sacred or revered texts of various kinds — the Old Testament, the sayings of Jesus, and even famous Greek texts. The proclaiming of the Good News could include many other stories, though the focus would most often be on explaining the story of Jesus. It is in the speeches in Acts 2 and 13 that we see most clearly an overlap with the summaries about Christ's career found in the creedal remarks, the prayers, and the hymn fragments. The reverence for the Old Testament and its use in an eschatological manner, indicating fulfillment, are evident throughout.

Conclusions

In this chapter we have sought to delve into the period behind the texts of the New Testament in a cursory manner. We have discussed both the means and meaning of communicating the Story in this period, and we have emphasized how remarkable indeed it is that there are these twenty-seven books from Christian authors, in an age when the vast majority of ordinary people were illiterate, could not afford documents, and in any case lived in a culture that was decidedly and definitely oral in character.

28. See my *The Acts of the Apostles*, pp. 610-12.

The Story existed, and was told in a variety forms before it ever became sacred text. It was even written down to some extent before it ever became sacred text. Its focus was on the story of Jesus the Lord, the Savior, the Messiah. We must turn now to other sorts of traditions and texts that existed before the creation of the earliest New Testament documents.

Exercises and Questions for Study and Reflection

→ Pick a chapter of the Bible that you enjoy. Take a pencil and a piece of ordinary notebook paper and then copy the entire chapter by hand onto the paper. Do your best to stay within the lines and write in a neat hand. How long did this take you? Did you make any mistakes? Is the document legible? What did you do when the pencil began to get dull? Now imagine being the scribe who copied Luke's Gospel for the first time — all twenty-four chapters. How long would it take you to copy just that one New Testament book? Do you begin to sense now the amount of time and effort that went into producing these books?

→ What is a scribe? What role did such a person sometimes play in the production of a New Testament document?

→ What is an oral culture? What role do written documents have in such a culture? What do we make of the fact that the New Testament was written in and for such a culture? What is meant by calling Paul's letters "oral" documents?

→ What does it tell us about the New Testament writers that many of them could read and write in a culture where only 10 percent of the population was capable of such things?

→ What does it mean to call the New Testament documents part of a conversation in a larger context? It has been said that a text without a context is just a pretext for what you want it to mean. How important is context to getting at the meaning of the New Testament?

→ What did the earliest oral proclamation about Jesus look like? How important was the preached Word? How important to Christianity is it today in a text-based (and computer-based) culture?

2 | The Pedagogy and the Passion: Sayings and Passion Stories about Jesus

In our last chapter we examined the tools of writing and discussed some of the liturgical elements such as hymns and creedal fragments and prayers and sermon summaries that may well have been put into writing early on in the telling of the Good News. In this chapter we want to examine more lengthy traditions such as collections of Jesus' sayings and stories (for example, miracle stories) and Passion narratives as we make our way toward an examination of the finished products — the documents in the New Testament. What the sources in this chapter have in common is that they seem to have been used for teaching purposes, and not just in and for worship. Their function seems to be a little different than that of the materials we examined in the last chapter.

Right on Q: The Sayings of Jesus

Thus far we have only been discussing materials found in the New Testament that appear to scholars to be sources for the later composition of New Testament documents. This will be the case in this chapter as well. Besides summaries of the story of Jesus' life, particularly its end, which we saw in hymns, creedal statements, and sermon summaries in the last chapter, there seem also to have been collections of other materials by or about Jesus. In particular, most scholars believe there was an early written collection of Jesus' sayings, which may first have been made while the sayings were still in an Aramaic form, and then later were translated into Greek when the Good News began to be spread beyond the context of Judea and Galilee.

In order however for us to discuss the source of the sayings, which came to be called Q,[1] we must first deal briefly with the issue called the Synoptic Problem. Scholars have long recognized that there is some sort of interrelationship between the first three Gospels. Which one came first? Is there a case of literary dependency of one or more Gospels on another? Did the Gospel writers ever independently use the same source? It is the answer to this last question that brings Q into the picture.

It is the general consensus of the vast majority of scholars that our earliest actual Gospel is Mark. Why? There are several reasons for this conclusion and taken together they are convincing. In the first place, it has often been noted that the most troubling and offensive form of various sayings of Jesus is found in Mark. For example, in Mark 13:32 we hear that not even the Son knows the timing of the second coming. Luke leaves out this saying altogether, and various manuscripts when recording Matthew 24:36 omit the clause "not even the Son." Another example of whittling off the hard edges of sayings found in Mark is in Mark 10:18 and parallels. A man comes to Jesus and calls him "Good Teacher," but Jesus responds rather abruptly: "Why do you call me good? No one is good but God alone!" This was obviously too much for the First Evangelist, who has Jesus say "Why do you ask me about the good?" (Matt. 19:17). The matter is depersonalized, and the issue becomes something other than whether Jesus might be good or God.

Another good example of the ameliorating tendencies of the later handling of the Synoptic tradition can be found when one compares Mark 10:37 and parallels. In Mark, James and John (the sons of Zebedee) ask in essence for box seats in the Kingdom, on the right- and left-hand side of Jesus when he comes into his glory. In what appears to be an attempt to spare the image of these disciples, Matthew 20:21 does not have the disciples but has the mother of the Zebedees making this request. One final example will have to do. In Mark the disciples are frequently portrayed as having no faith, and are upbraided for this. In Matthew the phrase that regularly crops up is "O you of little faith" (see Matt. 16:8 — the Greek is *oligopistoi*). The evidence above suggests clearly the priority of Mark over Matthew.

1. So called because it is an abbreviation for the word *Quelle,* which is the German term for "source."

Very few scholars have ever argued for the priority of Luke's Gospel. There are several reasons for this. In the first place Luke tells us that he had predecessors who had written down the story of Jesus (Luke 1:1-4), and he admits to using sources to compose his document. He does not claim to be an eyewitness or an apostle, but he claims to be in touch with some of the eyewitnesses and early preachers of the Good News. Nor does Luke have the same emphasis on future eschatology that we find in both Matthew and Mark, and we know from Paul's letters that this was a strong emphasis in the earliest period of the Jesus movement. With these general considerations we may turn to more specific data that help us sort out the interrelationships of the Synoptic Gospels.

First of all, some sort of literary relationship between Matthew, Mark, and Luke seems certain, and not just because Luke admits to using sources. Out of a total of 661 verses in Mark only 55 are not found in some form in Matthew. In other words, 95 percent of Mark also appears in Matthew. Over half of Mark's material is also found in Luke's Gospel. Even more telling is the fact that of the material Matthew and Mark have in common, 51 percent of Mark's exact words are also found in Matthew's version of the material. Of the material Mark and Luke share, Luke has 53 percent of the exact words found in Mark. This did not happen by accident or chance. If three of my students were to produce term papers with that much commonality, including exact verbatim use of the same words and phrases over and over again, I would have to assume some sort of literary relationship was involved.

Furthermore, if we examine closely the miracle stories that Matthew, Mark, and Luke share in common, we find that almost without exception, Mark has the longest version of the story even though his is the shortest Gospel. Now it is understandable how later Gospel writers might edit down the length of such stories to make room on a single scroll for other source material, such as the material we call the Sermon on the Mount. But it is inexplicable if Mark was following Matthew or Luke why he would leave out all the rich material found in the Sermon on the Mount in order to allow for mere verbal expansion of some miracle stories. Mark does indeed want to portray Jesus as a teacher (see Mark 4 and 13), but he has none of the Sermon on the Mount material. We must assume he did not have access to that source. This brings the issue of Q to the fore, and we must consider it now.

Just as we must account for the similarities in the accounts shared by

Matthew, Mark, and Luke, so also we must account for the repeated similarities found in material that only Matthew and Luke share in common (i.e. it is not found in Mark). This material is called Q. There are some forty-nine or fifty passages, or 230 or so sayings, that Matthew and Luke share and that are not found in Mark. In other words we are talking about well over two hundred verses of material, which is far too much similar material to be ignored. It is possible that Luke used Matthew, or vice versa, but this seems unlikely for three reasons: (1) Luke's version of the various Q sayings (cf., e.g., the Beatitudes in Matthew and Luke) often differs in ways that do not suggest mere editorial adjustment of what is found in Matthew; (2) Matthew's version of the material often appears more Jewish than Luke's (e.g., he uses the phrase Kingdom of Heaven rather than Kingdom of God), and yet clearly enough Luke does not have an anti-Jewish agenda, though he does Hellenize his source material somewhat; and (3) there is some material in Matthew that Luke would have been very likely to use, given his agendas and tendencies, and yet he does not do so. For example, with his penchant for telling Jesus' parables it is hard to believe that Luke would leave out some of the distinctive parable material we find in Matthew, for instance, the parable of the Wise and Foolish Virgins (Matt. 25:1-12) or the parable of the Laborers in the Vineyard (Matt. 20:1-16). Much more could be said along these lines, but this must suffice to show that it is likely that: (1) Matthew and Luke used Mark's Gospel independently of each other and (2) the non-Markan material Matthew and Luke have in common likely comes from their drawing on an earlier collection, or some earlier collections, of Jesus' sayings, which we call Q.

Scholars have sometimes suggested that Q existed as a written document because of the existence of the later Gospel of Thomas, which is indeed a collection of sayings attributed to Jesus. But there are several problems with this line of reasoning. In the first place, unlike Thomas there are some narratives in Q: for example, the story of the temptations of Jesus. There is also an interest in miracle stories in Q, which is not the case with Thomas. Q is not simply a collection of sayings, though that is its character in the main.

In the second place, Q does not reflect the later Gnostic and ascetical tendencies that we find in Thomas. It is particularly the Gnostic tendencies that probably led to the denuding of sayings from their narrative contexts. The story did not matter to Thomas's author, only the esoteric and secret wisdom that the sayings contained. Furthermore, there is an interest in di-

The current Capernaum synagogue ruins date to the third century A.D., but its foundations appear to go back to the time of the first-century synagogue in which Jesus' words were heard.

alogue in Thomas that is not manifested in Q. It must be remembered that Thomas is the only collection of sayings arising out of early Judaism that manifests a Gnostic tendency. Q, in contrast to Thomas, has a definite interest in eschatology, which is to say, in the historical future. It is therefore inappropriate to try to draw conclusions about the earliest state of Q on

the basis of Thomas. It is also probably a mistake to draw too many conclusions about the original form of Q on the basis of the more Hellenized
and de-eschatologized form of the Jesus material found in the latest of the
Synoptic Gospels, Luke's Gospel. However, the original form of a Q story
or saying must be judged on a case-by-case basis. The genre of Q needs to
be determined on the basis of the collection's content, not on the basis of
analogy with Thomas or some other document.

It will be well to list first the content of Q. Most scholars think that
Luke better preserves the order of Q because he tends toward alternating
between sources rather than combining them, whereas Matthew arranges
his material topically combining source material (a collection of parables,
a collection of miracle stories, etc.). But in fact one of the most telltale
signs that Luke and Matthew are drawing on a common source is the fact
that the order of Q material in Matthew is almost entirely the same as the
order of the Q material in Luke, even when there is intervening material
inserted from some other source in either one of these Gospels.

It is clear that the Q material was not solely focused on Christological issues, and in fact primarily on pedagogical ones, though there were
texts in Q that depict Jesus as God's Wisdom.[2] In fact, I have argued elsewhere at considerable length that not just a few passages but the entire editing of Q was done with certain sapiential agendas in mind, part of which
intended to portray Jesus not only as a great sage who told numerous parables and aphorisms but as God's Wisdom.[3] This can be seen from a glance
at the following table:

A. **The Story of Jesus the Sage/Wisdom**

1. The Forerunner and the Announcement of the Sage's Coming
   (by John) — Luke 3:2-9/Matt. 3:1-10; Luke 3:15-17/Matt. 3:11-12

2. The Anointment of the Sage with the Spirit — Luke 3:21-22/
   Matt. 3:13-16

3. The Testing of the Sage — Luke 4:1-13/Matt. 4:1-11

4. The Sermon of the Sage — Luke 6:20-49/Matt. 5–7

---

2. See pp. 37-40 below.

3. See my *Jesus the Sage: The Pilgrimage of Wisdom* (Minneapolis: Augsburg/For-
tress, 1994), pp. 211-36.

5. The Wonder Working of the Sage — Luke 7:1-10/Matt. 8:5-13

6. The Questioning of the Sage (by John) — Luke 7:18-23/Matt. 11:2-6

7. The Response of the Sage — Luke 7:24-28/Matt. 11:7-11

8. The Rejection of the Sage by "This Generation" — Luke 7:31-35/Matt. 11:16-19

Part One ends with the revelation of Jesus as Wisdom — "yet Wisdom is vindicated by her deeds" — Matt. 11:19

B. **Discipleship to Jesus the Sage — Its Character and Mission**

9. Discipleship's Cost — Luke 9:57-62/Matt. 8:19-22

10. Discipleship's Mission — Luke 10:1-24/Matt. 9–11 (portions)
    a. The Mission Speech — Luke 10:1-12/Matt. 9:37-38/10:5-16
    b. Woe on Galilean Cities — Luke 10:13-15/Matt. 11:20-24
    c. Authority of Missionaries — Luke 10:16-20/Matt. 10:40
    d. Thanksgiving and Blessing — Luke 10:21-24/Matt. 11:25-27; 13:16-17

11. The Disciple's Prayer and Praying — Luke 11:2-4, 5-13/Matt. 6:7-13; 7:7-11

Part Two ends with disciples urged to seek help from above

C. **The Wars and Woes of the Sage/Wisdom**

12. Struggling with Satan — Luke 11:14-26/Matt. 12:22-30, 43-45

13. Signs of Trouble I — Luke 11:29-32/Matt. 12:38-42

14. The Light of One's Life — Luke 11:33-36/Matt. 5:15; 6:22-23

15. The Woes of Wisdom — Luke 11:42-52/Matt. 23 (portions)

Part Three ends with "the Wisdom of God said" — seventh woe on those who would be sages (cf. Luke 11:52/Matt. 23:13)

D. **The Revelations of Wisdom**

16. Hidden and Revealed — Luke 12:2-3/Matt. 10:26-27

17. Wisdom's Persecuted Followers — Luke 12:4-7/Matt. 10:28-31

18. Acknowledging the Sage and the Spirit — Luke 12:8-12/Matt. 10:19, 32-33

19. Wisdom in Nature — Luke 12:22-31/Matt. 6:25-33

20. The Treasures of Wisdom — Luke 12:32-34/Matt. 6:19-21

21. Preparation for Wisdom's Feast — Luke 12:35-40/Matt. 24:43-44

22. Preparation for Wisdom's Return — Luke 12:42-48/Matt. 24:45-51

23. Wisdom's Second Baptism — Luke 12:49-50

24. Divisions over Wisdom and Her Demise — Luke 12:51-53/Matt. 10:34-36

25. Signs of Trouble II — Luke 12:54-56/Matt. 16:2-3

26. Time to Settle Accounts — Luke 12:57-59/Matt. 5:25-26

27. The Lament of Wisdom for Jerusalem — Luke 13:34-35/Matt. 23:37-39

Part Four ends with rejection of Wisdom at the heart of the nation; Jerusalem's house is forsaken, and Wisdom won't return until a beatitude on Wisdom is pronounced

E. The Narrative Parables and Aphorisms of the Sage/Wisdom

28. Seed and Leaven — Luke 13:18-21/Matt. 13:31-33

29. Gate and Door — Luke 13:23-27/Matt. 7:13-14, 22-23

30. East and West/Last and First — Luke 13:28-30/Matt. 8:11-12; 20:16

31. Wisdom's Banquet — Luke 14:15-24/Matt. 22:1-10

32. The Cost of Discipleship — Luke 14:25-27/Matt. 10:37-38

33. Old Salt — Luke 14:34-35/Matt. 5:13

34. Lost Sheep — Luke 15:3-7/Matt. 18:12-14

35. Lost Coin — Luke 15:8-10

Part Five ends with Wisdom's search for the lost

F. **Discipleship at the Turn of the Era**

    36. Choosing Whom to Serve — God or Mammon — Luke 16:13/Matt. 6:24

    37. The End of Torah's Era? — Luke 16:16-17/Matt. 11:12-13 (cf. 5:18)

    38. The End of a Marriage — Luke 16:18/Matt. 5:32

    39. Sins and Forgiveness — Luke 17:1-4/Matt. 18:7, 21-22

    40. Mustard Seed Faith — Luke 17:5-6/Matt. 17:20

Part Six ends with the assurance to disciples that even small faith can work great miracles

G. **The End of the Age**

    41. Against False Hopes — Luke 17:22-23/Matt. 24:26

    42. Like Lightning — Luke 17:24/Matt. 24:27

    43. Like Vultures — Luke 17:37/Matt. 24:28

    44. Like Noah's and Lot's Time — Luke 17:26-30/Matt. 24:37-39

    45. No Turning Back — Luke 17:31-32/Matt. 24:17-18

    46. Find Life by Losing It — Luke 17:33/Matt. 10:39

    47. Division of Laborers — Luke 17:34-35/Matt. 24:40-41

    48. Parable of the Talents — Luke 19:11-27/Matt. 25:14-30

    49. At Tables and on Thrones in the Kingdom — Luke 22:28-30/Matt. 19:28

Part Seven is an eschatological discourse, ending with a promise of reunion and roles with Jesus[4]

Only a glance at this material and at the chapters and verses of Matthew and Luke which are listed makes evident we are dealing with a substantial amount of material, substantially presented in the same order in these two Gospels. This is surely not a coincidence. As we have suggested, the Q material is basically grouped into two kinds of data, os-

4. This table appears in a slightly different form in *Jesus the Sage*, pp. 219-21.

cillating between a focus on Jesus as sage or Wisdom and a focus on discipleship, until we get to the final section, where we have an eschatological discourse.[5] It is in this discourse that we find the roles of Jesus and the Disciples coming together, and we discover the moral results of rejecting or following Jesus. Sections B and F focus more on discipleship, A, C, D, and E more on the presentation of Jesus as sage or Wisdom. Notice that A, C, D, and E all end with a personification of Wisdom or Jesus speaking as Wisdom.

The significance and preeminence of Jesus are established in the Q tradition in two ways: (1) by the identification of Jesus with Wisdom, who has already come and been rejected, and (2) by the identification of Jesus as Son of Man, in particular the future Son of Man who is yet to come. The two concepts often come together, for instance, in the present saying of the Son of Man about nests. If one takes all of this material together, the overall impression is that Jesus is a prophetic sage, one in whom the sapiential and prophetic/eschatological traditions come together and come to full expression. He is one like, yet greater than, Solomon. He is anointed with the fullness of the Spirit, resists every temptation, and performs wonders and miracles that surpass what Jewish folklore predicated of Solomon. Most significantly at the conclusion of several of the major sections of Q, Jesus is rather clearly identified as Wisdom come in the flesh, Wisdom who is vindicated by her deeds, Wisdom who seeks the lost or laments over Jerusalem as a mother over her children.

It is precisely the Son of Man and Wisdom combination that assures us that we are at an early stage in the thinking about Jesus, a stage in which this material is being handled by Jewish Christians steeped in the Old Testament and intertestamental prophetic and sapiential literature. It will be worthwhile to look briefly at some of the Son of Man material in Q a little more closely. First, in the Son of Man material in Q we find both the present Son of Man who eats and drinks with sinners but also the future Son of Man who will intervene at the close of the age.[6] There is also considerable

5. We have followed the conventional scholarly wisdom that Luke better preserves the order of Q. It is also my view that Luke has tended to edit the Q material more for the sake of his Gentile audience, and so often, but by no means always, we find the earlier more Jewish form of a text or saying in the Matthean form of the material. It is intriguing to note that Mark as well concludes the teaching of Jesus with an eschatological discourse, found in Mark 13.

6. See G. N. Stanton, "On the Christology of Q," in *Christ and the Spirit in the*

stress on sorting out the relationship between Jesus and John in collections of material like Luke 7:18-35 and parallels. It is interesting that by the end of this collection of material John is clearly distinguished from Jesus as not the Son of Man, just as at the beginning of the collection he is distinguished from Jesus as not a miracle worker.

G. N. Stanton points to the association of Isaiah 52:7 and 61:1 in the Qumran scroll 11QMelchizedek identifying the proclaimer of the Good News with God's Anointed One. Reading this Q material in the light of this information suggests that the author of Q is also portraying Jesus as the Messiah who has finally come to bring in the New Age. In other words, this material tries not only to answer the question about the relationship of Jesus and John, but also to make a statement about who Jesus himself was. Thus, despite disclaimers by some scholars, Q does reflect an interest in important Christological questions.

This conviction can only be strengthened when we examine the Q material on the baptism and temptation of Jesus where the issue of whether Jesus is the Son of God is repeatedly raised. Notice that in the Q material the voice at Jesus' baptism is confirming Jesus as God's Son, even to the public in the Matthean form of the text (cf. Matt. 3:17 and parallels), and there is no hint of adoptionist notions about the begetting of the Son at this point. In Luke's version at Luke 3:21ff. John the Baptist's name is not even mentioned, and in the Matthean form of the text a clear attempt is made to portray John as a lesser figure, unworthy to baptize Jesus.

Another major stress in Q with Christological implications is that in and with the ministry of Jesus the dominion of God is dawning. One may compare Matthew 12:28/Luke 11:20 to the Q beatitude in Matthew 5:3/Luke 6:20b. Most scholars regard Matthew 11:2-6/Luke 7:18-23 as the first Q passage, and here we find the theme of Jesus bringing the eschatological and messianic blessings. The theme of Jesus as bringer of the climactic age or revelation or blessing is also apparent in Matthew 13:16-17/Luke 10:23-24.

Stanton sums up as follows: "The Q material answers the questions 'Who was Jesus?' 'With what authority did he act and speak?' In other words it does contain Christological material — in the broadest sense of the term." Q also stresses "that the one anointed with God's Spirit, whose

New Testament: Studies in Honour of Charles Francis Digby Moule, edited by Barnabas Lindars and Stephen S. Smalley (Cambridge: Cambridge University Press, 1973), pp. 27-42.

words and actions marked the dawn of God's age of salvation, was rejected by those to whom he was sent."[7]

It is not at all clear to me that we should talk about a Q community, if by that we mean a community which had no traditions about Jesus except for those we find in Q. Rather, we should likely think in terms of early Jewish Christian communities that used collections of sayings, such as we find in Q before the Gospels were written beginning in the late 60s A.D. and afterward. In view of the skillful sapiential arranging and shaping of the materials reflected in Q it is believable that the collection was put together and edited by a Jewish Christian scribe (or scribes) who was something of a sage himself. This person was steeped in Jewish Wisdom material and sought to highlight the traditions that portrayed Jesus as sage and Wisdom. The lack of a Torah-centric orientation to Q does not discredit this notion as there were many kinds of early scribes and not all were Pharisaic Torah scholars.

In order to show how Jesus differed from previous scribes or sages, our author of Q presented Jesus as not only sage but Wisdom, as not only wise man but Son of Man. In other words, the Christological fruit we find in Q has not fallen far from the tree of Jesus' own self-presentation that bore it. Something greater than Solomon had come into Israel's midst. Indeed, something greater than just another son of man had come into Israel's midst. Wisdom, the Son of Man, had come in person. This is what the editor or editors of Q brought to the fore.

There is no good reason to think that Q was ever intended to be a summary of all that was believed by a particular group of Jesus' followers. The absence of a Passion Narrative, for example, would be telling only if Q represented an exhaustive faith statement of some group of persons. But there is no reason to think that it does. Indeed, the focus on discipleship and Christology makes it reasonably clear that Q was intended for the training of those who already knew the story of Jesus, those who were already his followers. It was not intended as a tool for evangelism, much less an evangelistic tract to be handed out. We have seen in the previous chapter that summaries of the story of the end of Jesus' life occurred in a wide variety of early Christian materials — in creedal statements, in prayers, in hymns, in sermons. It was then not necessary for this summary of the gospel story to appear in all Christian sources or documents. Let us consider some of the notable features of some of this Q material.

7. Stanton, "On the Christology of Q," p. 41.

First of all, if we begin with the material found in the narratives about the temptation of Jesus, we find a very high Christology indeed. The temptations Jesus is presented with, which occur at the beginning of the Q material (see the chart above), are not the temptations of ordinary mortals, who did not struggle with decisions about whether to turn stones into bread and the like. No, Jesus is being tempted as the divine Son of God to so use his divine powers that he will act in ways that his followers could never emulate. The response given by Jesus to the Devil shows that he chooses to respond to temptation in the same way all his disciples could — by relying on the Word of God. Elsewhere in Q Jesus is depicted as relying on the Spirit of God in order to perform miracles (e.g., "If I by the Spirit of God cast out demons . . .") rather than as drawing on some inherent powers resident in his divine nature. In other words, in Q Jesus is depicted as being the divine Son of God, but as choosing to live on the basis of the guidance and power of the Word and the Spirit, an example others could follow. The practical bent even of the more Christological sections of Q needs to be borne in mind.

Certainly another notable feature of the Q material is the stress on the fact that Jesus intensified the Law, went beyond the Law, and in some cases suggested that the Law had been fulfilled and/or superseded by going against it. Each of these tendencies can be illustrated from the Sermon on the Mount material. There is of course the famous saying about adultery of the heart (Matt. 5:28) and the guilt that accrues from it. This can be said to be an intensification of what the Law states, without going against anything the Law says. Second, there is the famous teaching about turning the other cheek, coupled with the counsel about loving enemies. These teachings not only are not found in the Old Testament, but they in fact go against the *lex talionis,* or law about taking revenge (an eye for an eye . . .). This is made especially clear in the Matthean form of the teaching which uses the contrastive formula "You have heard it said . . . , but I say to you." The Old Testament not only doesn't counsel Israel to love its enemies, it also sanctions a degree of violent response to them at various points in the Pentateuch and at various parts of the rest of the Old Testament. Jesus in Q, it will be remembered, also said "Blessed are the peacemakers," not "Blessed are the warmongers." Then there is the matter of oaths. The Old Testament actually encourages oaths of various sorts, and Jesus forbids his followers to swear oaths. The contrast is both striking and clear. One gets the impression that the compilers of Q were not interested in an unnuanced picture of Jesus and his teachings. Rather they chose to show how he affirmed, enhanced, intensified, and even dismissed some of the teaching of Moses in light of the new eschatological situation. What we see is Jesus' freedom and authority exercised in relationship to the tradition. This portrait seems to be somewhat toned down by the First Evangelist, who stresses the continued validity of the Mosaic Law until all of it is fulfilled.

The Q material certainly highlights Jesus' wisdom teaching, including some of his parables and aphorisms, but no more so than Mark or the First and Third Evangelists. In fact this is one of the interesting points of agreement in these four sources. In material unique to Matthew, and in material unique to Luke, and in Q, and in Mark, we find a stress on Jesus' wisdom sayings and parables. The parable of the Lost Sheep, found only in Q, aptly illustrates Jesus' concern for seeking out, finding fellowship with, and redeeming the lost, but this is a theme we find in other Gospel source material as well.

The Q material also underscores Jesus' dealings with and mastery of the powers of darkness. Not only do we have the visionary saying that Jesus saw Satan fall like lightning (Luke 10:18), but we also hear about the struggle with Satan (Luke 11:14-26 and parallels), and about Jesus casting out demons by the Spirit or finger of God (Luke 11:20). The portrait of Jesus in Q is close to Mark but far from John in this respect. The Jewishness of Jesus is clear in Q, but also clear is how radical some of Jesus' Jewish views were. Much more could be said along these lines, but we need to press on.

While there is not space here to go into any depth on this subject, it is worth pointing out as a sort of afterword to the discussion of Q that if there was such a thing as a Q collection it would in no way be surprising that there were also early collections of Jesus' parables or miracle tales before the Gospels were written. For example, in Mark 4 we find not only the parable of the Sower but also the parable of the Mustard Seed and of the Seed Growing Secretly. This may suggest that parables were grouped together on the basis of common or similar themes. Luke 15 suggests the same thing, where we have the parables of the Lost Sheep, the Lost Coin, and the Lost Son.[8] Scholars have often suggested that the seven Sign narra-

8. I am suggesting that perhaps before there was a Q, which also has the Lost Sheep and Lost Coin together, there may have been a collection of paired or similarly themed parables.

tives we find in John 2–11 reflect an earlier source which involved a collection of miracle tales. The plethora of miracle tales in Matthew 8–9 might also suggest a pre-Gospel miracle collection, though we must accept being uncertain of this as we know the First Evangelist's penchant for collecting and arranging parables and other narratives together in clusters.

The Passion and the Glory

Was there a pre-Gospel, written-down Passion Narrative? Many, if not most scholars today think it is likely there was,[9] or at the very least that there was a rather fixed oral tradition that Mark drew upon when he composed the first Gospel.[10] In fact, many think it may have been some of the earliest Jesus material to reach a somewhat fixed and written form. This is so for a variety of reasons, not the least of which is the closeness of all four Gospels on various elements and the basic sequence in the Passion and Resurrection narratives. There is a sequence of events found in all four accounts which Raymond Brown has divided into four acts: (1) Act I — Jesus in Gethsemane, the prayer and arrest; (2) Act II — Jesus before the Jewish authorities; (3) Act III — Jesus before Pilate; and (4) Act IV — the crucifixion and burial of Jesus. The Resurrection narratives in the four Gospels manifest much less common material than the Passion narratives.

It is readily apparent what an important role the citation and allusion to the Old Testament plays in the Passion Narrative. But should we see the Passion Narrative as largely created out of certain Old Testament texts, or should we view the role of the Old Testament as largely interpretative of this portion of the Jesus story? To use a phrase coined by J. D. Crossan, are the Passion narratives largely prophecy historicized, or history prophesied and seen as fulfilled?

The answer to this question must be the latter, for a series of important reasons: First, we find no historical precedent in early Judaism for historicizing prophecy in this sort of whole-scale manner. Second, the use

9. See the survey by J. B. Green, "Passion Narrative," in *The Dictionary of Jesus and the Gospels,* edited by Joel B. Green and Scot McKnight (Downers Grove, Ill.: InterVarsity, 1992), pp. 601-4.

10. The latter view is espoused in the magisterial work by R. Brown, *The Death of the Messiah,* 2 vols. (New York: Doubleday, 1994).

of the Old Testament in this material does not seem to be midrashic. There is no contemporizing of the Old Testament text, but rather an attempt to explain events in the story of Jesus' demise, even odd events, on the basis of Old Testament texts. It is the odd story of Jesus' demise that caused early Christian interpreters to search the Scriptures for understanding of how Jesus' life could have come to such an end. Underlying this search is an attempt to answer the question, Could these events that led to crucifixion really have been God's plan for his Anointed One? This was a pressing question considering the fact that early Jews did not really read Isaiah 53 as being about the Messiah, nor were they looking for a crucified Christ. Third, there are frankly too many elements in the Passion Narrative that cannot be accounted for on the basis of the use of Old Testament texts (e.g., the anointing at Bethany, the sword incident at the arrest, the mention of Simon of Cyrene and his sons, the tearing of the Temple veil). Fourth, it is striking that some obvious Old Testament texts were overlooked if this Passion story was being made up out of prophetic texts. For example, it was widely known in Jesus' era that victims of crucifixion were regularly nailed to crosses. Yet this fact is not mentioned in any part of the Passion Narrative directly (cf. the Easter story in John 20:25 and Acts 2:23), nor is Psalm 22:16, which reads "They pierced my hands and feet," cited to this effect even though Jesus is said to have cited the beginning of this Psalm from the cross. This is almost completely inexplicable if the Passion Narrative is an example of prophecy historicized.[11] One should conclude that whether it was oral or written down, there was a historical story which required interpretation and explanation on the basis of the use of the Old Testament. Those who would have formed such a compelling and highly allusive narrative were surely Jews who cared deeply about demonstrating that Jesus' demise was no tragic accident. On the contrary, it needed to be shown that it was God's preordained plan.

What was likely contained in this pre-Gospel Passion Narrative? We get something of a glimpse of a portion of it in the tradition that Paul passes on in 1 Corinthians 11:23-25, a tradition he astoundingly says he got from the Lord. Probably he means that the sayings in these verses go back to Jesus himself. But notice how the story starts — "On the night when he was betrayed. . . ." Paul clearly knows a passed-down form of the story of the last twenty-four or so hours of Jesus' life, even though he only quotes it

---

11. See Green, "Passion Narrative," pp. 602-3.

very briefly (for example, here is the only place he mentions Judas's role, which elsewhere he says nothing about). I agree with Brown that we probably see the major lines of the primitive form of the story in the events mentioned in all four Gospel writers' Passion accounts. Especially significant is the agreement in numerous places between John and the Synoptics since it is unlikely that John is dependent on any of the Synoptic accounts. Rather the Fourth Evangelist knows the same pre-Gospel story as the other Gospel writers.

It is possible that the primitive Passion story should be pushed back to Jesus' action in the Temple, which seems to have precipitated the Jewish trial and ensuing events. It would then include not only the Temple action but also the Last Supper, the events in the Garden of Gethsemane, the Jewish hearing or trial, the Roman trial, the execution by crucifixion, and the burial. If there was ever a particular portion of the story that early Christians needed to get straight and be able to explain in detail, it was this portion of the story, since crucifixion was not viewed as a noble or honorable way to die, much less as a martyrological way to die. And since the ancients also believed that how one dies most reveals one's true character or nature, there was necessarily a lot of explaining of this story required. The Old Testament is used in an attempt to explain and do apologetics for those who would be skeptical that God would have anything positive to do with such an event, much less that he would use such a hideous death to redeem the world!

Conclusions

The earliest Christians had a viable concern that the story of Jesus and the interpretation of that story might be lost if it was not passed on in a relatively fixed form, first orally, then in writing. Not only worship but pedagogy drove these Christians not only to pass on but eventually to write down various of the things that were later to show up in both the Gospels and the Epistles. Since they were Jews, it is not surprising they passed the materials on as Jews normally did, handling them as sacred traditions, and not just as tales worth retelling. The teaching of Jesus and the ending of Jesus' life came in for especial attention and concern, as these Christians wanted not only appreciation but also worship of and discipleship to Jesus to follow from hearing the story.

No one genre or type of literature would be used to convey the Good News. Sometimes it would be fiction like the parables, sometimes it would be historical narrative like the Passion story, sometimes it would be a collection of sayings like Q, sometimes it would involve creedal fragments, sermon summaries, hymns, and the like, as we saw in the last chapter. The sayings would have had to be translated from Aramaic, and it may even be that some of the narratives were as well, perhaps especially the Passion Narrative if it was written down early on.

We can see the transition from early to late just in the way the Aramaic is handled in the Synoptics. Mark knows both Aramaic and Greek as well as some Latin, and so he translates a few Aramaic terms and phrases for his audience, who were surely Gentiles and some Jews who lived outside of the Holy Land and did not know Aramaic. The First Evangelist seems to have a similar capacity and assumes his audience should know samples from the language of Jesus as well. Luke, however, the latest of the Synoptic writers, says he is relying on sources and deliberately omits the Aramaic he finds in his Markan source. He probably does not understand the language any more than Theophilus would, and indeed Luke probably does not know Hebrew either since he regularly uses citations from the LXX in both Luke and Acts. We should not assume that the Gospel traditions were simply in flux prior to the writing of the Gospels, because they were surely already being used in worship and for teaching and for evangelism well before A.D. 60. The writing of letters led to some sayings and traditions being quoted or used in print well before the compilation of the Gospels.

The preservation of the Jesus traditions did not happen in a vacuum. If we ask the question where it is likely that these traditions were first written down, several factors must be considered. Surely the translation of Aramaic sayings of Jesus, or that of any major Aramaic source, most likely transpired in an environment where Aramaic was spoken. This narrows things down to either the Holy Land or very nearby in a place like Damascus or Antioch where there were probably a good number of Aramaic-speaking Jews. If we ask the question, Where did Paul get his Jesus materials? including the narrative about the Last Supper, again there is no place more likely than Jerusalem, or nearby cities like Damascus or Antioch which we know Paul visited. This is of no small importance because whether it is creedal fragments or hymnic material or an Aramaic prayer like *marana tha* or a collection of sayings or a Passion narrative, all of which Paul uses or seems to know, the crucial question is, Where he would have gotten such material? The answer must be from the earliest Jewish Christians, people like Peter and James and John with whom Paul visited on more than one occasion in Jerusalem. Less likely, but certainly possible, is that Paul received instruction in Damascus or in Antioch about such matters from someone like Ananias or Barnabas.

Does Paul ever quote or use Jesus sayings that are found in Q? Yes he does! Does Paul ever use summaries of the Passion and Resurrection story? 1 Corinthians 11 and 15 show that he does. Does Paul ever use creedal or hymnic or prayer material that reflects a Jewish and sapiential orientation that likely reflects the thinking of the earliest Jewish Christians about Jesus? Yes he does. As it turns out, Paul is the crucial figure in understanding the prehistory of the Gospel story and how it came to be assembled. Already in the 50s, and well before the Gospels were written, Paul was using such materials. This suggests that at a minimum collections of sayings, Passion and Resurrection narrative summaries, and the like were already extant in a relatively fixed form by the time Paul began writing his letters in the middle of the first century A.D. That is to say, such traditions already existed, perhaps even in a written form, within twenty years of Jesus' death, and during the lifetime of the eyewitnesses of the ministry of Jesus.

The story of the New Testament is a story that arises out of the story of Jesus and his followers, which is to say it arises out of the story of a historical and historic movement. The Gospels were not literary fictions created in a social vacuum. They were the literary residue of living communities of faith and worship grounded in early Judaism and carefully and yet creatively preserving Jesus' story because their own stories were continuations of and dependent on that story. We must keep this constantly in mind as we turn to the earliest New Testament documents, the letters of Paul, James, and others.

....

Exercises and Questions for Study and Reflection

→ Take two Bibles, preferably the same translation, and turn to the Sermon on the Mount in Matthew 5–7 and the Sermon on the Plain in Luke 6. Write down the similarities between these two texts, and also write down the differences. Are these passages from the same material, or do you think they involve material taken from several different but similar teaching occasions of Jesus? If they are not from different sources, how do you account for the differences?

→ What is Q, and why is the question about its existence important if we have all of its material in either Matthew or Luke or both?

→ Is Q simply a collection of sayings of Jesus, or is there more to it?

→ What does the Q collection tell us about Jesus and how he was portrayed by the earliest Christians?

→ What language did Jesus speak? What language is the New Testament written in? What difficulties does this present when we are dealing with the sayings of Jesus?

→ Was there a written-down Passion Narrative before the Gospel of Mark was written? If so, what stories did it contain?

→ Do we find any trace of sayings of Jesus elsewhere in the New Testament but not in the Gospels? If so, where? What does this tell us?

3 | Letters and Homilies for Converts

The earliest canonical writings that we have are the various letters of Paul.[1] They predate not only works like the Book of Acts and John's Revelation but also in all likelihood the Gospels as well. The earliest letter we have from Paul's pen however does not date to earlier than about A.D. 49. This is why we did not begin this study with the letters of Paul. A good deal of time and teaching and preaching had already transpired by the time Paul wrote Galatians. The gospel was by no means invented by Paul, any more than the early Christian movement was invented by Paul. Yet Paul in the end contributed more documents to the New Testament than any other single figure. Almost half of the documents, an amazing thirteen documents out of a total of twenty-seven in the New Testament canon, are attributed to Paul. In pages, some fifty-one pages out of a total of two hundred and eighty-six New Testament pages are attributed to Paul. We must consider his efforts and that of other letter writers and preachers in this chapter.

Let us first consider Paul as a letter writer. All of the letters we have from him, like all other letters in the New Testament, are written to one or more Christians or groups of Christians. We have no letters to those out-

1. There are numerous full-scale treatments of the questions of New Testament introduction in English. Three of the best are: P. J. Achtemeier, J. B. Green, and M. M. Thompson, *Introducing the New Testament: Its Literature and Theology* (Grand Rapids: Eerdmans, 2001); L. T. Johnson, *The Writings of the New Testament* (Minneapolis: Fortress, 1999); and R. E. Brown, *An Introduction to the New Testament* (New York: Doubleday, 1997). At a more popular level but in more detail than this study, see J. Drane, *Introducing the New Testament* (Minneapolis: Fortress, 2001).

side the Christian circle in the New Testament. Thus we must reconcile ourselves to the fact that what we will find in these letters is insider communication. We do not really know what a letter to a non-Christian would look like in this early period, and more particularly we do not know what an apologetic letter, introducing the faith to a non-Christian, would have looked like.

Paul, on all accounts, was an extraordinary person. In the first place, he was multilingual. Galatians 6:11 shows that Paul could not only understand Greek but also write it. Philippians 3:5 probably demonstrates he knew Hebrew, and 1 Corinthians 16:22 bears witness to his knowledge of Aramaic. In addition to all that, Paul reflects an extensive knowledge not only of the Old Testament, but also of Greco-Roman rhetoric. The attempt to paint Paul as just another unsophisticated early Christian preacher will not work. Paul was surely one of the great minds, great educators, and great communicators of his era. A later Christian writer says, "Bear in mind that our Lord's patience means salvation, just as our dear brother Paul also wrote to you with the wisdom God gave him. He writes the same way in all his letters, speaking in them of these matters. His letters contain some things that are hard to understand, which ignorant and unstable people distort, as they do the other Scriptures, to their own destruction" (2 Pet. 3:15-16). This comment, written not only after Paul's death but also apparently after a collection of Paul's letters is circulating through a considerable portion of the Church, bears witness to the considerable impact of Paul's writings, and also to the level of their content. So far as we can tell, Paul was the first profound and profoundly persuasive Christian writer to interpret the Christ event.

Letters in a largely oral culture are by and large surrogates for a direct conversation the author would rather have had in person. They have various oral and aural features to them. Paul, like some other ancient writers, takes the oral dimension a step further by writing in a rhetorically effective way, which is to say, Paul follows the Greco-Roman conventions on speeches as he writes his letters. One of the reasons Paul's letters, with the exception of their beginnings and endings, do not look much like most other ancient letters in either content or length is that they are in fact long-winded speeches written down, speeches Paul would rather have delivered in person but instead must have one of his coworkers, or another rhetorically adept Christian, perform for him at the letter's destination. Colossians 4:16 makes evident that Paul's letters were meant to be read aloud at their destination and in the congregation.[2] This is even true of a document like Philemon. Only the so-called Pastoral Epistles (1 and 2 Timothy and Titus) may originally have fallen into the category of purely personal and private letters, and yet even they became part of the sacred texts of the early Christian movement, read and learned by one and all.

To judge not only from Paul's letters but from other New Testament documents, Christianity seems to have been led by a literate elite who at least in terms of their education were of higher social status than many involved in the movement. E. A. Judge says that "far from being a socially depressed group . . . the Christians were dominated by a socially pretentious section of the population of big cities. Beyond that they seem to have drawn on a broad constituency, probably representing household dependents of leading members. . . . The peasantry and persons in slavery on the land were the most underprivileged classes. Christianity left them largely untouched."[3]

Paul had an urban ministry strategy, largely focusing on major cities like Ephesus, Philippi, Thessalonike, and Corinth, and he seems to have had particular success in cities where his own status as a Roman citizen would have opened numerous doors, which is to say in Roman colony cities like Philippi and Corinth. He deliberately couched his message in ways that would have attracted a cross-section of the population of the ancient world, attempting to be all things to all persons so that by all means he might win some (1 Cor. 9:19-23). Paul turned to letter writing to nurture and correct distant converts, and even, as in the case of Romans, to address those who were not Paul's converts but with whom Paul wanted to associate and wield some influence. J. Murphy-O'Connor has rightly underscored that "oratorical skills were the key to advancement in an essentially verbal culture. The acquisition of such skills fell into three parts . . . the theory of discourse which included letter writing[, t]he study of the speeches of the great masters of rhetoric . . . [and] the writing of practice speeches."[4] Paul manifests in his letters that his own education involved all three of these activities.

2. Almost all ancient reading was done aloud, even when one intended to read alone (see Acts 8:30).

3. E. A. Judge, *The Social Pattern of Christian Groups in the First Century* (London: Tyndale, 1960), pp. 52, 60.

4. J. Murphy-O'Connor, *Paul: A Critical Life* (Oxford: Oxford University Press, 1996), p. 50.

It is fair to say that Paul had few peers when it came to writing long and profound letters. Even his opponents recognized his letters as weighty and strong (2 Cor. 10:10). How very different they were in comparison to ordinary letters of the day such as the following one which was written at about the same time in the mid-century that Paul was writing 1 Corinthians: "Mystarion to his own Stoetis: Greetings. I have sent Blastus to get forked sticks for my olive gardens. See that he does not loiter, for you know I need him every hour. Farewell" (written September 13, A.D. 50).

It is important to bear in mind that letters were essentially private communications prior to the time of Cicero in the first century B.C. Letters were not meant for public consumption much less publication prior to Cicero. Cicero was the first to begin to publish letters, and sometimes to write public letters that were group communications, as almost all of Paul's letters are.

Letters during the New Testament era tended to follow the stereotyped format of the period, which involved most of the following features, which are the regular features of Paul's letters:

1. Opening, sender, addressee
2. Initial greeting
3. Thanksgiving or blessing
4. Body, complete with introductory formula, body proper, conclusion, sometimes a travelog
5. Parenesis or ethical remarks
6. Closing greetings
7. Writing process and signature
8. Closing benediction

Apart from no. 8 and the fact that Paul tended to close the body of the letter with an eschatological conclusion followed by ethical remarks, things not usually found in a pagan letter (though Cicero did on occasion give ethical advice in his letters), Paul's letters manifest the same general form as other ancient letters. It was just that the bodies of Paul's letters were much longer. We should remember that Paul's letters were only ad hoc documents, written to be words on target dealing with particular matters of importance at the time, and they were written as part of a larger communication effort involving Paul being present and speaking directly to his converts, Paul sending oral messages through coworkers and other traveling Christians, and Paul writing letters. The letters then are only the visible tip of the iceberg of communication that we can still see today.

Galatians — The Earliest Extant Christian Letter

There is debate about which of Paul's letters is the earliest. Some scholars think it is 1 Thessalonians, while others think it is Galatians. Much depends on when one thinks Galatians was written in relationship to the Apostolic Council meeting recorded in Acts 15. In my view, the better argument is made by those who say Galatians was written to converts in south Galatia (Pisidian Antioch, Iconium, Lystra) and so was written after the first missionary journey of Paul (Acts 13–14) and before the Council in A.D. 50.[5] We have no letters of Paul from the period of time between his conversion in the mid-30s and A.D. 49, and in fact Galatians is the only letter addressed to converts that Paul made on his first missionary journey. The rest of his letters come from a period of time after the second missionary journey, which transpired in A.D. 50-52. Obviously, letters written to the churches founded on that mission would have to date from no earlier than about A.D. 52.

Galatians is a crucial letter in many regards, not least because it enunciates some of Paul's major themes such as righteousness by grace through faith, "Christ and him crucified," the fruit of the Spirit, the law of Christ, Paul's view of the Mosaic Law, the imitation of Christ, Abraham as an exemplar, the role of the Spirit in the Christian's life, Paul's apostolic authority, the importance of the Gentile mission, Paul's relationship with Peter, James, and Barnabas among others, Paul's conversion, the faith/faithfulness of Christ, and the freedom believers have in Christ. It also reveals Paul at his most polemical, and so gives some real insight into what drove the man, what his passions were. In this same letter we have the remarkable statement found at Galatians 3:28 about the baptismal unity of all believers in Christ which transcends and is intended to transform all social, sexual, and racial or ethnic distinctions or divisions. This letter also clearly enunciates the notion of what was later called orthodoxy, namely, that there are right and wrong conceptions of and representations of the

---

5. See the discussion at length in my *Grace in Galatia: A Commentary on St. Paul's Letter to the Galatians* (Grand Rapids: Eerdmans, 1998), pp. 8-48.

gospel, and there are nonnegotiable truths involved. This orthodoxy involves both theological and ethical matters. One can go beyond the pale not only in how one thinks about the gospel but also in how one behaves. Paul is most exercised in this letter to prevent the Galatians from submitting to circumcision and the requirement of obeying the Mosaic Law, which was being urged on them by Jewish Christian agitators who likely came from Jerusalem.

One of the keys to reading this letter or any Pauline letter is to analyze the rhetorical structure of the letter and find the basic proposition or thesis statement (known in rhetorical terms as the *propositio*). In Galatians this thesis statement is found at 2:15-21, which reads:

> We by nature are Jews and not sinners from the [Gentile] nations, and seeing that a human being is not acquitted from works of the Law but through the faithfulness of Jesus Christ, even we began to believe in Jesus Christ, in order that we might be set right by the faithfulness of Jesus Christ and not by works of the Law, because "by works of the Law no one will be set right." But if seeking to be acquitted by Christ we ourselves were found to be at the same time sinners, then is Christ a servant of sin? Absolutely not! For if I build up again what was once destroyed, I show myself to be a transgressor. For I through the Law died to the Law in order that I might live to God. I have been crucified with Christ. I no longer live, but Christ lives in me. But now living in the flesh, I am living in the faith — that of the Son of God who loved me and gave himself for me. I do not render invalid the grace of God, for if through the Law there is righteousness, then Christ died for nothing![6]

Paul seems to be concerned with two major things. First, what are the implications of the fact that believers are saved by grace through faith (subjectively) and (objectively) through the faithfulness of Christ even unto death on the cross? Second, how then should Christians live in view of the basis and fact of salvation? It is this latter matter that Paul spends most of his argumentative verbiage on in this letter. In a world where the essence of religion was seen as having to do with priests, temples, precisely performed liturgies, and sacrifices, Paul is enunciating a religion which has right thinking and right living as the essence of the matter, and rituals

6. The translation is my own.

playing only a secondary role.[7] The issue of behavior and rituals comes up again in the second earliest letter we have from the pen of a New Testament author, namely, the letter of James to Gentile converts in the Diaspora written at the Apostolic Council in A.D. 50 (and found in Acts 15) and taken along by Paul and his coworkers on the second missionary journey. We turn now to this letter, as well as to the canonical letter of James.

The Letters of James

I like to see just how alert my students are, and so I regularly ask them how many letters of James we have in the New Testament. Of course they almost always respond, "Only one." This however is not quite correct. The ruling of James found in Acts 15:19-21 is turned into a letter from James and the other apostles and elders in Jerusalem written in A.D. 50 (Acts 15:23-29). The letter is important as it passes along a ruling that in essence requires Gentiles to avoid going to pagan temples and so avoid the sort of idolatry and immorality associated with that venue.[8] The letter recognizes that Gentile converts were being pestered by Judaizing Christians, and it also recognizes the need not to burden Gentiles with a lot of Jewish requirements. The essence of what is required of them is to do what the heart of the Ten Commandments requires — avoid idolatry and immorality. Neither circumcision nor food laws per se are being imposed on the Gentiles. The issue is eating food sacrificed to idols and served in temples, and so it is more a matter of venue than menu. It is my view that once this ruling was circulated in letter form to the Pauline (and other Gentile) churches in Syria, Cilicia, and presumably elsewhere, Paul then made a good faith effort to implement the decree in places like Corinth and Thessalonike, as well as in Galatia.[9]

The other and more familiar letter of James comes from slightly later but seems to have been written within a few years of the Apostolic Council

7. Notice how very little Paul says about baptism in this letter, and how much he emphasizes life in the Spirit (cf. Galatians 3 and 5).

8. See the book I coauthored with H. Shanks, *The Brother of Jesus: The Dramatic Story and Meaning of the First Archaeological Link to Jesus and His Family* (San Francisco: HarperCollins, 2003), pp. 132-39.

9. On which see pp. 60-62 below.

in 50, and may well date to about the same time as Paul's next letter, the first letter to the Thessalonians (or possibly just a little later). In fact it is not so much a letter as a homily, or sermon, drawing on a plethora of Jesus' sayings and other wisdom teachings and creatively reworking them for a new audience. In his canonical letter, James is writing to Jewish Christians outside the Holy Land. Interestingly then, the only two written communiqués we have from the first head of the earliest church in Jerusalem are two documents written first to all Gentile converts outside the Holy Land, and then to all Jewish converts outside the Holy Land.

To write to either Gentiles or Jews outside of Israel, James had to be able to write in Greek, which means that James was bilingual or used a good scribe who was bilingual. One of the telltale signs that he might well have been bilingual like Paul is that in Acts 15:16-18 James chooses to quote the Greek version of a text from Amos which best supports his case. This was a normal early Jewish practice, going with the version that helps make one's point, and as Richard Bauckham has demonstrated there is no reason why James himself could not have done such a thing.[10]

But did James, the brother of Jesus, really write the Epistle of James we find in the canon? The matter is disputed by scholars, but probably a majority of scholars now think James is responsible for this letter. The self-effacing way that the author presents himself as the servant of Jesus, rather than as the brother of Jesus, supports this line of thinking, as do the many allusions to the Sermon on the Mount found in James. Notice that the use of the heading "to the Twelve Tribes of the Diaspora" means not only that it is written to Jews, but also from Israel, in this case likely from Jerusalem. On first blush, it might appear that the letter was written to all Jews, including non-Christian ones, but once one reads through the letter it becomes apparent that only followers of Jesus are being addressed. "Early Jewish Christians thought of themselves, not as a specific sect distinguished from other Jews, but as the nucleus of the Messianic renewal of the people of Israel, which was under way and would come to include all Israel. . . . What James addresses in practice to those Jews who already confess the Messiah Jesus, he addresses in principle to all Israel."[11]

---

10. See R. J. Bauckham, "James and the Gentiles (Acts 15.13-21)," in *History, Literature, and Society in the Book of Acts,* edited by B. Witherington (Cambridge: Cambridge University Press, 1996), pp. 154-84.

11. R. J. Bauckham, *James* (London: Routledge, 1999), p. 16.

This letter seems in part to have been written not long after Paul's ministry had begun to have a considerable impact in the Diaspora, and was raising doubts and concerns among Jewish followers of Jesus who lived outside the Holy Land. This letter was intended to give ethical guidance and to help some Jewish believers sort out and not be confused by some garbled reports about Paul's message. Let us be clear that while Paul and James differed as to whether Jewish followers of Jesus ought to be obligated to keep the Mosaic Law, they did not differ on either salvation being a matter of grace and faith or on the importance of obedience and good works once one was a Christian. Genuine Christian faith works, it could be said.

The canonical Letter of James reflects the stream of early Jewish tradition known as Wisdom literature, and it is much like the teaching of Jesus in this and other respects. Aphorisms, riddles, proverbs, parables, and the like are used to convey a truth which aids one in leading a life pleasing to God. It is telling that James is so indebted to his brother's teaching, particularly the teaching as it is found in the Matthean version of the Sermon on the Mount. Consider the following texts: James 1:4/Matthew 5:48; James 1:5/Matthew 7:7; James 1:17/Matthew 7:11; James 1:22/Matthew 7:24; James 2:5/Matthew 5:3, 5; James 2:10/Matthew 5:18-19; James 2:13/Matthew 5:7; James 3:12/Matthew 7:16-18; James 3:18/Matthew 5:9; James 4:2-3/Matthew 7:8; James 4:11/Matthew 7:1-2; James 5:2-3/Matthew 6:19-21; James 5:12/Matthew 5:34-37. There are more parallels than these, but these are sufficient to demonstrate the connection. In general James does not directly quote his brother; he uses the concepts in similar ways but makes the ideas, the Jesus tradition, his own.

James is basically enunciating a sort of community ethic, and giving samples of the sort of conduct he has in mind. He is mainly concerned about how Christians relate to each other. Some of his main concerns include caring for widows and orphans, avoiding "friendship" with the world, fulfilling the commandment to love one's neighbor as oneself, bridling one's tongue, persevering in the midst of trials, confessing sins, and praying for the sick and suffering. The ethics James teaches, he teaches with one eye on the eschatological horizon, looking for the second coming of the Lord who is also the Judge (see James 5:3-7). Like his brother he believes that the eschatological situation has upped the ethical ante. Thus he too speaks about wholeness, perfection, wholehearted loyalty to God, and fulfilling the whole royal Law. The opposite of this is double-mindedness or saying one thing and doing another.

It is clear that, like his brother, James is a sage, and he is concerned about the followers of Jesus not losing their sense of identity. This is why he is concerned to carefully set up boundaries of speech and behavior and relationships. To use sociological terms, he is inculcating a high-group but low-grid type of community, by which is meant a community with a clear sense of identity but without a highly stratified or hierarchical leadership structure. Some of James's wisdom is of a counter-order, going against the flow of conventional wisdom found in Proverbs about wealth and poverty, and some of it would seem to be counterintuitive in the Greco-Roman world where humility and becoming a servant of others was not seen as a plus or a desirable course of action.

Jude

Servanthood is also on the mind of Jude as is clear from the very first verse of this brief missive. Most scholars think that the author of this document was indeed the brother of Jesus and of James. It is noteworthy that he identifies himself as the brother of James without further clarification, which surely indicates that the James in question was so well known that further explication was not required. The Jude in question then is mentioned as the next oldest, after James, in the holy family in the Gospels (Matt. 13:55; Mark 6:3, the lists would normally be in descending order from eldest to youngest), and like his brother James, he was not a follower of Jesus during Jesus' earthly ministry (see John 7:5). Servanthood to Jesus for both James and Jude came after Easter, not before. This document reflects the sort of Jewish-Christian eschatology and even apocalyptic thinking we find in Paul's early letters and in Mark. Jude writes at a time when false teachers have infiltrated the group of Christians to whom he writes, and in this regard this document bears some resemblance to Galatians and to 2 Corinthians.

The letter of Jude is quite polemical, attacking the false teachers using various examples — they are like the fallen angels of Genesis 6, or like Cain and Balaam or Korah. The judgment that will come on them is enunciated using both a tradition from 1 Enoch 1:9 (quoted in Jude 14-15) and also apostolic tradition. Jude, like James, is striving to inculcate a high group sense of identity, but he does so by using historical examples and eschatological teaching rather than relying primarily on wisdom material. He wishes his audience not merely to keep the faith, but to contend for it. It is difficult to know to whom exactly this letter is addressed in particular, but Jewish Christians are a likely bet, and probably Jewish Christians found in some city near to the Holy Land, such as Damascus or Antioch. This letter also reflects the particularism or ad hoc character that is especially a hallmark of Paul's undisputed letters.

1 and 2 Thessalonians

By the time Paul wrote 1 Thessalonians from Corinth, where he stayed for about a year and a half in A.D. 50-51, he had already pretty much completed his second missionary journey, and he was writing to recent converts made on that selfsame trip. It will be noted immediately that Paul in the very first chapter of 1 Thessalonians reminds his converts how they have turned from idols to worship the one true God (1:9-10) and have adopted an eschatological outlook that involves eagerly anticipating the return of Christ. Here, at least in verse 9 it seems we have an echo of the Decree of James, which indicates that Paul made it a priority to insist that his largely Gentile audience make a clean break with paganism.

Both 1 and 2 Thessalonians are coauthored documents from Paul, Silas, and their coworker Timothy to the converts in Thessalonike. How much this really affects the content (for example is there really any non-Pauline material in these letters, much less un-Pauline material) has been debated by scholars, as has the Pauline character of 2 Thessalonians in general. 1 Thessalonians 3:6 would appear to suggest that Paul and Silas are the main authors of this material. Both of these letters indicate that the Thessalonian Christians had been suffering and continued to suffer for their commitment to Christ. This probably explains some of the polemics we find at 1 Thessalonians 2:13-16. It may also help explain the heavily and explicitly eschatological content of both these letters. It is also probably a further clue about the ethnic extraction of almost all the audience that: (1) Paul speaks polemically of "the Jews," by which he may mean Jewish officials or missionaries; and (2) he never cites the Old Testament in either 1 or 2 Thessalonians, unlike many of his other letters. When we add this to 1 Thessalonians 1:9, it seems clear that Gentiles are the focal audience of these documents. One gets the impression not only from 1 Thessalonians 4–5, but also from 2 Thessalonians 2 that Paul's initial eschatological teaching (see 1 Thess. 1:10) had not only raised questions but led to some misunderstandings about topics such as the timing of the second coming and whether those who died before Christ's return would participate in the resurrection. The eschatological beliefs of some of these new converts had apparently also affected their willingness to work.

Since Paul's return to Thessalonike was hindered or prevented (1 Thess. 2:18), Paul had to suffice with sending Timothy back (1 Thess. 3:2). It would appear that these letters are written after Timothy's return to Corinth with his report about the stability and issues the congregation still faced. Paul is very thankful indeed for the essentially positive report that Timothy brings back. This may be why only in these two Pauline letters do we find at least two thanksgiving sections (1 Thess. 1:2-10; 2:13-16; 2 Thess. 1:3-4; 2:13-14), and in fact it can be said that there is a third such section in 1 Thessalonians 3:9-10.

The usual objections to 2 Thessalonians being post-Pauline have been shown to be weak in recent treatments of these letters in commentaries.[12] In the first place both in early Judaism and also in the Jesus tradition language about a possibly imminent end of some sort was often juxtaposed with a discussion of preliminary events (Mark 13). There is no conflict between what one finds in 1 Thessalonians 4–5 and what one finds in 2 Thessalonians 2. The difference in tone between the two letters may be because the situation had changed between the writing of 1 and 2 Thessalonians. The reason for the lack of personal references in 2 Thessalonians is uncertain, but perhaps we should see 2 Thessalonians as more of a general homily and 1 Thessalonians as more of an ad hoc document. In any case the other stylistic differences between 1 and 2 Thessalonians are not significant enough to warrant the conclusion that it is likely 2 Thessalonians is by someone else. Perhaps Silas had more of a hand in 2 Thessalonians than in 1 Thessalonians. This might explain some of the minor differences. It is also possible, as some have conjectured, that 2 Thessalonians was chronologically the first of these two letters, and thus 1 Thessalonians reflects some of the reaction to the earlier letter.

---

12. See, e.g., C. Wanamaker, *1 and 2 Thessalonians* (Grand Rapids: Eerdmans, 1990).

1 and 2 Corinthians

There is somewhat of a gap of time between when the Thessalonian correspondence was written and when the Corinthian correspondence was
written. Paul returned to Antioch from Corinth and then proceeded on his
third missionary journey. This series of movements especially is not really
just a journey since it lasted from A.D. 53 to A.D. 57 and furthermore en-
tailed the time Paul spent in one place, namely, Ephesus, for more than two
years. In addition, this period in Paul's life does not really involve much
church planting except perhaps in Ephesus and its environs. It is more a
matter of Paul strengthening churches he had already founded in Galatia,
Macedonia, Achaia, and elsewhere. The pattern of Paul often staying in
one place until he is driven out and must go to another city repeats itself at
the end of his time in Ephesus. In Ephesus he had a considerable period of
time to write letters, and we know of at least four letters that Paul wrote to
Corinth from that locale. Unfortunately we have only two of them, known
to us as 1 and 2 Corinthians.

1 Corinthians 5:9-10 refers to a letter, now apparently lost, which Paul
wrote to the Corinthian Christians. Of course not all documents, even by
apostolic figures, made it into the New Testament. 1 Corinthians seems to
be the second letter Paul wrote to the converts in Corinth in either A.D. 53
or 54. If we may characterize Paul's letters to congregations as either
problem-solving letters or progress-oriented letters, 1 Corinthians is definitely a problem-solving letter. The problems have become so exacerbated
that the congregation is in danger of splitting apart. Already there are divisions and factions apparently along house church and social lines.[13] Paul
then decides to write a letter of unitive rhetoric, trying to produce peace
and concord and reconciliation in a fractured congregation. The proof
that this is the aim of Paul's rhetoric in 1 Corinthians is clear enough from
the thesis statement in 1 Corinthians 1:10-11 where Paul appeals to the Corinthians that they might all be of one united mind, no longer nurture divisions, stop quarreling, and agree with one another. The rhetorical question in 1:13 — "Is Christ divided?" — is meant to imply another one —
"Should Christ's Body be divided?" What we find in 1 Corinthians is a tour

13. See my discussion of these matters in *Conflict and Community in Corinth: A
Socio-Rhetorical Commentary on 1 and 2 Corinthians* (Grand Rapids: Eerdmans, 1995),
pp. 1ff.

Paul's two-year ministry in Corinth made a considerable impact there, and it resulted in the conversion of a high-status Corinthian official named Erastus (see Romans 16:23), who is mentioned in this inscription in stone found in front of the Corinthian theater. It reads, in essence, "Erastus, for the office of aedile, paved this."

de force argument trying to produce unity on both theological and ethical and social grounds and terms.

Paul has to fight on a variety of fronts in order to deal with the problems in Corinth. On the one hand, in 1 Corinthians 1–4 he must deal with their desire for knowledge and wisdom, or more appropriately for their desire to appear to be people in the know and wise. He must also deal at length with the residual influence of their pagan background not only in regard to matters of sexual immorality but also in regard to their using secular law courts, eating in pagan temples, and the like. In particular, there seem to have been some higher status Corinthian Christians who were refusing to sever their ties with their social milieu even when it conflicted with their Christian faith. Paul then decides not only to call for a church disciplinary action against someone who married his father's wife, but he chooses to implement the Decree of James in a lengthy argument in 1 Corinthians 8–10, insisting on no more fraternizing in pagan temples. On top of all this Paul chooses to tell the Corinthians how they should run their married or single lives (1 Corinthians 7), how they are to partake of their fellowship meals including the Lord's Supper (1 Corinthians 11), and how they are to exercise their spiritual gifts in worship (1 Corinthians 11–14). His discourses are framed with a discussion of baptism and the death of

Paul worked with his hands in Corinth, making tents. It is here that he probably first met Erastus, who was collecting money as the city treasurer, and it is also probably here that Paul did some of his writing of letters, perhaps including Romans.

Jesus at the outset (1 Corinthians 1) and resurrection and a different sort of practice of baptism at the conclusion of his arguments (1 Corinthians 15).

However much we may be impressed with Paul's rhetoric in 1 Corinthians, it is a sobering fact that this letter must not have had the full effect that Paul wanted or we would not have what we find in 2 Corinthians. 2 Corinthians 2:3-9 tells us that after the writing of 1 Corinthians, Paul made a short painful visit to Corinth, was rebuffed, and then wrote a sharp letter of anguish that some scholars have identified with 2 Corinthians 10–13. This is probably incorrect since this material refers to a past visit by Titus to Corinth (12:18), nor is there any reference in 2 Corinthians 10–13 to the person who accosted Paul during his brief, painful visit. 2 Corinthians may be a composite letter, but most scholars are in agreement that the parts are all Pauline. It would appear that none of it was written before A.D. 55, and probably it was composed a bit later than that. This suggests that

Paul's relationship with the Corinthians continued to be tumultuous for some time, not least because the Corinthians were only partially socialized Christians with one foot in the pagan world and one foot in the Church.

Romans

The letter to the Roman Christians seems to have been written from Corinth in about A.D. 56 or 57. Unlike the earlier letters of Paul, this letter is not written to those who were Paul's own converts, and this somewhat affects Paul's rhetorical strategy in this letter. That however does not make this a theological treatise or a generic letter. Paul is well aware of the various issues which are percolating in the Roman church, and he addresses them in various ways, doing so quite directly from Romans 9 onward.[14]

Romans cannot be seen as a summary of Paul's gospel, not least because many of the major Pauline themes are missing from this letter, such as a treatment of resurrection (cf. 1 Corinthians 15) or the Lord's Supper, or a variety of other subjects. What we do find is a rhetorically adept and masterful treatment of certain key themes Paul thought would be germane to share with the Roman Christians prior to visiting them. The central theme or thesis is not difficult to find — Paul is not ashamed to proclaim the gospel for it is the power of God for the salvation of everyone, to the Jew first and also to the Gentile, because in the gospel a righteousness from God is revealed, a righteousness that is from faithfulness to faith just as Habakkuk said, "The righteous will live by faith" (Rom. 1:16-17). There is clearly enough an overlap between Paul's earlier treatment of righteousness by and through faith in Galatians, and what we find in Romans, even to the point that Paul uses the Abraham example in both acts of persuasion, though with differing emphases and nuances. Paul here, as in 1 Corinthians, is concerned about helping to unite a very divided group of Christians in Rome, and to make especially clear to the Gentile majority that they need the Jewish minority and are indebted to them and to Judaism in general for their faith heritage.

There was indeed a very difficult and touchy situation going on in Rome, for Jews had been marginalized and some Jewish Christians even

14. On this letter see the work that Darlene Hyatt and I have done in *The Epistle to the Romans* (Grand Rapids: Eerdmans, 2003), pp. 1ff.

sent into exile (see Acts 18) when Claudius wrote his decree in A.D. 49, and they were only beginning to come back into the city and reestablish themselves beginning in A.D. 54. Paul is writing in the wake of that devastating series of events and trying very hard to help the Jewish Christian minority in Rome be more fully accepted by the Gentile majority. The tensions bubble to the surface of the argument in Romans 9–15. Paul is also countering the latent and sometimes overt anti-Semitism of Roman life in the capital city as well. God had not forsaken his first chosen people or replaced them with Roman Gentiles.

A careful reading of Romans will show that Paul deals first with Gentiles, then turns to Jews, then deals with Christians in the various arguments found in Romans 1–8. Of course there are also comments about Christians all along throughout this portion of the discourse; the general trajectory of the arguments needs to be recognized. By the time Paul gets to the ethical portion of the letter he wants to address how all Christians should live (see Romans 12–15).

Philippians, Philemon, Colossians, Ephesians

About the authorship of Philippians and Philemon there is little debate. Paul wrote them. There is more debate about whether he penned Colossians, and even more as to whether Ephesians came from Paul's hand. There is also debate in regard to all of these letters as to when and where they were written. Some scholars favor a date in the 50s for two or more of these letters and connect them with Paul's being in prison in Ephesus. This latter suggestion is largely an argument from silence since neither Paul's letters nor Acts tells us that Paul was imprisoned in Ephesus, and 1 Corinthians 15:32 should probably not be taken literally as a reference to Paul being taken captive and thrown to the lions in the Ephesian arena. Even if we did take the reference literally, it would have to refer to an imprisonment before Paul wrote 1 Corinthians, which is to say before A.D. 53 or so. And where do we have evidence of Paul being in such a situation in Ephesus? The answer is we have no such evidence. In fact there is a strong reason to take the reference to struggling with wild beasts as a metaphor for a struggle with other human beings in Ephesus. The phrase *kata anthropon* in 1 Corinthians 15:32 likely means to speak according to a human metaphor or as we would put it, "as they say." The phrase is used in later literature as a metaphor as well (see Ignatius Rom. 5.1; Plutarch *De virtute morali* 439). It is understandable that an incident like the one described in Acts 19:23-41 might be referred to in the way Paul uses the metaphor in 1 Corinthians 15. The Ephesians were acting like wild beasts in response to the preaching of Paul. Sometimes 2 Corinthians 1:8-10 is brought into the picture, but this also refers only to an affliction, not to an imprisonment.

Sometimes it is suggested that Philippians or these other captivity epistles could not have been written from Rome because Rome is too far away from Philippi or the Lycus Valley in Asia Minor for Paul to be saying things like "prepare a guest room for me" (Philemon 22). This underestimates the mobility of Paul and other early Christians. It also forgets that had Paul been in prison rather than just in chains (as Phil. 1:7, 14; Col. 4:18; Eph. 6:20), prison was only a holding pattern prior to judgment, but during such a time it is unlikely Paul would have been able to write and send letters the way that he did, or have so many visitors the way these letters suggest he did during that time. Even Philemon says Paul is a prisoner only of Christ (vv. 1, 10, 13, 23) not a prisoner of Rome. Paul's remarks about the Praetorian guard in Philippians 1:13, and about Caesar's household in 4:22, are more naturally taken as spoken from Rome. This in turn means that if these letters are from Paul's hand, they were likely written while Paul was under house arrest in Rome, which is to say, during the period A.D. 60-62.[15]

There may be some sort of literary relationship between Colossians and Ephesians since Colossians 4:7-8 and Ephesians 6:21-22 are nearly word for word identical in the Greek, and most scholars would argue that Ephesians is dependent on Colossians, not only here but also in the household code material found in Colossians 3-4 and Ephesians 5-6. The personalia mentioned in Philemon and Colossians are basically the same, which suggests that the letters were written at about the same time (and by the same person as well). In my view these documents were composed as follows: (1) Philemon and Colossians were written concurrently and deliv-

15. It has sometimes been suggested that perhaps Paul wrote these letters from Caesarea Maritima when he was under house arrest there. But there is an atmosphere of danger in these captivity epistles that is not commensurate with the situation we find Paul in at Caesarea. Paul was a Roman citizen, and he could always appeal to the emperor if he did not like the way things were going in Caesarea. It is more likely that these letters were written from a locale where Paul's case was going to be resolved one way or another.

ered at the same time to the household of Philemon and then the latter document was circulated to Laodicea and perhaps elsewhere. (2) Ephesians was written after these two documents and is in fact not really a letter but rather a homily meant to circulate through several churches. As a homily it is written in the popular style of Asiatic rhetoric famous for its ornamental character and long periods. It also reflects epideictic rhetoric (in praise of the nature of God's creation of a people — Jew and Gentile united in Christ) on a scale hitherto not found in Paul's letters (though see 1 Corinthians 13). It is not at all impossible that Ephesians is a sermon from Paul done in a rhetorically effective way in order to grab the attention of Asian Christians very familiar with Asiatic rhetoric. The epistolary elements in Ephesians were added to Ephesians possibly after the fact, or when Ephesians became a homily that also circulated through these churches. All of these documents were likely written in A.D. 60-61. Philippians, which is clearly written to a very different audience in Macedonia, is probably the last of these documents to be written (A.D. 62), for it is the one document which most reflects an atmosphere of imminent danger or release.[16]

There are common themes in these letters such as the discussion of slavery in Philemon, Colossians, and Ephesians, or the discussion of the Christological core of the faith brought out by quoting one or another Christological hymn (cf. Colossians 1 to Philippians 2) or creedal statement (Col. 3:11; Eph. 4:4-6) to reemphasize what the addressees have been taught previously. The theme of knowledge is also emphasized in both Colossians and Ephesians. There may be a reason for this. In Philippians Paul is addressing his own converts, but this appears to be only partially true when it comes to the other captivity epistles. Philemon is certainly Paul's convert, but did Paul go and found the church in Colossae or was it Tychicus, one of his coworkers? It appears to be the latter. But still, if these churches were founded by Pauline coworkers, they are in a different relationship with Paul than is the church in Rome. In the captivity epistles Paul is able to play a pastoral role to a degree not possible with the Romans.

---

16. See the discussion in my book with Darlene Hyatt, *Colossians, Ephesians, and Philemon* (Grand Rapids: Eerdmans, forthcoming), and my *New Testament History: A Narrative Account* (Grand Rapids: Baker, 2001), pp. 326-29.

1 Peter

Both Peter and Paul seem to have lost their lives during the Neronian crackdown after the fire in Rome in A.D. 64, which continued on through A.D. 65-66. 1 Clement 5.4 indicates that this was the case, though we have no evidence that Peter and Paul were ever in Rome at the same time. The vast majority of scholars are quite convinced that 2 Peter was not written by Peter, not least for the following reasons: (1) it quotes Jude at length; (2) it refers to a collection of Paul's letters, which surely did not happen prior to Paul's death, especially when it is added that they were being treated as Scripture; and (3) there are a variety of sources and styles in 2 Peter — it is a composite document. It does seem possible or even likely that 2 Peter quotes an earlier Petrine source, for the style and substance of 2 Peter 1:12-18 is consistent with what we find in 1 Peter, and a reasonable case can be made that Peter is the author of, or mind behind, 1 Peter. It is highly probable that 2 Peter is one of the latest if not the latest New Testament document, written at a time when there had already been for some time a collection of Paul's letters being used by various churches. I would judge it comes from near the end of the first century A.D.

1 Peter by contrast can well be seen as a document from Peter written in the mid-60s not long before his execution. In 1 Peter 5:1 the author speaks of himself as an old man and also as one who saw the sufferings of Christ, which to judge from this letter left a profound impression on Peter since 1 Peter more than any other New Testament document reflects a theology of the Christ as the Suffering Servant and Christians as imitating that pattern (cf. 1:11, 19; 2:21-24; 3:18-19; 4:1). It appears that Silas has helped Peter with this document (1 Pet. 5:12-13), and Peter also has with him John Mark, with Silas perhaps serving as his scribe as he may have done for Paul with 1 and 2 Thessalonians. 1 Peter is written from Rome, as 1 Peter 5:13 makes evident (cf. Rev. 18:2-14). This letter is written to Jewish Christians in the western and middle portions of what we would call Turkey (including the provinces or regions of Pontus, Bithynia, Galatia, Asia, Cappadocia). It is thus a circular letter. These regional names may suggest where Peter went when he left Jerusalem. When Peter writes his audience, they are undergoing suffering and persecution, and they are exhorted to honor the emperor, an exhortation probably needed in the mid-60s with Nero on a tear. Notice that the reference to leaders in these Asian churches is to elders. There is nothing in 1 Peter that suggests a later stage of Christian his-

tory beyond the 60s. Like Galatians 2:7-8 this letter suggests Peter preached to the Jews, while Paul concentrated on Gentiles.

Hebrews

The provenance of this document is difficult to pin down, not least because it is anonymous. There of course have been numerous conjectures about who authored this document. In the early church it was sometimes thought to be by Paul. This is not a surprising conjecture as there is an apparent indebtedness of this document to several of the earlier Pauline letters, especially Galatians and 1 Corinthians and perhaps Romans as well.[17] These echoes of other letters help in the dating of the document, but they do not really clarify its authorship. The style and a good deal of the substance of this document are so non-Pauline that it is unlikely to be by Paul, but it may be by a Pauline associate. A reasonable case can be made for Apollos being the author of this document in light of what is said in Acts 18 and in 1 Corinthians about the man, but we cannot be certain, and in any case the author wished to remain anonymous.

The simplest way to read Hebrews 13:24b is that the author is writing to Christians in Italy, and sends greetings from various Italian Christians, presently elsewhere, to them. The dating of this letter is difficult, but in light of the Pauline echoes, the statement in 13:7 about remembering past Christian leaders who died for their faith is very possibly a reference to Peter and Paul (noting that 13:7-8 echoes the Hall of Faith passage in 11:1–12:2, which certainly discusses past martyrs among others). Calling leaders *hēgoumenoi* points to Rome as this document's destination (cf. 1 Clem. 1.3; 21.6; 37.2; Hermas *Vis.* 6.6; 17.7). Clement of Rome seems to have been the first known user of Hebrews (1 Clem. 36.1-6). The references in Hebrews to persecution and suffering and potential martyrdom among the audience (cf. 2:15; but they had not yet experienced shedding blood-12:3-4) suggest a time in the 60s for the writing of this work. The reference to the Temple being entered year after year (9:25) would surely seem to place this letter before A.D. 70 since the author is addressing Jews, in particular Jewish Christians, who care about the Temple in Jerusalem.

17. See my "The Influence of Galatians on Hebrews," *New Testament Studies* 37 (1991): 146-52.

What is the character of this anonymous document? Is it really a letter? Nothing at the beginning of the document suggests that it is, and only Hebrews 13:22-25 at the very end of the document suggests otherwise. It appears likely to be a homily. Hebrews 13:22b in the Greek does not say "I have written you a brief letter," but rather "I have written to you briefly," a comment that is perhaps somewhat tongue in cheek since whether this is seen as a letter or as a homily, it is certainly not brief.

The strongly Jewish character of this document reminds us, as did the homily of James, that there were indeed a goodly number of Jewish Christians in various cities of the Greco-Roman world, and not just in Jerusalem. In this case we should probably correlate the remarks in Hebrews with the remarks we find in Romans about Jewish Christians. The document has as a major part of its aim an attempt to convince the audience that Christ is the believer's high priest, that the perfect sacrifice has already been made by Christ, and so no more sacrifices are required, and that heaven is the true sanctuary that Christ has entered. Earthly ones are no longer required. This message might well have been a timely one if the destruction of Jerusalem and the Temple there loomed on the horizon as the Jewish War wound down to its conclusion at the end of the 60s. The high Christology of this document, and in general the highly theological content of the document, shows that Jewish Christians were by no means just interested in matters of praxis, though the concern for perseverance in the faith shows there was also a practical focus to this exhortation. This homily is one of the most rhetorically adept and skillful Greek compositions in the New Testament and reveals to us an author with gifts equal or almost equal to those of Paul when it came to exhortation and the art of persuasion.

The Pastoral Epistles

Most scholars do not believe Paul wrote these letters, but for them to not be entirely artificial compositions they would need to have been sent to their audiences at the end of or just after the end of the Pauline era, which is to say, before the end of the A.D. 60s. In my view it seems likely that these documents were composed at or just after the death of Paul, perhaps by his sometime companion Luke or another such companion, based on authentic notes and/or oral comments from Paul while he was in Mamertine prison in Rome in the mid-60s. The person who penned these letters did so in his own hand and style (there is a uniform style that these letters share), not attempting really to imitate the Pauline style, though at times (e.g., in 2 Timothy) we seem to hear the voice of Paul directly.[18] The letters are basically personal letters, and despite the views of some older treatments there is no evidence of "early Catholic" tendencies in them. The ecclesiology manifested in these letters is not like that found in the letters of Ignatius, where we find evidence of monarchial bishops. Notice that when Church functionaries are spoken of, what we have is more of a character description than a job description in texts like 1 Timothy 3.

The ethical advice in these letters is consistent with the sort of pastoral advice Paul would likely have given at the end of his life to close coworkers like Timothy and Titus. Furthermore, the more conservative character of some of the ethical advice in these letters may reflect the fact that the author knows that the apostolic era is about over, and the Church leaders that were to follow apostles like Paul would not have the same authority as those who had either known Jesus during his earthly life or had seen the risen Lord. These letters could be said to help Pauline coworkers make the transition to a situation beyond the time of Paul. They are certainly closer in length and in character to other ancient personal letters than the rest of the Pauline corpus. It appears they were written from Rome in the mid to late 60s.

Conclusions

It should be already clear that there was no single or singular human hand guiding and guarding the composition of the books of the New Testament. These books were written by various persons at various times in various places to differing audiences, and their authors would no doubt be surprised to find such occasional documents as letters and homilies as part of a sacred canon of Scripture called the New Testament. There are after all no real letter documents or expository sermon documents in the Hebrew Scriptures, and so we find no precedent there.

---

18. L. T. Johnson makes a reasonable case for 2 Timothy being dictated by Paul. See L. T. Johnson, *The Writings of the New Testament* (Minneapolis: Fortress, 1999), pp. 423-49.

The documents we have explored in this chapter reveal living Christian communities that have leaders vitally concerned about the well-being of the converts in these congregations. It appears that all the authors of all these documents were Jews, and all reflect indebtedness to their Jewish heritage, though they draw on it in differing ways. James is just as Jewish a document as Hebrews or 1 Peter and all three address Jewish Christians, but oh how very different these documents are. We have seen in this early period that letters and sermons seem to have been the vehicles of choice to personally address converts in various places. There are both a practical and a profoundly theological bent to most of these documents. They are largely ad hoc in character, addressing specific situations and specific times in the life of one church or another.

In an era before a written gospel there was an oral gospel that bubbles to the surface, and is quoted or echoed in a variety of these texts. None of these documents are however addressed to non-Christians. They all reflect insider discourse between Christians. They also reflect quite clearly that the structure of early Christian communities was to some degree hierarchical. There were apostles and elders and others who had great authority and power and were not afraid to wield it in order to guide, goad, and guard these churches. To judge from these documents, the leaders of the earliest Christian movement were: (1) some members of Jesus' family (James and Jude); (2) various apostolic figures (e.g., Paul); (3) at least one of the Twelve, namely, Peter; and (4) those who became coworkers of one or more of the above-listed leaders (e.g., Silas, Timothy, Mark, Aquila and Priscilla, Phoebe, etc.). We have no evidence in these documents of an attempt to begin collecting them, copying them, and distributing them more widely to churches. Perhaps while there were still living eyewitnesses and apostles there was not felt to be a need for such a collection. Yet as we shall see, by the last third of the first century, such a felt need did arise, and the process of collection and copying and distribution was already set in motion. In our next chapter we must consider the Gospels themselves, written during that last third of the first century A.D. They, more than any other documents save perhaps Paul's letters, were the driving force, so far as texts go, that led to the formation of the New Testament.

Exercises and Questions for Study and Reflection

→ Find a letter you have received recently from a Christian. Notice where the names of the addresser and addressee appear in the letter. Find the greetings in the letter. If the letter contains travel information, notice where it appears in the letter. Notice where the letter is signed. From this draw up a skeletal outline of the modern letter, and compare it to the skeletal outline of an ancient letter in this chapter. What are the similarities and what are the differences? How do you explain the differences? Why do you think it was important in ancient letters to put both the name of the addresser and the addressee at the outset?

→ During what time frame were Paul's letters written? How long had Paul been a Christian before he wrote Galatians? Were any of the letters written when Paul was a new Christian, or were they all from much later in his life?

→ It has been said that Paul's letters fall into two categories: problem-solving letters and progress-oriented letters. Draw up a list and put Paul's letters into one or the other category. Which category has the most letters? What does this tell you about his churches?

→ What is a homily? Do we find any of these in the New Testament? Cite some examples. How do they differ from letters, and how can you distinguish them if epistolary elements have been added to the ends of them?

→ Why do you think it is that we have so many letters in the New Testament?

4 | All the Good News That Was Fit to Print

The term "gospel" comes to us from the Old English term *goodspel*, meaning "good story" or "good news," later shortened to *godspel* (meaning "God's story"). It was intended as a translation of the late Latin term *evangelium* which meant "tidings." *Evangelium* is the Latin near transliteration of the Greek *euangelion*, which again means "news" or more specifically "good news." We are so used to the term gospel having religious significance, and even sometimes being thought of as a particular genre of literature, that we have difficulty coming to grips with the fact that *euangelion*, which is the first major noun in the earliest Gospel (Mark 1:1), was a term widely used about the emperor being a cause of good news before it was ever used of Jesus. Furthermore, it is unlikely that the term *euangelion* was already some sort of technical term for a particular kind of literature by the time Mark wrote his work. The Gospels would have appeared to the ancients as much like other ancient historical or biographical works, only in this case about a figure of religious significance. It is important to note that in the last decade of the first century A.D. we already have references to written documents called Gospels in the *Didache* (8.2; 11.3; 15.3-4). In other words, this confirms that these works were composed before the end of the first century A.D. and circulated in print.[1]

This raises the question, What then are the Gospels? Whatever they

1. The *Didache* shows particular familiarity with Matthew, but the author seems to know other Gospels as well.

are, as we have already previously discussed in this book,[2] they are documents which drew on pre-Gospel sources in the process of composition. Furthermore, three of these documents have some sort of literary relationship, leading to the likely conclusion that Mark was written first and then used by Matthew and Luke. These two Gospel writers also used other sources, including Q,[3] but also both the First and Third Evangelists used distinctive sources, M in the case of the first Gospel, and L in the case of the third Gospel. But what are we to make of the finished products? Again, what are the Gospels? In my view three of the Gospels, Matthew, Mark, and John, appear to have been intended to be seen as ancient biographies, while Luke-Acts appears to have been an ancient two-volume historical monograph. Let us explore these possibilities further, one Gospel at a time.

Mark

It needs to be kept in mind from the outset that there are various features of an ancient biography that are also found in an ancient historical monograph. The basic difference is that a biography focuses on a single person and deals with stories that are deemed to be revealing about the person's character or nature, whether the events involved were historic or not. Historical monographs by contrast focus on events and the flow of cause and effect, and are seldom interested in personal anecdotes that are not of any historic significance. We will discuss Mark in the context of considering which Gospels might be seen as ancient biographies and which might not.

It can be said about Mark's Gospel that it shows little interest in historical causality. Apart from the Passion Narrative, he makes little attempt to link one event to the next or one story to another. He simply selectively presents episodes in the life of Jesus.[4] Mark also shows no interest in synchronisms, by which is meant linkages between world events and one or more of the Gospel stories. This is quite different from what we find for instance in Luke 3. People are mentioned in Mark's narrative only because of their connection, direct or indirect, with Mark's central character — Jesus.

2. See pp. 28-34 above.

3. See pp. 31-41 above.

4. On all of what follows see my *The Gospel of Mark: A Socio-Rhetorical Commentary* (Grand Rapids: Eerdmans, 2001), pp. 1ff.

This is true even of major figures like Peter or John the Baptist or Caiaphas the high priest. There is in addition the fact that the way the disciples and crowds are presented suggests that the author has certain ethical purposes — he wants his audience to follow certain examples and avoid others that he presents. This comports with ancient biographical works like Plutarch's famous *Parallel Lives* far better than it does with the function and focus of ancient historical monographs.

Mark's Gospel is written in Greek though there is evidence that the author knows some Aramaic, Hebrew, and Latin. It was written well after the rise of both the Greek and Roman biographical traditions. The Roman tradition which came to the fore in the first century A.D. is especially germane for our study because it added certain features to its adaptation of the Greek tradition — there was a greater concern for family traditions, and most tellingly there was sometimes a focus on the hero's patient suffering and death at the hands of some tyrant (see Thrasea Paetus's *Life of Cato*). These sorts of biographies were en vogue during the reigns of Nero and Domitian especially. In other words, the Gospels were written in an atmosphere where there would be sympathy for telling the story of a virtuous man who suffered unjustly and had an untimely demise. It is not by accident that the Gospels have been called Passion narratives with a long introduction. Some 30 percent of Mark's narrative is devoted to the Passion Narrative, while John's account devotes more than 40 percent to the events of the last week of Jesus' life.

There are certain indicators that Mark, Matthew, and John would all have appeared to be biographies. First, they all introduce their main protagonists at the beginning of the document, whereas in Luke's Gospel Jesus does not come to the fore until after Luke 1. A person perusing the beginning of Luke's scroll would not have recognized it to be a biography of Jesus. Second, these documents are the right length. Mark has 11,242 words, Matthew has 18,305 words, and John has 16,150 words. The longest of all the Gospels is Luke's, which has 19,428 words, which puts it right at the upper limits of what a scroll could hold. Even at a glance all these documents are some sort of prose narrative or story; they are not plays, speeches, or the like. In Mark's Gospel, Jesus is the subject of over 44 percent of all the verbs.

All three of these Gospel writers follow the convention of indirect portraiture — Mark, Matthew, and John all let the deeds and words of Jesus speak for themselves without a lot of intrusion into the story of analysis of one kind or another. Mark and Matthew in fact follow the rhetorical convention of using *chreiai,* short pithy narratives, which conclude with a dramatic pronouncement or memorable deed. John's Gospel offers monologues and dialogues and is more like the life of a philosopher or sage than the life of a prophet or preacher. All the Gospels however go out of their way to portray Jesus as both a proclaimer/teacher and a healer.

Biographies were popular literature in the first century A.D. They were not necessarily for a high-brow audience, since they could be read aloud profitably, containing as they did selected short episodes from a life. They did not intend to compete with classics like Homer's *Odyssey* or Virgil's *Aeneid* in terms of literary merit or sophistication. Historical monographs, by contrast, tended to be for the well-educated — for politicians and movers and shakers in society who were both literate and involved in major affairs. That Luke-Acts appears more like the work of Thucydides or Polybius than Plutarch's *Lives* must surely tell us something about Luke's audience (see below).

A few of the conventions of ancient biographies need to be kept in mind: (1) These were never exhaustive accounts of a person's life. The mere limitations of scrolls and of the means of researching and writing prohibited anything that might be comparable to a modern thorough biography. (2) Ancient biographies were not written in the post-Freudian, post-Jungian era. By this I mean they did not operate with certain developmental personality models. Most ancients seemed to believe that you were born and stuck with the personality you have, and that it is eventually revealed over time, not developed. They also believed that how one died most revealed one's character, which is the very reason why the Gospel writers had to explain in detail the demise of their hero Jesus. He died in the least honorable way possible. How could this be explained if he was a virtuous man? In the Roman tradition there was an answer to this question, as the *Lives of Julius Caesar* showed. One's death revealed also what God or the gods thought of a person. The Passion narratives had to come to grips with this basic ancient assumption. (3) Ancient biographies tended not to spend much time on the youth of a person. The focus was normally on the adult life of the person in question. This is the case in all three of the more biographical Gospels, although Matthew and John do speak briefly about the antecedents to Jesus' adult life. (4) Ancient biographies were not really all that concerned with the physical appearance of the person in question unless it was particularly striking. The biographies of Jesus are no different in this regard. (5) Ancient biographies were not greatly concerned about either precise chronology (in an age before watches where even seconds are counted) or the issue of proportionality. By the latter I mean that an ancient biographer might well spend an inordinate amount of time on some particular period in a person's life, not offering a womb-to-tomb balanced portrait. (6) Ancient biographies were certainly more like portraits than photographs. They were tendentious in character, presenting and interpreting a life from a particular point. Such writers wanted to tell the truth, but they were not laboring under the modern anxiety about objectivity.

The particulars about Mark's Gospel are both interesting and to some degree allusive. Since no one ever claimed that Mark was one of the Twelve or one of the original apostles, or even an eyewitness of much of Jesus' life, it seems inherently unlikely that later Church tradition would make up the notion that John Mark wrote a Gospel. He is after all only a minor figure in Acts and Paul's letters. What we do know of him is that his mother had a house in Jerusalem, and so he was based there, and that at one juncture he traveled with Paul and Barnabas, being a relative of Barnabas. Later, apparently in the 60s, he seems to have had associations with both Paul and Peter in Rome. If Mark is the young man who makes a cameo appearance in the Passion Narrative in the interesting vignette of Mark 14:51-52, then Mark may have been very briefly an eyewitness to some of the events at the close of Jesus' life. More cannot be said.

As for the provenance of Mark's Gospel, it seems to have been written for an audience of Gentile Christians in the western part of the empire, possibly in Rome. There may well be a clue to the dating of the book in Mark 13:14, which has the phrase "let the reader understand." This phrase suggests that Mark is writing at a time when the demise of the Temple could be foreseen as possibly imminent. In other words, it would appear that this Gospel was written sometime in A.D. 68-69 after the Jewish War was well under way but shortly before its climax in Jerusalem.[5]

The structure of the Gospel of Mark is both simple and profound. Basically it falls into three parts and reflects both something of a chronological and a theological outline. Part One encompasses the whole first half of the Gospel where who and why questions are raised about the identity and ministry of Jesus. The who question is finally answered by Peter at

5. See my *Gospel of Mark*, pp. 1-62.

Caesarea Philippi at Mark 8:27-30 in a way that matches up with the beginning of the Gospel at Mark 1:1. Jesus is both Christ and Son of God. After this Mark then, in three straight chapters, has Jesus present the nature of his mission — he is the man who was born to die. We hear that the Son of Man must suffer many things, be killed, and rise again. This way of putting the mission statement comes to a climax in Mark 10:45 where we hear about the one who came to give his life as a ransom for many. Thereafter in Mark 11–16 in his Passion Narrative Mark records how the mission was successfully accomplished. Mark's Gospel is also noted for having various disclosure moments, such as at the baptism and transfiguration of Jesus, which serve as a counterpoint to the messianic secret motif we also find in Mark.

Matthew

This Gospel is a composite of several known sources, including 95 percent of Mark, a wide range of Q material, and some material unique to Matthew called special M (such as what we find in the birth narratives). It may appropriately be asked why one of the original twelve disciples who was an eyewitness to the life of Jesus would need to be so profoundly dependent on a Gospel written by a non-eyewitness, namely, Mark. This is why most scholars do not think that Matthew the tax collector wrote the first Gospel. It is however quite possible that Matthew did contribute the unique material found in this Gospel and no other, and the book came to be named after its most famous contributor, which was not uncommon in antiquity. This makes some sense of the tradition of attributing this Gospel to Matthew, which otherwise seems an odd choice since he is a minor figure among the Twelve in all four Gospels, including in Matthew. It must in any case be remembered that the superscript of each of the four Gospels is not an original part of the document written by the Evangelist. It was likely later appended to the scroll for identification. Formally speaking, all four canonical Gospels are anonymous since their author's names are not mentioned anywhere within the context of the verses of the Gospels themselves.

Since Matthew's Gospel is so clearly dependent on Mark, it must then have been written later than Mark's Gospel, perhaps sometime in the 70s or 80s. This Gospel is however different in numerous ways from Mark's Gospel although it fits the description of being an ancient biography. Consider the following. Matthew's Gospel is the most Jewish of the Gospels in various ways, is very concerned about the fulfillment of the Scriptures, including the Law, as the Kingdom comes on earth. It is also a Gospel which emphasizes tradition and gives a special focus to the teaching of Jesus, presenting us with five or six blocks of teaching material (Matt. 5–7; 10; 13; 18; 23 and 24–25), much more than we find in Mark. It is often argued that Jesus is presented as a new Moses in this Gospel, but it would be better to say that he is presented as a new Solomon, since his form of teaching is sapiential over and over again in this Gospel. He does not lay down the Law; rather, he picks up the Gospel and presents it in a manner that is in accord with the Jewish Wisdom tradition. Picking up on hints and ideas found in Q, our Gospel writer presents Jesus as both a sage and the embodiment of Wisdom, the very mind and presence of God on earth.[6] There is then an understandable interest in Jesus as the Son of David, which is to say, both a messianic figure and one cut in the mold of the other famous son of David — Solomon. The author of this Gospel seems to see himself as a teacher who is to bring out of his treasury both the wisdom of old and new wisdom as well (see Matt. 13:52), highlighting how Jesus can be both sage in the line of other great Davidic Jewish sages, and at the same time the Wisdom of God and indeed the Son of God. Jewish kings were to be characterized by Wisdom, and Jesus is the exemplar of both in this Gospel.

It would appear likely that Matthew's Gospel was written to a largely Jewish Christian audience, one that had concerns about the ongoing role of the Mosaic Law in Christian life. This Gospel also seeks to highlight the role and importance of Peter in various ways, perhaps because he was the apostle to the Jews, as Galatians 2 makes evident. The overall tenor of Matthew suggests a time when the Jewish Christian community had to define itself over against the synagogue, and was struggling because it could no longer shelter under the protective umbrella of the recognized religion known to us as Judaism. This consideration as well points us to a time at least in the 70s if not later, after Judaism was reorganizing itself at Jamnia. Even so, our author wants to demonstrate that his audience has more than enough Jesus tradition to sustain their community without having to turn back to the synagogue. Jesus is the sage and master teacher. He is also the

---

6. See my *Jesus the Sage: The Pilgrimage of Wisdom* (Minneapolis: Augsburg/Fortress, 1994), pp. 348-68, and my *The Gospel of Matthew* (Macon: Smyth and Helwys, forthcoming).

Son of David, the Son of God, and even Immanuel, God's presence and Wisdom with his community always.

Luke-Acts

This two-volume historical monograph probably antedates the Gospel of John by as much as twenty years. Most scholars think it is unlikely that the Church would have attributed a Gospel to as minor a figure as Luke is in the New Testament if he hadn't written one. He is not an apostle, he is not an eyewitness of the life of Jesus, he was not one of the Twelve, and he is only a sometime companion of Paul toward the end of Paul's missionary journeys. He may well, however, have been a doctor, and so literate in his own right.[7] Is it an accident that in his carefully crafted prologue in Luke 1:1-4 he follows the model of how prologues to scientific treatises were written? Probably not. That prologue also tells us something else about Luke. It tells us that he knows that he has predecessors and that perhaps he wants to write something different than what we find in Matthew and Mark, or for that matter in Q. Luke realized that a more strictly historical account following the rules for Hellenistic historiography was in order. Notice the emphasis in this prologue on: (1) investigating things for himself (i.e., doing research); (2) having examined things from the beginning (i.e., backing up far enough to see where Jesus comes into the historical nexus of cause and effect); (3) writing an orderly account. This prologue, plus the fact that we have multiple volumes in this work, plus the synchronisms (cf., e.g., Luke 2:1-3; Acts 18:2), makes it evident that Luke is serious about his attempt to write historical monographs that will follow a careful, mostly chronological ordering of things. They will also follow the convention of dealing with materials region by region as well.[8]

Theophilus is probably the real name of a real person, namely, Luke's patron.[9] Luke-Acts is as close as we come to real high-brow literature in the New Testament. It is written primarily if not exclusively for a person of high social status who is apparently a recent convert and needs to have

---

7. See pp. 5-9 above.

8. See my discussion in *The Acts of the Apostles: A Socio-Rhetorical Commentary* (Grand Rapids: Eerdmans, 1998), pp. 1-101.

9. See pp. 8-10 above.

some confirmation and assurance about what he has been taught before, as well as some illumination about salvation history and Jesus' and his followers' roles in it.

The structure of Luke-Acts is quite interesting. In the Gospel there is an orientation that is toward Jerusalem, but in Acts we have an orientation from Jerusalem to the rest of the empire. In other words, there is something of a geographical as well as chronological ordering of these volumes. But Luke is interested in more than just mundane history and causation. He is interested in the divine guiding of and interfacing with human lives and events. He wants to show how God, God's Word, and God's Spirit are alive and active in the process of human history. It is not an accident that Luke presents the quotation of Isaiah and Jesus' sermon in the synagogue in Luke 4 as in essence giving a preview of coming events in Jesus' ministry; likewise the quotation of Joel and the speech of Peter similarly foreshadow events in Acts. God has a plan for human redemption that he works out by the activities of the Word and Spirit through human lives and processes. Salvation history is a very apt description of what Luke records in his two-volume monograph. Luke's Gospel chronicles how the Good News is spread from Galilee to Samaria to Judea and Jerusalem and up and down the social scale from the least, the last, and the lost, to the first, the most, and the found. Jesus must go up to Jerusalem, and the Disciples must wait there for power from on high before they take further action. But once Pentecost happens in Acts, Luke wants to show the spread of the Good News from Jerusalem to Rome, for he is concerned to show the universal scope of the Gospel to all persons, to all kinds of persons, to all races of persons, to all of whatever social status, gender, and ethnic origin. The Gospel focuses mostly on the vertical universalization of the salvation while Acts focuses on the horizontal spread of salvation across all geographical and ethnic boundaries. Jesus is the one savior for all peoples. Salvation comes from the Jews and from Jerusalem, but it is for everyone, for as it turns out, God is no respecter of persons; God is impartial. There is a special interest in the poor, oppressed, possessed, disenfranchised receiving Good News — help, healing, and salvation — but equally Luke shows how salvation comes to the well-to-do just as it comes to the ne'er-do-well. In a Church that was becoming increasingly dominated by Gentiles, it is understandable how Luke's work underscoring universal salvation and concentrating on the work of Paul for the most part in his second volume would have served an important purpose for new Gentile converts like

Theophilus, who might have worried about the legitimacy of this new religion, and also about its political implications.

John

As different as the Fourth Gospel is from the First Gospel, it nonetheless shares in common with Matthew a wisdom orientation to Jesus and his teachings.[10] Only the Fourth Evangelist has chosen to present Jesus as Wisdom Incarnate, discoursing on earth as Personified Wisdom does in Proverbs 8–9 and in sources like the Wisdom of Solomon. The Fourth Evangelist does not seem to be dependent on any of the earlier Gospels, though clearly he knows some of the same Gospel traditions. Rather he pursues an independent line of presentation of the biography of Jesus. Like the other Evangelists his presentation is somewhat chronologically ordered, but the author is not afraid to rearrange episodes in order to conform to a certain theological agenda he wants to emphasize (see, e.g., John 2, where we find the episode of the Temple cleansing retrojected from the Passion Narrative material).

Can we know who wrote this wonderful and profound Gospel? Like the other Gospels the document is formally anonymous, but there are clues in John 19 and 21 that the source of this Gospel material is the Beloved Disciple, an eyewitness of at least some of the conclusion of Jesus' ministry, and perhaps more broadly of his Judean ministry. John 21:24 says that the Beloved Disciple is the one who testifies to at least some of the Gospel happenings and indeed wrote them down in some form. His community vouches for his testimony ("we know his testimony is true"). John 19:35 indicates that he was present at the death of Jesus, and this selfsame chapter claims only one such man was present — the Beloved Disciple to whom Jesus bequeathed his mother as he died.

It seems highly unlikely that the Fourth Gospel was written by John son of Zebedee. It includes only one of the Galilean miracle sequences we find in the Synoptics (the feeding of the five thousand and the walking on water), and absolutely none of the episodes from the ministry of Jesus in which the sons of Zebedee play a significant part. We have no story about

10. On all of this see my *John's Wisdom: A Commentary on the Fourth Gospel* (Louisville: Westminster/John Knox, 1995).

the calling of the Zebedees to follow Jesus, nothing about their presence at the raising of Jairus's daughter or at the Transfiguration, nothing about them requesting special seats in Jesus' coming Kingdom, and so on. Instead we have all these unique traditions, most of which center on Jerusalem and its environs, whether we are thinking of the raising of Lazarus or the healing of the man born blind, or the episode of the lame man by the pool. We also have the story in John 13 about the Beloved Disciple reclining with and beside Jesus, and Peter having his feet washed, neither of which is mentioned in the Synoptic Gospels. All in all it appears that we should think of the Beloved Disciple as the source of much of this material, and that he was a Judean follower of Jesus, not one of the sons of Zebedee, even though his name may have been John.

The author of this Gospel focuses so intensely on Jesus that the Twelve just about disappear into the background. They are hardly ever mentioned. This Gospel presents us with a Jesus who is not said to perform miracles and who is not presented as teaching mainly in parables. It presents us with the powerful paradox of a divine and also truly human Jesus who both can say "Before Abraham was, I am," and in the same breath indicate that he can do nothing unless his Heavenly Father gives him the go-ahead. The key to understanding Jesus' identity in this Gospel is to know where he came from (which is to say, to know the content of the prologue) and where he is going (returning to the Father as John 14–17 stresses). Those who think Jesus has merely human origins or a merely human destiny cannot properly understand his identity.

The Gospel can be divided up into two major parts, a book of signs (John 2–11), and the Passion and Resurrection stories (John 12–20) framed by a prologue (John 1) and an epilogue (John 21). The Sign narratives are seven in number, as are the "I am" sayings and discourses. This highly schematized presentation is deliberately selective, as John 20:30 makes perfectly clear. There is something of a crescendo of the miraculous from Sign One through Sign Seven, and the Seventh Sign, the raising of Lazarus, in fact foreshadows what is to happen to Jesus in the last week of his life. There is also a crescendo of confessions, with the only one that fully matches up with the prologue's high Christology found paradoxically on the lips of Thomas who, when he sees the risen Jesus, proclaims Jesus "My Lord and my God," which not coincidentally is also what Emperor Domitian asked to be called. This provides a clue that suggests that this Gospel was written at a time when the emperor cult was going strong, and Domitian was its focus.

This in turn means that this Gospel was likely finally assembled in the 90s, though its traditions from the Beloved Disciple may go much further back.

The author of this Gospel goes out of his way to shed light, indeed glory, on the cross. The cross in this Gospel is seen as the first stage of Jesus' exaltation. When Jesus is lifted up on the cross, he will draw all persons to him. Furthermore, there is no agony on the cross in John. Instead, we are told from the very first chapter of this Gospel that Jesus is the Lamb of God who takes away the sins of the world, and that he will finish or accomplish this glorious task. The cross is when Jesus reaches his "hour" in prime time for the redemption of humankind, and is in his element — even forming his new community from the cross in the persons of the paradigmatic male and female disciples — the Beloved Disciple and Mary. This Gospel is a very different sort of masterpiece than Mark or Matthew, but it is no less compelling. To judge from John 20:31, this Gospel was written to aid the task of evangelism, not as a tract to be distributed, but as a tool for teachers of unbelievers. It is the Gospel where all sorts of seekers, ranging from the Baptist, to Nicodemus, to the blind man, to the Greeks, to Mary and Martha, search for Jesus, and in their seeking he finds them and calls them by name (see John 20 and the story of Mary Magdalene). This Gospel writer does not confine himself to short pithy sayings of Jesus or short pithy narratives. Rather, he often offers extended treatments of discourse and narrative. It is a Gospel that has been said to be shallow enough for a baby to wade in, but deep enough for an elephant to drown. The Gospel of John is a constant reminder that Jesus was a figure who fit no one formula and was a larger figure than any one portrait could convey. We should rejoice there are four Gospels and not just one.

In the end we may say that like the Gospel of Luke, the Fourth Gospel has a universal flavor to it. It seems to have been written at a time and in a place where salvation is being readily offered to all sorts of people, and the universal nature of the Gospel needs to be underscored (see John 3:16). The tradition that it comes from Ephesus may well be true. There is certainly nothing against such an idea; the book of Revelation may support this general locale for the source of the Johannine corpus. The community being addressed has heard portions of the Gospel story before (see John 11:2 referring to a story not mentioned until John 12). Under the impetus of the death of the Beloved Disciple (see John 21:22-23) someone, whom we may call the Fourth Evangelist, has assembled the man's memoirs and shaped them into a Gospel of the ancient biographical sort. This docu-

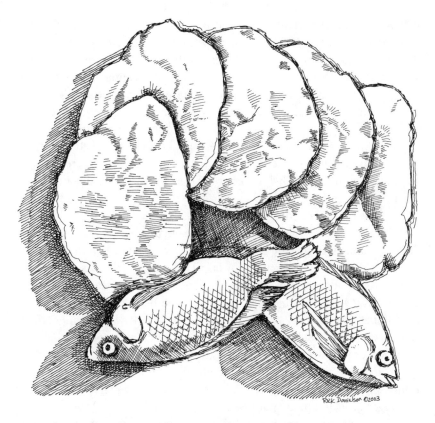

The one miracle narrative that all four Gospel writers felt they must include is the story of the feeding of the five thousand, the miracle of the loaves and fishes.

ment would need to have been written later than the Johannine Epistles if they are by the same person. We must consider the other Johannine documents at this juncture.

Johannine Epistles and the Apocalypse

Letters continued to be written by Christians long after the time of Paul, but it is noteworthy that few were able to use them in so full or dynamic a way as Paul had done. Some writers who wrote at the end of the first century A.D. chose to imitate Paul in both style of writing and in substance and audience (see 1 Clement), others wrote personal letters that were indeed more like normal personal letters of the period both in style and to some degree in content. 2 and 3 John are such letters, and it appears probable that we should see 1 John as a homily rather than a letter.

We are told in the heading to 2 and 3 John that they are from the "elder" or "old man." In view of the similarities of style and content between this material and the material in the Gospel of John it is likely that these documents are also by the Beloved Disciple, now an elderly person and writing to churches he helped establish that are at some distance from where he currently resides.

If the Gospel of John was written during the height of the reign of Domitian, then we would need to put these documents at a somewhat earlier date, namely, in the late 80s A.D. They reflect a time when there are difficulties in these churches caused by false teaching, and there is not enough of a local orthodox or apostolic presence to prevent such teachers from entering congregations and wreaking havoc. The Beloved Disciple is trying hard to reaffirm the core Christological truths as well as the proper ethical response to false teaching while not dousing the flames of love between members of the community. The situation does not seem to be too different from some of the complaints made about the seven churches mentioned in Revelation 2–3, particularly those combating false teachers and in danger of losing their first love.

It is hard to know which of these documents was written first. 2 John is apparently a document to a Christian community (called the elect lady, though it could be addressed to an individual). The clue that this is the correct conclusion is found in the last verse of the letter, where greetings are sent from another congregation's members called "the children of your sister." Notice verse 12: "I have much to write you but I do not want to use papyrus and ink. Instead I hope to visit you. . . ." As was true during the Pauline era, letters were only surrogates for, and indeed preparations for, a visit (cf. Philemon and 2 John). Some of the members of this congregation have remained faithful to the Gospel that Jesus has come in the flesh and has called his followers to love one another, and some have not. Orthodoxy and orthopraxy are both at stake, and so a visit seems required to sort things out.

3 John is clearly a personal letter to a friend named Gaius. Traveling evangelists have informed the Beloved Disciple that Gaius has remained true to the Gospel, but he seems to be on the outside of the leadership

structure. Diotrephes seems to have the church meeting in his house, but Diotrephes will have nothing to do with the author of these documents. It appears he has sought to become the chief leader of the church at the expense of their loyalty to the Beloved Disciple. By contrast there is Demetrius who is still holding on to the truth. In other words, the church is divided about the message and the leadership the Beloved Disciple seems to have offered them in the past.

1 John should be seen as a homily about core theological and ethical values that the Beloved Disciple wants to reiterate to a divided and troubled group of Christians. This may be the sermon he wanted to deliver to the church he was writing to in 2 John, but we do not know if he actually got the opportunity to do so. One of the more neglected and interesting features of this homily is found in its very last verse. There is an exhortation to stay away from idols. This could be an attempt to reinforce the Decree and Letter of James which had long since been circulated to the largely Gentile churches in what we today call Turkey.[11]

Some of the themes in 1 John are also covered in the Gospel of John: discussions about love and loyalty and obedience and sin and walking in the light. The homily begins in a way that sounds at first glance much like what we find in John 1, until one looks more closely and discovers that here the Beloved Disciple is talking about "*that* which was from the beginning" rather than the One who was from the beginning. In other words he is talking about the word about the Word, or the Message that included Jesus but was not limited to him. 1 John has some of the same theological depth conveyed in beguiling simple words that one finds also in the Fourth Gospel. If we had any illusions that first-century Church life was less troubled or contentious than Church life today, all we need to do is read some of the letters found in the New Testament to make clear this is not so. The remedy the Beloved Disciple offers for the Church's ills is speaking the truth boldly about the Incarnate Christ and the way Christians should live an ethical lifestyle, but speaking that truth in love. It was then, as always, a hard thing to balance. These Johannine documents do not reflect the same rhetorical skills we see in Paul's letters, but they are no less compelling. They reflect an ethos in which individual congregations were not assumed to be autonomous and were not allowed to go their own way when it came to matters of either orthodoxy or orthopraxy.

11. See pp. 54-57 above.

Though it may not be the very last book written that made it into the New Testament (2 Peter may be from about the same time or a little later), the Revelation of John was certainly one of the last documents written. We have come to the end of the discussion of the creation of New Testament books, and it is only now that we have come across a book of prophecy among these documents. This ought to strike us as odd. The Hebrew Scriptures were replete with prophetical books of various lengths and foci. Yet the New Testament, written almost entirely by Jews (Luke may be the lone exception, though he may have been a God-fearer before following Jesus), has no books of prophecy apart from the Apocalypse. Why?[12]

We do of course have prophetic portions in some of the earlier New Testament documents, for instance, in Mark 13, but we do not have an entire prophetic book written before Revelation. It is my guess that the reason for this is that the earliest Christians believed they had already arrived in the age of fulfillment, the eschatological age, and therefore they were more exercised with discerning the fulfillment of the Scriptures in Jesus and within the movement he spawned (see, e.g., Luke 24:26-27) than in offering up new prophecies about the future.

Jewish prophecy had in any case largely taken a unique turn ever since the Exile, when books like Ezekiel and then later Daniel were written. Prophecy had taken on an apocalyptic form involving dramatic visions. It had become the Word made vivid and visible. The book of Revelation stands in that tradition of Jewish prophecy rather than in the tradition of the oracular prophets like Jeremiah or Hosea and others. Revelation is a collection of visions set within an epistolary framework and addressed to seven churches in Asia Minor. It reflects a time when churches had existed for some time, but more recently had come under pressure and in some case persecution from the nonbelievers among whom they lived. The dangers of apostasy and unfaithfulness were considerable, and John the Seer writes to them so they will both continue to believe and behave, and persevere in the midst of suffering and difficulties. His visions are meant to galvanize the audience, undergird the ethical exhortations in Revelation 2–3, and reassure the converts that though all manner of things seem to currently be going wrong, God in Christ is still on his throne, and he will sort things out in the long run. Justice will be done on earth, as it is in heaven,

12. On all of what follows see my *Revelation* (Cambridge: Cambridge University Press, 2003).

and salvation will come to earth, in the form of the millennium followed by the New Jerusalem, in due course. It is God, not the emperor and his minions, that is truly in control of the historical process that is leading to an eschatological climax. Revelation is not a call to arms, but rather a call to perseverance and trust and faithfulness, allowing God and God alone to mete out justice and deal with problems the largely pagan world created for Christians.

There is no reason to doubt that this book was indeed written by John the Seer, as in fact Revelation 1 suggests. Therefore, this is not a pseudonymous document, a document claiming to be by a worthy ancient but in fact written by an anonymous contemporary. We do not have history written up and masking as prophecy from long ago in this work.

John the Seer is on the island of Patmos off the coast of Asia Minor (see Rev. 1:9). He has been exiled to this locale, presumably because of his vigorous presentation of the Gospel in that region, to which someone, or some group of persons, objected. There has been enough contact between himself and the churches that he knows of and has been involved with in Asia Minor that he has become concerned that they are buckling under cultural pressure of various sorts, and have become discouraged because some Christians there, like Antipas, have been martyred. John cannot go and visit them directly, but somehow he must give them hope and share something of the glorious vision. So he chooses to set down in writing some of the visions he had while on the island of Patmos.

Apocalyptic literature is by its very nature visionary literature, and so it often has both a vertical and a horizontal dimension, by which is meant it unveils something of what is going on up there in heaven, and also out there in the historical future. As the word *apokalypsis* suggests this is revelatory literature. It is about the unveiling of secrets known only to God; it is not about sharing shrewd deductions based on detailed knowledge and analysis of the historical process. Revelation is just that, revelation, not speculation.

Another feature of apocalyptic literature is that it is also always mediated revelation. Notice the chain of communication in Revelation 1:1-2. This is a revelation from God through Jesus given to an angel who then communicates it to John who in turn shares it with the seven churches. We are dealing with top secret information that would be seen as subversive if the secular authorities could only decode the symbols, for it suggests that the emperor, after all, is not a God upon the earth; there has been only one

Ephesus was one of the cities to which John addressed his Apocalypse, or he addressed at least the Christians in that city. The city was a center of commerce, religion, and erudition, as the impressive Celsus library suggests.

of those, Jesus, and the emperor and his evil empire are in for a real shock in the future. The emperor is not in control of his own domain and does not grasp or control the future. Only God in Christ has such sovereignty. Furthermore, it is not the emperor who can dispense real lasting benefits to those who dwell in the empire. No, salvation and real community, and health and healing and immunity from further harm or suffering or disease, decay, and death, are only in the hands of God. The emperor not only has no royal clothes; his promises and rhetoric are false. It is hard to imagine a much more subversive document penned by a Christian than this document. No wonder it is written using apocalyptic symbols and metaphors.

It appears likely that Revelation was written during the dark days of the 90s A.D. when Domitian was on the throne, touting himself as *Deus et dominus noster,* "our Lord and our God," and when Christians in Asia Minor were suffering consequences for not participating in, indeed for even protesting against, the emperor cult, which was alive and well in various of the seven cities to which John writes. Domitian is depicted in John's Revelation as a sort of Nero come back from the dead, Mister 666, the conveyor of chaos and an anti-Christ figure. John wants to tell his charges — "this too will pass in God's good time." Notice too that John is unable to appeal to local apostles or leaders or true prophets in the seven churches to help give them guidance. This work was written after the apostolic age and during a time when there were not that many figures like John around who had the authority and experience to give guidance to churches under duress.

John the Seer is not likely the same person as the Beloved Disciple, not least because he would have needed a vocabulary and grammar transplant at some juncture to have written all of these documents. The Johannine Epistles and the Gospel can reasonably be said to be from the same source, the Beloved Disciple, but it is difficult if not impossible to account for what we find in Revelation on the supposition that it too is written by the same person. Because this is an exceedingly complex matter, we must briefly go into some detail.

The linguistic study of the Johannine Gospel, Epistles, and Revelation makes it quite unlikely that these five documents were all written by the same person. These differences were noticed as early as Dionysius of Alexandria in the mid-third century A.D., who is quoted favorably by Eusebius. While it is certainly possible to argue that Revelation reflects Semitic interference (i.e., the Greek of someone who thinks in a Semitic language and struggles to translate), and it is even possible to argue that the author is deliberately archaizing (in this case Semitizing)[13] because of the nature of this document which stands in the tradition of Jewish apocalyptic, these suggestions do not adequately explain all the differences in grammatical habits between Revelation and the other Johannine writings. Consider the following details: (1) In Revelation *axios* is followed by the infinitive, while in the Gospel it is followed by *hina*. (2) In the Gospel we find *mē* used with the participle eleven times and with the genitive absolute frequently, but the author of Revelation uses neither, when there were opportunities to do so. (3) The author of Revelation frequently uses different words than the Gospel writer to refer to the same concept. Thus, *arnion* is used for "lamb" some twenty-nine times, but not at all in the Gospel. Instead *amnos* is used there (twice). (4) Jerusalem is spelled *Hierousalēm* in Revelation, but *Hierosolyma* in the Gospel. (5) For exclamations Revelation uses *idou* some twenty-six times, but the Gospel uses *ide*. (6) In so simple a matter as whether to use *kaleō* or *legō* to speak of what something is called or named, Revelation always has *kaleō* and the Gospel always has *legō* (cf. Rev. 16:16; John 19:13). (7) Even more striking is when the writers of these documents use the same word to mean very different things. Thus, for example, *alēthinos* means "true" as opposed to "false" in Revelation, but the same word means "authentic" or "genuine" in the Gospel. (8) *Ethnos/ethnē* means "Gentiles" or "all nations" in Revelation, but in the Gospel it refers exclusively to the Jews (five times). (9) *Kosmos* in Revelation means the created world, while in the Gospel it means the world of humanity. (10) *Laos* means "Gentiles" or "Christians" in Revelation, but in the Gospel of John it means "Jews," except perhaps in one case. (11) *Proskynein* with the dative means "to worship" in Revelation, while with the accusative it means "to do homage." This is just the reverse of the usage in the Gospel.

These differences in diction rather strongly favor the conclusion that the person who produced the final form of Revelation did not also produce the final form of the Gospel of John (or the Johannine Epistles for that matter, which are similar in diction and grammar to the Gospels). Yet it is also true that there are terms, such as *logos*, which are applied to Christ only in the Fourth Gospel and in Revelation. There are in addition passages where there is similarity of diction and usage between the two works (cf. Rev. 20:6 to John 13:8; Rev. 22:15 to John 3:21; Rev. 22:17 to John 7:37).

13. This is unlikely in view of the fact that the author finds it natural to use the Hebrew Old Testament as his major external resource for this document.

The question then is how to explain the similarities as well as the differences between these works. While style does evolve, a total change in style and usage is most unlikely. Furthermore the Gospel is written in rather plain and simple Koine Greek, whereas in Revelation the vocabulary is much more complex and the grammar is often prolix. For example, one out of every eight words in Revelation is found nowhere else in the New Testament. While some of this can be explained by different subject matter in the two works, not all of it can be. On the whole this internal evidence strongly favors the conclusion that the person who wrote Revelation did not also write the Fourth Gospel or the Epistles, yet John the Seer has some sort of relationship with those who wrote the rest of the Johannine corpus and/or with their communities.

In order to understand the book of Revelation one must understand early Jewish and Christian apocalyptic literature. One must recognize that while visions do not describe things literally, they are often referential using symbols and analogies and metaphors to convey meaning. The seer must resort to describing what he sees using the phrase "it was like. . . ." Furthermore, the seer often uses multivalent symbols, symbols that can apply to more than one person or thing. Mister 666 could be Nero; it could also be Domitian. The symbols indicate the character of the person or thing referred to. Rome is not really the whore Babylon, but the city has the character early Jews and Christians often associated with Babylon. John is operating with a disclosure model of communication, revealing aspects of the truth using what we might call political cartoons (e.g., he is not really concerned about actual dragons pursuing a woman; he is concerned about the Devil tormenting God's people on earth). One of the most flagrant examples of misunderstanding Revelation comes when one forgets that a text like Revelation 4:1-3 is not about a literal trip in the flesh to heaven, but about a spiritual and visionary experience in which John of Patmos, still on terra firma on that island, "sees" into heaven through the inspiration of the Spirit. The description of this experience is much like that found elsewhere in early apocalyptic literature (cf., e.g., the description even in 2 Cor. 12:1-5).

It is a fitting thing in the end that Revelation turned out to be the last book in the canon of the New Testament, as it is certainly the most complex, and as a book of prophecy it points the Church forward into the final future God has in mind. One should not begin to study the New Testament by studying its most complex book. But one should also not neglect the one powerful prophetic text we have in the canon.

Conclusions

The last third of the first century A.D. saw the composition of the Gospels, Acts, a few more letters and homilies, and an apocalypse. We have considered briefly in these last four chapters the usual data about authorship, audience, date, and the like of the twenty-seven New Testament documents. But this does not in any way tell us how these documents came to be collected and placed together in what we would later call the New Testament. We begin to have an inkling of this process in 2 Peter 3:15-16, where we hear of Paul's letters being treated as sacred texts or as a part of the Scriptures. At a minimum this suggests that there was already a collection of Paul's letters (how many letters we do not know) by the end of the first century A.D. that were circulating as sacred Scriptures for Christians. In our next chapter we must consider the rather surprisingly long process of collecting and sifting and debating, which led finally in the fourth century to something we call the canon of the New Testament. For now, it must suffice to say that paradoxically enough there was no New Testament in the New Testament era, but by the end of that period at least some books that were later included in the New Testament had begun to be treated as sacred texts or Scripture. The rest of the story must await our next chapter.

....

Exercises and Questions for Study and Reflection

→ The first three Gospels are called the Synoptics, meaning those that see with one eye. Sit down and draw up a list of stories that you can find in all three Gospels. Reflect on why it is that all three Evangelists chose to include these events. Write down your reflections. Are there events not on this list that you think should have been included? List them.

→ What does the term "Gospel" actually mean?

→ What kind or kinds of literature are the Gospels? How do they differ from modern biographical or historical writings? Are these differences a drawback or an asset?

→ Why do you think it is that the Gospel of John is so different from the first three Gospels? Do you find this troubling or refreshing?

→ Draw up a chart of the probable authors, dates, and audiences of the four Gospels. What do you make of the fact that at least two of these

Gospels were written by non-apostles who were also not eyewitnesses of the Gospel events?

→ Who was the Beloved Disciple? Is he the same person as John, son of Zebedee? Why or why not? Does it really matter if we don't know the name of the Beloved Disciple if his Gospel does not reveal it?

5 | The Selection, Collection, and Rejection of Texts

It has been rightly said that the "formation of the canon represented the working out of forces that were already present in the primitive Christian community and that would have made some form of canon virtually inevitable."[1] Right from the outset of this chapter then we need to rule out the mistaken notion that the canon is something the early medieval Church leaders imposed on their constituency. This is historically untrue.

Equally untrue is the anonymous comment one of my friends pulled off of a website recently and sent to me with the query — Is it true? It claimed:

> When Constantine commissioned new versions of these documents, it enabled the custodians of orthodoxy to revise, edit, and rewrite their material as they saw fit, in accordance with their tenets. It was at this point that most of the crucial alterations in the New Testament were probably made. The importance of Constantine's commission must not be underestimated. Of the five thousand extant early manuscript versions of the New Testament, not one predates the fourth century. The New Testament as it exists today is essentially a product of fourth-century editors and writers.

Besides the error of fact about there being no manuscripts or partial manuscripts of the New Testament from before the fourth century

---

1. Paul J. Achtemeier, Joel B. Green, and Marianne Meye Thompson, *Introducing the New Testament: Its Literature and Theology* (Grand Rapids: Eerdmans, 2001), p. 589.

A.D.[2] (our earliest text is a papyrus from the second century A.D. with a small portion of John's Gospel on it; see below), there is also the error of judgment that some sort of whole-scale alteration of earlier manuscripts was undertaken in the fourth century which produced a New Testament quite different from what the original New Testament writers had in mind for their own works. The historical evidence does not support this claim either.

It is wise to speak first for a moment about the canon of the Hebrew Scriptures. This collection of sacred texts which was in fact the Bible of the earliest Christians seems to have come to a point of final closure during the New Testament era, though mostly it was a closed collection well before that point in time. There seems to have still been some debate in the first century A.D. about the authority and inspiration of some texts (e.g., Esther) and whether they should be included in the third division of the Hebrew Scriptures (the Writings), but generally speaking, the Hebrew canon, especially of the Law and the Prophets, was fixed by the time the translation of the text into Greek (the Septuagint [LXX]) was undertaken in the second century before the New Testament era. It can not be said however that the Old Testament canon was truly closed before about 90 A.D., when the deliberations at Jamnia took place. It may be that knowledge of that process, and recognition that Christians also needed a written collection of sacred texts, may have provided some impetus at the end of the first century A.D. to collect a parallel Christian canon of books.

Since all, perhaps save one, of the New Testament writers were Jews, it is understandable that they would not only know and embrace the concept of canon and of inspired writings but also might well believe they were at the least offering inspired writings to their audiences, precisely because they believed the Holy Spirit had been given in full measure to Jesus' followers and that all sorts of people would be fulfilling the prophetic roles described by Joel and reiterated as coming to pass at Pentecost in A.D. 30 by Peter (see Acts 2). It was not just that Jesus was seen as the fulfillment of Old Testament hopes and prophecies but that those hopes were coming to fruition in the community of Jesus as well. A sense of inspiration and authority comes across especially strongly at the conclusion of Revelation 22,

2. See K. Aland and B. Aland, *The Text of the New Testament: An Introduction to the Critical Editions and to the Theory and Practice of Modern Textual Criticism,* translated by Erroll F. Rhodes (Grand Rapids: Eerdmans, 1987).

but it is also present in the way Paul's writings are spoken of in 2 Peter 3. It was not just in the fourth century that the Church came to recognize these documents as inspired by God and profitable for reproof and training in righteousness.

It appears that already by the period of time 2 Peter was written or a little later (A.D. 125) there was circulating a collection of four Gospels together, the four Gospels we know as the canonical Gospels.[3] The impetus to create such a collection was in part the rise of the use of the codex in place of the roll, which the second-century evidence suggests Christians adopted as a practice quite eagerly. H. Gamble chronicles this for us quite helpfully:

> Almost without exception, the earliest Christian books known have the form not of the papyrus roll but of the papyrus codex, or leaf book, which is the model of the modern book. The evidence of this fact has been furnished by archaeological discoveries of the twentieth century. . . . The earliest of the Christian texts belong to the second century. Privilege of age belongs to ℙ52, a small fragment of the Gospel of John, paleographically dated to the first half of the second century. A number of other Christian papyrus fragments are not much later . . . ℙ64 + ℙ67 from a codex of Matthew and Luke; ℙ77 from a codex of Matthew; ℙ66 and ℙ90 from codices of John, and ℙ32 from a codex of Pauline epistles. All these, not to mention some Christian copies of Jewish scripture may be placed in the second century.
>
> The comparative evidence is instructive. Of the remains of Greek books that can be dated before the third century C.E., more than 98% are rolls, whereas in the same period the surviving Christian books are almost all codices. . . . Together the relevant evidence indicates that early Christianity had an almost exclusive preference for the codex as the medium of its own writings and thus departed early and widely from the established bibliographic conventions of its environment.
>
> To appreciate how peculiar this step was one must realize that a codex was not recognized in antiquity as a proper book. It was regarded as a mere notebook, and its associations were strictly private and utilitarian. The humble origin of the codex is enshrined in its name: the Latin *caudex* means "a block of wood" and referred to a wooden tablet used for writing. . . . From an early time it was customary to link two or more of these together by passing a string or thongs through holes

3. See below, pp. 99-100.

along one edge, thus constructing a series of loose leaves of wood. The proper Latin name for such a collection of wooden tablets was *codex*.[4]

In my view it was the need to circulate groups of texts from early Christian writers that pushed the Church in the direction of using the codex. We know from both Clement and Ignatius as well as 2 Peter 3 that there were early collections of Paul's letters circulating. But what of the Gospels? It is likely that the superscripts to the Gospels give us a clue. We have in p66 a papyrus that has as its heading "Gospel according to John," a document which dates to no later than A.D. 200. Now there is no reason to have the phrase "according to . . ." unless there are well-known Gospels in circulation in the same region that are "according to" someone else. This is why M. Hengel has argued both that from the early portion of the second century there was a collection of the fourfold Gospel and that the title "Gospel according to . . ." had become customary.[5] Thus now we appear to have clear manuscript evidence already in the second century for the four-fold collection of the Gospels.[6] For there to be a collection of letters or a collection of Gospels circulating in the Church in the early second century, the codex form of presentation was necessary. G. N. Stanton is likely partially right when he urges that the four Gospels circulating together precipitated the prevalent use of the codex in Christian circles, for no one scroll could contain even two Gospels.[7] Equally, no one scroll could contain a collection of more than two of Paul's longer letters. What this bears witness to is that the Church in the postapostolic era was very concerned about both the preservation and the circulation of its foundational documents in as convenient and economical a means as was then possible.

In regard to the collection of the four canonical Gospels together it is important to bear in mind Irenaeus's witness before the end of the second century A.D. to and defense of the notion that there was only one Gospel in only four specific presentations (*Against Heresies* 3.11.8, written about A.D.

4. H. Gamble, *Books and Readers in the Early Church: A History of Early Christian Texts* (New Haven: Yale University Press, 1995), pp. 49-50.

5. M. Hengel, *Studies in the Gospel of Mark* (Philadelphia: Fortress, 1985), pp. 64-84.

6. See T. C. Skeat, "The Oldest Manuscript of the Four Gospels?" *New Testament Studies* 43 (1997): 1-34.

7. G. N. Stanton, "The Fourfold Gospel," *New Testament Studies* 43 (1997): 317-46.

180). He had rightly seen that there were certain implications to the circulation of these four Gospels together such as the fact that, unlike Marcion's view, one Gospel was not deemed sufficient. Equally rejected was the notion that a harmony of these four Gospels (and others?) was sufficient. There was also an implicit suggestion at the least that other Gospels were not equally valid and valuable. This last supposition is made explicit in Irenaeus.

There was however also some negative historical impetus toward canonization as well. The dying off of the eyewitnesses and apostles was one impetus, but we must speak of other more pressing ones in the second century A.D. Clearly the first major wake-up call came when Marcion in the middle of the second century A.D., who had come to Rome in about A.D. 144 from Pontus and had joined the Roman church, separated from that church because of his beliefs and drew up his own list of inspired and authoritative New Testament books. He rejected the Hebrew Scriptures as proclaiming a vengeful God and instead urged that the Gospel of Luke and the letters of Paul (minus the Pastorals) should be the standard or measuring rod of Christian belief. But this was not enough. Marcion decided that even these texts needed some editing to purge them of elements of the older Jewish beliefs about God and the Law. He deleted, for instance, Luke 1–2 as too Jewish and Old Testamental in character. It is to the credit of the Roman church (and other churches) that they did not reject these books on the basis of a guilt-by-association sort of thinking. Instead, they continued to affirm the value of these writings. "The Christian community therefore did not create what came to be called canonical literature to combat Marcion. Rather, it simply reaffirmed that its basis of authority was broader than one Gospel and one apostle, and it reaffirmed the authority of the writings of the Jewish community of faith as well (i.e., the Old Testament)."[8]

It was not just Marcion however that provided a negative impetus toward creating a canon; there were also the Montanist movement and the Gnostic movement, which had their own collections of authoritative texts (e.g., the Gospels of Philip and of Thomas). These documents remind us however that the early Christian movement was not struggling to produce enough documents to form a canon. Rather there was a whittling down of the possible candidates for inclusion. Gospels and epistles and other sorts of documents (e.g., the Shepherd of Hermas) were being produced already be-

8. Achtemeier, Green, and Thompson, *Introducing the New Testament*, p. 594.

fore the end of the first century A.D. and right through the second century A.D. Some of these documents contained the same trajectories of thought we find in the twenty-seven documents, and some of them contained notions that were antithetical to what was being taught in the foundational documents. Some documents were seen as unobjectionable but not necessary for inclusion in the canon of Scripture. There were in fact dozens of documents, some Gospels, some epistles, some other sorts of documents, in circulation in the second-century and third-century churches. "Given the mass of literature that was circulating and even being produced on into the second century and beyond, it is surprising how quickly agreement was reached on a core of writings acknowledged to be authoritative."[9] The issue really proved to be *not* whether our canonical Gospels should be included in the collection but whether there were other Gospels that should be added to the collection (e.g., the Gospel of Peter).[10] Justin Martyr suggested already in the second century that the fourfold collection of Gospels was held widely by Christians to be of equal value with the Hebrew Scriptures.

It was also probably in the second century that the so-called Muratorian canon list was composed.[11] The very beginning of the document is missing but seems to have listed Matthew and Mark. After that we have the other two canonical Gospels, Acts, the letters of Paul (including the Pastorals), 1 and 2 John, Jude, and the Apocalypse. In other words twenty-two of the twenty-seven documents later listed as canonical are included. Also included are the Jewish document the Wisdom of Solomon, which was very popular in the Early Church, and the Apocalypse of Peter (though with the warning that not all agree that this last document should be read in church). The Shepherd of Hermas is discussed, but the conclusion is reached that it is not among the writings of the apostles and proph-

9. Achtemeier, Green, and Thompson, *Introducing the New Testament,* p. 598.

10. It needs to be noted that the Gnostic books, such as the Gospel of Thomas or the Gospel of Truth, were never seriously considered for inclusion. They were recognized already in the second century as beyond the pale and contradictory to the fourfold collection of Gospels in various ways. The Gospel of the Hebrews and the Gospel of Peter, however, were not viewed in the same negative way as the Gnostic texts were.

11. There is some debate about this, with some scholars thinking it comes from the fourth century. However, though the document we have is in Latin, it seems clear that an older Greek document stands behind the Latin one. See Luke Timothy Johnson, *The Writings of the New Testament: An Interpretation* (Philadelphia: Fortress, 1986), pp. 600-601.

ets. It can be read by believers but should not be read aloud in church. "From this we see how the key factor for canonization is not whether documents can be read or used by individuals but whether they are to be read publicly in worship"[12] and so would be seen as sacred and inspired texts.

If we move forward just a little more than a century later (about 320-330), we encounter the remarks of Eusebius, the so-called Father of Church History. Eusebius was the bishop of Caesarea, and he was the first person to formally talk about "the writings of the New Testament." He says in the early fourth century that they include "the Holy Tetrad" (i.e., the four canonical Gospels), Acts, the letters of Paul, 1 John, 1 Peter, and, though he hesitates on this one, the Book of Revelation. These, he says, are the universally recognized books. He then lists as disputed James, Jude, 2 Peter, 2 and 3 John. Together, these two lists make up our twenty-seven-book canon. He then gives a list of works that are considered "nongenuine," including the Shepherd of Hermas and the Apocalypse of Peter, as well as all Gospels and Acts that bear names of apostles but, he says, are put forward by heretics. It is clear that the notion of orthodoxy well precedes the closing of the canon in this process. Indeed the notion of orthodoxy is already evident in various places within the twenty-seven books written in the first century (cf., e.g., Galatians 1, 1 and 2 John). Eusebius in this same discussion enunciates three criteria for acceptance of such writings: use in the Church, apostolic origins, and theological consistency with the clearly apostolic documents (*Hist. eccl.* 3.25.1-7).

In the East we have similar testimony to these twenty-seven books in the 39th Easter Letter of Athanasius, who was bishop in Alexandria. He wrote a few decades after Eusebius in A.D. 367 and lists the twenty-seven canonical books, calling them "wellsprings of salvation." From yet another place, Carthage in northern Africa, we have in A.D. 397 a list put out by a church council that lists these twenty-seven books and no others, with the final comment "Let the church across the sea [i.e., in Rome] be consulted for the confirmation of this canon."[13] The church across the sea is the church in Rome. This in turn makes clear that by the end of the fourth century A.D. in both the East and the West and in three different seats of authority there was agreement of what should be included in the canon.

What we see here is not a process where some particular church

12. Johnson, *The Writings of the New Testament*, p. 601.
13. See Johnson, *The Writings of the New Testament*, p. 603.

called a conclave of representatives of all churches to decide the issue. Rather, we should see that the process of discernment and discrimination was going on throughout the second through fourth centuries, and agreement and conclusion without collusion or even consultation was finally reached. Certain books had been recognized since the end of the first century as inspired and authoritative, such as the fourfold Gospel and the letters of Paul, and others came to be recognized through the process of discernment that lasted about two hundred years.

Nor was it just a few individuals under the instigation of Constantine or anyone else who determined what was in and what was out. On the contrary, as Eusebius says, certain books were almost universally accepted from very early on, and even the disputed books were widely accepted. It was not so much a process of deciding in the fourth century what was in and authentic at the end of the day as of recognizing and ratifying what the Church and God's Spirit had long been saying about certain books, and then realizing that this meant that certain other books had to be excluded from the canon since they were not consistent with the core foundational documents that the Church had almost always affirmed. As my professor at Princeton B. M. Metzger once said, the canon was not so much chosen as recognized, and the books that were left out were not excluded by an arbitrary decision. They excluded themselves because under careful scrutiny by many different Christians it was recognized that these documents were in some way inconsistent and lacked agreement or harmony with the sacred texts which all respected. Orthodoxy preceded canon, and helped the process of discerning what the canon should look like. Consider the concluding remarks of L. T. Johnson:

> Thus by the end of the fourth century not only had the organic process of canonization been accomplished for some time, but ratification was complete. Apart from the remaining dissidents of a gnostic persuasion this was the canon of all Christians for the next millennium. In response to Luther's reopening the issue of canonicity by his demotion of Hebrews, James, Jude, and Revelation from "the proper books," and to Ulrich Zwingli's rejection of Revelation, the Council of Trent in 1546 reaffirmed a canon of twenty-seven writings, as did also the articles of the Church of England (1562/1571) and the Westminster Confession (1647).[14]

14. Johnson, *The Writings of the New Testament*, p. 603.

This statement should be compared to that of Achtemeier, Green, and Thompson:

> One can say therefore that the formation of the canon was coterminous with the life of the Christian community during its first three centuries of existence. It is not the case that some synod or council of bishops decided which books should be normative and thereafter required for Christians to accept. Rather, the books that were finally included in the canon were included because over the centuries Christians had come to use them in their worship and instruction and to revere them for the power they displayed in engendering, enriching, and correcting Christian faith. The canon thus represents the collective experience and understanding of the Christian community during the formative centuries of its existence.[15]

Conclusions

The story of the New Testament is not the story of something done by a few for the many. Nor is it a story about the orthodox co-opting of the tradition in the fourth century A.D. for self-serving purposes, to the exclusion of the historical losers. It is the story of the impact of the Jesus movement on literate Christians who chose one way or another to write to various audiences about their faith. It is a story of courage and perseverance against great odds, and a story of faithfulness to the traditions already begun to be passed down by the very first Jewish Christians in Jerusalem who prayed *marana tha* and sang praises to Christ the divine and yet human Son of God and who believed the narrative when it said that he was crucified, dead, and buried, and on the third day arose (see 1 Cor. 15:1-4), ascended into heaven, and is poised to come again. Through the toil of writing on papyri and then codices these texts were formed, copied, circulated, collected, and finally canonized. But thus far we have only told the tale of the formation of the documents which became New Testament books, and then the collection and canonization of these books as Scripture. We have not really spoken of the story and stories within the New Testament. To this task we must devote the rest of this study.

15. Achtemeier, Green, and Thompson, *Introducing the New Testament*, p. 608.

Exercises and Questions for Study and Reflection

→ Draw up a list of your favorite New Testament books. Then write down why you have picked these books.

→ Would your life of faith be any different if you focused more on some of the other books of the New Testament? Take the time to read through at least two or three times one of the books of the New Testament you have seldom if ever read. Write a journal about what you have learned from this exercise both about the New Testament and about yourself.

→ What is a canon? Why was it important for the canon to finally be defined? What historical factors do you think were most important in leading to the canonization of the twenty-seven books and not others?

→ What were the earliest books of the New Testament that were put into a collection together? What role did the invention of the codex play in this process? Why do you think Christians were such major users of codices instead of scrolls?

PART II | The Stories in the New Testament

6 | Borrowed Tales from the Earlier Testament

I was in the lobby of a London theater and it was intermission. Alec McGowan was doing a stunning one-man production of the Gospel of Mark, entirely from memory. It was fun to be a fly on the wall and listen to the comments of the audience. One person said, "Where were the birth narratives? I missed that bit at the beginning of the show." Another said, "I thought the Sermon of the Mount would have been proclaimed by now. Is it in the second half of Mark?" At least these folks knew enough of the stories in the New Testament to recognize that some Gospel contained such stories. But alas, they did not have the story straight about Mark. This episode in my life made it clear to me that it would be worthwhile to retell some of the New Testament stories at some juncture, in some kind of reasonable order. So, in this half of our study we are embracing the task of examining and retelling some of the stories that are alluded to or told in the New Testament. We will try to tell the stories roughly in chronological order, and try to tell them as stories of discrete witnesses where possible, rather than making up our own composite sketch. Sometimes following the story line will not be possible or adequate due to the complexity of the material. But in the main we intend to follow the lead of the writers and their ordering of the material as story.

It has been said that a community is defined and refined (and confined) by the stories it tells.[1] Since there was no New Testament in the era

1. It is more than a little strange that we have so many New Testament introductions that tell you very little about the actual content of the New Testament books. This

when the New Testament was written, and since the authors were all Jews, with one possible exception, it is hardly a surprise that they would draw on the great wealth of stories found in the Hebrew Scriptures.

The truth is that most New Testament authors assume a lot of their audiences. They assume that at least some of their audience already knows the Old Testament stories.[2] This is why they almost never bother to retell the Old Testament stories at length. They allude to the stories, they draw on the stories, they sometimes quote the stories, but they hardly ever fully retell the stories. This is an important point because what in effect happens is that the old stories are taken up into the new Christian stories and re-configured in various ways. We see this in so many different places in the New Testament that it becomes apparent that one must emphasize the newness even more than the fact that old stories are being used.

For example, in Revelation 1:12-16 we have a remarkable vision of Christ that draws on the story about the Son of Man and the Ancient of Days in Daniel 7. Only what happens in Revelation 1 is that some of the imagery used to describe the Ancient of Days (e.g., the white hair like wool) is now used to describe the one who is the Son of Man and also the divine Son of God. While it is too much to say that the Old Testament is simply used as a quarry for images and ideas that are radically transformed in their new context, it is quite true that the Old Testament stories are used in a flexible manner in order to get the New Testament story straight. The Old Testament is stretched to fit and explicate the New Testament story in various ways.[3] Sometimes there is indeed a concern to show how the Old Testament stories have been fulfilled or come to fruition, but sometimes it is also true that Old Testament ideas and imagery are used in fresh ways and in fresh contexts. The throne chariot vision of Ezekiel 1 is reused in

---

half of the book seeks to remedy this a bit, with a narratological approach. I am hoping to answer the questions: What is the New Testament about? What story or stories is it trying to tell?

2. I emphasize the word "story." I am not attempting to deal with the use of the Old Testament writ large in these chapters, but only the use of Old Testament stories. This means I am not concerned for the most part with the reuse of laws or oracles or proverbs, or the citation of verses from the Psalms that do not tell stories. I am examining the influence of the Old Testament stories in the New Testament.

3. Sometimes the stretching is considerable. Matthew 2:23 would be a classic example. The Old Testament does not really say "he shall be called a Nazarene" — Nazarite perhaps, but not Nazarene.

Revelation 4, but it is clear that the chariot and its attendants had something of a makeover at the hands of John the Seer. The images are plastic and can be melded and mended in various ways. Yet we should not be deceived that our authors, just because they sometimes do not reveal clearly their dependence on Old Testament stories, are ignorant of such material. Chapters like Hebrews 11 make so very apparent how the New Testament writers looked to Old Testament figures as heroes and exemplars. Bearing these things in mind, let us consider how some of the Old Testament stories are used and retold in the New Testament.

The Old Testament Reloaded — Paul as a Master Storyteller

With almost half of the New Testament books falling under the heading of Pauline material, and in view of the fact that some of his letters are our earliest documents, we must begin with Paul. One of the features of the storytelling of all the New Testament writers is that they come at their material from an eschatological and often also a Christological viewpoint. By this I mean they do not read the Old Testament quite the same way as many early Jews would have done. While they sometimes share eschatological perspective with some of the Qumran writers, the persistent Christological perspective largely sets their work apart. This is very much the case with Paul. He certainly views the Old Testament in light of the Christ event.

Cultures that are largely oral in nature in terms of how they convey information are storytelling cultures. Paul was perfectly capable of retelling Old Testament stories in a rather full way (see Galatians 4; 1 Corinthians 10), but mostly such stories function as a subtext. Paul writes out of his storied world, but sometimes the stories are just presupposed or only partially surface in his letters. Yet it is the case that Paul's logic in his letters is basically a narrative logic for it has to do with the sacred stories of Adam, Abraham, Moses, Hagar and Sarah, Israel, Christ, and Christians. It also has to do with the story of God.

The formative narratives I see Paul grounded in, reflecting on, and using are in fact five interwoven stories comprising one large drama: (1) the story of God, the one who existed before all worlds and made them; (2) the story of the world gone wrong in Adam; (3) the story of God's people in that world, from Abraham to Moses and beyond; (4) the story of the

Jewish messiah, the Christ, which arises out of the story of both human-kind and Israel, but also in fact arises out of the larger story of God as creator and redeemer; and (5) the story of Christians, including Paul himself, which arises out of stories (2)-(4).

Paul's way of thinking about individuals is within the context of what they have done, or as we would put it, within the context of their various story lines. While it will be surprising to some, Paul does not spend much time on the story of God the Father. This is all the more shocking in light of the amount of space that is given to God's story in Paul's chief sourcebook — the Hebrew Scriptures. This is in part because for Paul Christ is divine and so is part of the story of God. But this is not all that dictates how Paul tells the story of God. His interest in salvation and other eschatological matters significantly affects how Paul tells the story of God in Christ.

Paul understands God the Father to be Abba, the one to whom Jesus prayed, and whom Christians are likewise to invoke (see Rom. 8:15). God is viewed as the Creator of the world who created all things good, including human beings, which God made male and female (cf. Rom. 1:19-20; 1 Cor. 11:8-12). 1 Corinthians 11:12 stresses that all things come from God. Paul does not make the later mistake of Gnostics who pit God and the spiritual realm over against the creation, nor does Paul affirm two deities in heaven.

1 Corinthians 8:5-6 makes quite clear Paul's commitment to monotheism and to passing along the faith that there is one God, the Father, and one Lord, Jesus Christ. God is not just the one involved at creation. God the Father is the one to whom Christ will turn the world over when he completes his work after the second coming (1 Cor. 15:28; Eph. 1:22). Paul's vision of God however is not merely of one who is present at the beginning and the end. God the Father is also the one who raised Jesus from the dead and sent the Spirit (cf. 1 Cor. 15:15; Gal. 4:6). God is also the one who set Paul apart from birth, called him, and equipped him for the ministry of reconciliation, a ministry in which God is always active (cf. Gal. 1:15-16; 2 Cor. 5:18). God is Creator, Sustainer, Reconciler, Ruler, and indeed Judge of the World (Rom. 1:18).

The story of humankind is, in Paul's view, the story of three universals. All live in this present age and are subject to its spiritual and even supernatural wickedness and problems. Even the creation itself experiences the fall (Rom. 8:19-22). All live in bondage to sin, so none can be set right by their own works (Rom. 3:23-25). All are subject to death. Outside of

Christ, one experiences the unholy trinity of the world, the flesh, and the Devil, and that trinity rules in a human being's life. There is only lostness outside of Christ, and a complete inability to save oneself.

But how had humankind come to be in such a drastic and dark state of affairs if God had in fact created all things good? Paul's answer is to tell the story of Adam. It is interesting that we do not find Paul saying much about original righteousness or the prefallen condition. He focuses on the world as he finds it since Adam, the world whose form is passing away (1 Cor. 7:31), and Adam is brought into the discussion only to explain the present malaise (Rom. 5:12-21; 2 Cor. 11:3). Of course Paul knows the story of man created from the dust and given a natural life-animating principle (1 Cor. 15:47-48) and the story of being created in the image of God with Eve originally coming forth from Adam, but man coming forth from woman ever since (1 Cor. 11:7-12). Paul does not say more about this precisely because his audience does not live in that world any longer. They live in a world of the dark shadows of disease, decay, death, and the Devil. To be sure humankind is not as bad as it could be — the mirror image has been bent or broken, but not entirely shattered or lost. The point however is that humankind has fallen and cannot get up on its own. Salvation is not for Paul a human self-help program.

Of primary importance to Paul about the story of Adam and Eve is the effect they have had on the rest of the race. Paul mainly holds Adam responsible for the fall (Rom. 5:12; 1 Cor. 15:21-22), for Eve was deceived (2 Cor. 11:3). Paul believes that the story of Adam and Eve is more than a personal tragedy; their story is representative and affects those that come forth after them. The original couple not only committed the original sin but also passed on both the inclination and the determination to go and do likewise. Paul concludes that "just as sin came into the world through one man, and death came through sin, so death spread to all *because all have sinned*" (Rom. 5:12). The progeny are like the parents in their sin.

One of Paul's most creative moves in telling the story of human fallenness is found in Romans 7:7-13.[4] He tells the story in the midst of commenting on the Law. Paul apparently thought that the original sin was a violation of the tenth commandment, the one against coveting. In Romans 7:7-13, Paul is dealing with the paradox that while God's commandments

---

4. See my detailed treatment of this crucial text in *The Epistle to the Romans* (Grand Rapids: Eerdmans, 2003), pp. 179-200.

are certainly all good, yet human beings would not have known what transgression amounts to had there not been commandments — "I would not have known what it is to covet if the law had not said, 'You shall not covet.'" A transgression is a willful violation of a known law or commandment.

For rhetorical purposes, Paul has chosen to retell the tale of Adam in the first person and has chosen to personify Sin as the snake. One can then read Romans 7:8-11 as follows: "But the serpent (sin), seizing an opportunity in the commandment, produced in me all kinds of covetousness. . . . But I (Adam) was once alive apart from the Law, but when the commandment came, sin sprang to life and I died, and the very commandment that promised life proved to be death to me. For sin [the serpent], seizing an opportunity in the commandment, deceived me and through it killed me." Here is the by now familiar primeval tale of life apart from sin, then come a commandment, deception, disobedience, and ensuing death.

There are strong reasons for reading Romans 7:7-13 in this fashion: (1) In verses 7-8 there is reference to one specific commandment, called *the* commandment in verse 8, and Adam was given only one. (2) Verse 9 says, "I was living once apart from the Law," but certainly the only persons Paul believed lived before or apart from any law are Adam and Eve. (3) In verse 11 sin is certainly personified as a living thing that seized an opportunity and deceived a human being. This is surely the tale of Eve and Adam and the snake. (4) The same verb used for deception here is the one used to speak directly about Eve being deceived in the garden in 2 Corinthians 11:3. (5) In verse 7 Paul says sin was not known except through the commandment, but everyone since Adam has had personal or experiential knowledge of sin. The view that best makes sense of all the nuances of Romans 7:7-13 is that Paul is reflecting back on the primeval story of Adam and how human sin and fallenness began.

If Romans 7:7-13, which involves all past-tense verbs, is about Adam, whose story is told in Romans 7:14-25 where we find present-tense verbs? I would suggest that it is a dramatic presentation of the present fallenness of all humanity who followed in Adam's footsteps, with perhaps the story told primarily from the point of view of a Jewish person outside of Christ. Paul has prepared for this discussion earlier in Romans 5:12 where he explained not only that sin entered the world through Adam, but also that all his progeny went on to sin as well, both Jews and Gentiles. Indeed, as Romans 2:9 says, judgment for sin will begin with the household of God. Romans 5:12 says sin and death came to reign over all humankind, and

Romans 6:16-17 says those outside Christ are slaves to sin, unable to avoid sin or escape its bondage.

It must be stressed that the context of the discussion found in Romans 7:14-25 is the discussion of the Law. Notice the important statements that prepare for this section in Romans 7:5-6 where Paul speaks of believers who in the past were in the flesh, and who now have been made in Christ (v. 6). Believers have been released from the Law, as the analogy with the death of the husband makes clear. One is no longer under its jurisdiction, no longer obligated to it. Notice too how in Romans 8:8-9 Paul uses the phrase "in the flesh," just as he did in Romans 7:5-6, to characterize what was true of a person before becoming a Christian. Yet the person described in Romans 7:14-25 is said to be fleshly and sold under sin (v. 14) and cries out for deliverance. This is not a person who is free in Christ.

I have discussed elsewhere in detail who Paul identifies the "I" to be in Romans 7:14-25, considering all of the major options,[5] and there are really only two that make sense of the context of Romans 7:14-25. Paul may be discussing the Jew who knows and strives to obey the Law, but the Jew as now seen by Paul with perfect hindsight and Christian insight. This person knows that the Law of God is good, but his fallen nature leads him to do what he ought not to do. The other possibility is that Paul is describing the plight of any person outside of Christ who is under conviction, having heard God's Word, in particular his Law, and yet is still in the bondage to sin. It must be borne in mind that Paul had earlier said in Romans 2:14-15 that the essence of what the Law requires is written on Gentile hearts. Thus Romans 7:14-25 would describe the person under conviction of sin and crying out for redemption, and Romans 8:1-15 would be the response of God to this cry and the description of the transformation that happens once one is in Christ.

Notice that Romans 8:1-10 makes clear not only that a verdict of no condemnation has been pronounced but that the Spirit has entered the person's life and has set him free from the bondage to sin. The spirit of such slavery has been replaced by the spirit of adoption, and what this Spirit prompts the person to say is not "Who will deliver me from the body of this death" but "Abba Father" (contrast 7:24 and 8:15). Paul is of course not saying that believers instantly become perfect or are not after conversion still tempted to sin. The point is that while the temptation to sin remains, it no longer reigns. But in fact having taken a journey through Romans 7–8, we

5. See my *The Epistle to the Romans*, pp. 187-90.

have given a preview of coming attractions. We have gotten ahead of the story and shown where it is leading. The next story after the story of Adam that is crucial in Paul's narrative thought world is the story of Abraham.

It comes as something of a shock that Paul, the former Pharisee, while devoting a great deal of time and space to the discussion of Abraham and his story (cf. Gal. 3:6-18; 4:21-31; Romans 4; 9:6-15; 11:1), gives Moses far less ink. For Paul, Abraham is the critical example of faith prior to the coming of Christ. Galatians 3:8 puts it this way: "And the scripture, foreseeing that God would set the Gentiles right by faith, declared the Gospel beforehand to Abraham." Abraham is the prototype or, as S. Fowl has put it, the exemplar of Christian faith because he heard the first preaching of the Good News about righteousness by faith and he responded appropriately. Abraham thus is seen as the ancestor of both Jew and Gentile. Even Gentiles share the faith of Abraham (Rom. 4:16) and become with Jewish Christians his heirs and the beneficiaries of the promises given to him through Christ (Gal. 3:14).

As is true with all the stories of the Hebrew Scriptures, Paul looks at the story of Abraham through eschatological, Christological, and, to a lesser degree, ecclesiological glasses. The elements in the stories that he stresses are those most germane for his Christian audience. Yet what Paul omits from his discussion (the sacrifice of Isaac, the Sodom and Gomorrah story, the entertainment of angels, the Melchizedek incident) is as telling as what he includes. Paul's concern is to show that Abraham is a paradigm of faith, and that the promises to him are fulfilled in his seed, Christ, and by that means to those who are in Christ. In part this means that one of the most crucial aspects of the Abraham material is its chronology.

It is crucial not only that Abraham is already promised many offspring in Genesis 12:2-3 but also that God's covenant with him is already initiated in Genesis 15. The most crucial remark is "And he believed God, and it was reckoned to him as righteousness" (15:6). All of this transpires *prior* to any discussion about circumcision as a covenant sign, which appears in Genesis 17. Note also that the discussion of Hagar and Sarah does not show up until after Genesis 15:6 (see Genesis 16 and 21:8-21). Paul in Galatians draws on the Hagar and Sarah story in a shocking allegory, the point of which is that the Law should be associated with the slave girl and the old Jerusalem, and therefore should not be followed. The order of events in Genesis allows Paul to appeal to God's original dealings with Abraham over against any later institution of circumcision whether Abrahamic or Mosaic.

This leads to conclusions such as we find in Romans 4:11-12 — circumcision is only the seal or sign of a righteousness or right standing Abraham had already obtained through faith in God. Paul also sees this order of events as implying that Abraham can be the father of Gentile believers as well as Jewish ones, for like them he believed without having already been circumcised, and he was accepted on this basis (see Rom. 4:1). He is not the forefather of all believers according to the flesh but on the basis of faith. This can also lead to a further corollary. Not all of Abraham's physical descendants are true children of God, true Israelites, for it is not the children of the flesh but those of the promise who are true descendants (Rom. 9:6-7).

The paradigmatic character of Abraham comes to the fore in a text like Romans 4:23-24. Abraham is exhibit A of relating to God on the proper basis of eschatological faith: "Now the words 'it was reckoned to him' were not written for his sake alone, but for ours also. It will be reckoned to us who believe in him who raised Jesus our Lord from the dead." This is not just any story but a scriptural story, and as such provides a normative model for the people of the Book. Abraham is not merely analogous to Christians; he is their scriptural model or paradigm.[6]

The story of Abraham takes a surprising turn in Galatians 3:16 where in a tour de force argument Paul will maintain that the term "seed" in the Abraham story refers in particular to Christ. It is right to stress the twists in the tale that Paul adds to his foundational Jewish stories.[7] Genesis 17:6-7 seems to lie in the background here. It is this version of the promise to Abraham that refers to the fact that kings will come from Abraham, and it is this version that also says that the covenant is between God and Abraham and his offspring. Romans 9:6-7 shows that Paul knows quite well that "seed" is a collective noun, but the larger context of Genesis 17 has provided Paul with the legitimate opportunity to talk about the most important Jewish king that was to be the descendant of Abraham. What we learn from this discussion is that in fact Paul sees the risen Christ as, like God, an inclusive or omnipresent personality, one in whom many can abide or dwell. Christ is the seed, and believers in Christ are also that seed if they are in him. They become heirs through being in the seed who is Christ. "Seed"

---

6. See S. Fowl, *The Story of Christ in the Ethics of Paul* (Sheffield: JSOT Press, 1990), p. 94.

7. See N. T. Wright, *The New Testament and the People of God* (London: SPCK, 1992), pp. 405-9.

then in Galatians 3:16 has both a particular and a collective sense (Christ and those in him) just as it did in the case of Abraham (Isaac and subsequent descendants are promised). What this means is that if Galatians 3 is read carefully in light of the larger context of Genesis 17, if one hears the intertextual echo, then Paul in the end is not guilty of exegetical legerdemain here.

Of crucial importance for understanding Paul's narrative thought world is the connection mapped out between the Abrahamic covenant and the new covenant in Galatians 3–4. The Abrahamic covenant is seen as being fulfilled in Christ, and thus the covenant that he began is the consummation of the Abrahamic one. Both of these covenants involved the circumcised and the uncircumcised. From Paul's perspective, circumcision is not the essential issue, faith is, for Genesis 15 precedes Genesis 17. Both these two covenants involve children given by the grace of God, both involve an everlasting covenant, and both have to do with the fact that in this context all the nations of the earth will be blessed (see Gen. 17:6).

In terms of the narrative flow of Paul's thought, the cost of closely linking the Abrahamic and the new covenant is high. It means that for Paul the Mosaic covenant must be seen as a temporary arrangement, a parenthesis between the promises given to Abraham and the promises fulfilled in Christ. This does not mean that the Law was a bad thing, just a temporary one, a temporary guardian to keep God's people in line until the Messiah should come.

When Paul thinks of Adam he thinks of the entire story of sin and fall; when he thinks of Abraham he thinks of a faith-based covenant and the promises that went with it; but when he thinks of Moses, he thinks of the Law, and in particular the Law as something given *pro tempore*.

Nowhere is this more evident than in Galatians 3–4, but Romans suggests the same thing.[8] Because Paul thinks Christologically about the timeline of salvation history, in his view when Christ came the situation with regard to the Law and God's people also changed — "But when the fullness of time had come, God sent forth his Son, born under the Law, in order to redeem those under the Law, so that we might receive adoption as children" (Gal. 4:4-5). The Mosaic Law is not seen as opposed to the prom-

8. See my more detailed substantiation of this line of argument in my *Grace in Galatia: A Commentary on St. Paul's Letter to the Galatians* (Grand Rapids: Eerdmans, 1998), pp. 197-341.

ises or as annulling the Abrahamic covenant (Gal. 3:17-21); it was simply given for different times and purposes.

Paul makes clear his views on the Mosaic covenant in 2 Corinthians 3. We have there a retelling of the story of Moses' visit to Mount Sinai, and if one does not know this story, one will not understand the nuances of Paul's interpretive moves. 2 Corinthians 3 can also be said to be a tale of two ministries of two called servants of God (Moses and Paul), which leads to comments on two covenants, the Mosaic one and the new one. This tale is clearly not about the Hebrew Scriptures themselves; nor is Paul suggesting we should adopt a particular hermeneutic here — spiritual versus literal — in the interpretation of the text. Nor is Paul pitting the written word, here written in stone because the Ten Commandments are alluded to, against the Spirit or even the spoken word. Rather, he is comparing and contrasting ministries and the covenants on behalf of which these two ministries were undertaken.

Moses ascended Mount Sinai and came back down with the Ten Words and trailing clouds of glory. The Ten Commandments, like the Law as a whole, was seen by Paul as holy, just, good, and even spiritual (Rom. 7:12, 14). Paul in no way disputes that the Law came attended with splendor. The fact is however that its glory or splendor and that of Moses have been eclipsed by the greater splendor of Christ and the new covenant. Thus not only the glory on Moses' face but the Mosaic covenant itself is being annulled (2 Cor. 3:10-11). Unfortunately, though the intent and purpose was otherwise, the direct effect of the Law on fallen human beings was death-dealing rather than life-giving. The problem with the Law was that it could not give life; it could not enable one to obey it, which means it could not but condemn human behavior over and over again. What was to be done about this?

The crucial verb in 2 Corinthians 3:7, 11, 13, 14 is *katargeō*. Twenty-one of the twenty-seven uses of this verb are found in the Pauline corpus, and always in other Pauline texts the word refers to something replaced, invalidated, abolished, not merely something that is faded. The deliberate contrast between the ministry of life and that of death in 2 Corinthians 3 strongly suggests we must interpret the verb similarly here. The coming of the glorious Christ has put even former glories in the shade, in effect making them obsolete. Paul's argument is one grounded in his reading of the way salvation history has progressed. It is not about human attitudes or approaches toward the Law; nor is the Law itself seen as defective. The defect lies in fallen human beings. The effect of the Law on such fallen ones is contrasted with the effect of the Spirit on them. The written code kills; the Spirit gives life. Galatians 3:19 then makes it clear that a change of guides or guardians was needed. The Law was only until Christ came. We must reserve the discussion of Paul's treatment of the story of Christ and those in Christ for a later chapter.

What really stands out in Paul's treatment of Old Testament stories is just how much his reading of those stories is controlled by his embracing of the story of Christ and of those in Christ. Paul says what he does about Adam because he believes the last Adam has appeared and put the first one in his shade. Paul says what he does about Abraham because he is able by historical analogy to see Abraham as a sort of prototype of a Christian, out of due season. Paul says what he does about Moses because he believes that Christ has overshadowed the glory of Moses and that the glory of the Law has been eclipsed by the new covenant. It is simply astounding that a former Pharisee could associate the Law with Hagar and with bondage, but this is because of Paul's great faith in Christ and the benefits he believes Christ brings.

The Old Stories Elsewhere in the Epistles

The appropriation of Old Testament stories elsewhere in the New Testament is sometimes sublime and sometimes very surprising. Consider for example the use of the story of the fallen angels found in Jude and 1 and 2 Peter.

Jude (v. 6)	2 Peter (2:4)	1 Peter (3:19-20)
"and the angels who didn't keep their own position, but left their proper dwelling, he has kept in eternal chains in deepest darkness for the judgment of the Great Day"	"For if God did not spare the angels when they sinned, but cast them into Tartaros and committed them to chains of deepest darkness to be kept until the judgment"	"[Christ] went and made a proclamation to the spirits in prison, who in former times did not obey when God waited patiently in the days of Noah."

Obviously, the first two texts are more similar to each other than they are to the third. The first two are not obviously of Christological import, though if the reference to Christ as Lord in Jude 4 prepares for verse 5 where the Lord is the one who saved the people from Egypt and then kept the angels in chains, then we have a comment on Christ's preexistence and role in Israel's history, drawing on Wisdom ideas not unlike what we find in 1 Corinthians 10:4 (cf. Wisd. of Sol. 11:4). The author of 2 Peter however would clearly seem to see God and not Christ as the one who chained the disobedient angels.

In all these texts the reference is to the story in Genesis 6:1-4 where God was so outraged by what the angels (sons of God) did with the daughters of humanity that God brought a flood upon the earth. This Genesis context is more obvious in the 1 Peter 3 use of this material, and it is in 1 Peter 3 that we find something of clear Christological importance. There Christ (v. 18 makes clear this is who it is) goes and preaches to these angels in prison. Though the 1 Peter 3 texts have been the basis of the credal statement "he descended into hell" and also the basis of various "second chance" theologies, it is doubtful this text has anything at all to do with such notions. Indeed nothing is said about Christ's "descent" anywhere. We are simply told that after Christ died and was "made alive in the Spirit" he went and preached or made a proclamation to these spirits or angels. There may be a trace of this whole theological development in the hymn fragment in 1 Timothy 3:16, where we hear that Christ was "vindicated in spirit," a remark that is immediately followed by "seen by angels." Commentators have always thought this remark was out of place. If it referred to Christ's entry into heaven, it would be better placed just before or after the last line of the hymn which reads "taken up in glory." This reference to being seen by angels however may not be out of place at all if it is about Christ's visit to Tartaros. It is also not impossible that Ephesians 4:8 is of relevance here as well, for there it is said of Christ, quoting Psalm 68:18 with alterations, "When he ascended on high, he led or made captivity itself captive."

To understand this material a certain knowledge of Jewish angelology and demonology is necessary. For our purposes it is necessary to say only that the powers and principalities and indeed Satan himself were believed to inhabit the realm between heaven and earth. This is one reason why the planets were sometimes assumed to be heavenly beings or angels ("the heavenly host") and is also why Satan is called in the New Testament "the Ruler of the Power of the Air" (Eph. 2:2). It would appear then that 1 Peter 3, far from being about a descent to humans, is about Christ's ascent to the angels on his way to heaven, at which point he proclaimed his victory over such powers and thereby made their captivity all the more permanent and their doom sure. What we have thus far failed to point out is that all three of these New Testament texts are not merely drawing on and retelling the story of Genesis 6:1-4. They also are drawing on even earlier readings of that story found in Isaiah 24:21-22 and 1 Enoch 104:4-6. The former text reads: "On that day the Lord will punish the host of heaven and on earth the kings of the earth. They will be gathered together like prisoners in a pit and they will be shut up in a prison, and after many days they will be punished." The text from Enoch reads: "the Lord said to Raphael, 'Bind Azaz'el hand and foot, throw him into the darkness' and he made a hole in the desert which was in Duda'el and cast him there; he threw on top of him rugged sharp rocks. And he covered his face in order that he might not see the light; and in order that he might be sent into the great fire on judgment day." It should also be pointed out that this very same story is told of the Devil himself in Revelation 20:1-3.[9] Knowing the story and its precursors would have prevented those who formed the Apostles' Creed from making the mistake of thinking 1 Peter 3 was talking about Christ descending to the dead, when in fact it was about his ascending to the prison of the fallen angels.

Another of the brief Old Testament stories that nonetheless comes in for some significant treatment and use in the New Testament is the story of Melchizedek. Here again we are dealing with a phenomenon that there is a history of use and interpretation of a text, in this case Genesis 14:18-20, which is taken up in Psalm 110:4. The mysterious Melchizedek is a priest from [Jeru]salem who blesses Abraham and to whom Abraham then tithes. In the Psalm the one addressed is said to be made a priest forever, after the order of Melchizedek's priesthood.

The author of Hebrews makes no small use of this Melchizedek material. He begins his discussion of the matter at Hebrews 6:20 in the context of his discussion of Abraham (see v. 15). It is the Psalm text that he alludes to first because he wishes mainly to make the point that only Jesus can be a forever priest (in the heavenly sanctuary), and, since he is such a priest, it has to be in the order of Melchizedek's priesthood in light of the Psalm text. Thus, amazingly enough, the Melchizedek story is

9. On which see my *Revelation* (Cambridge: Cambridge University Press, 2003), pp. 245-47.

used to explain not some earthly role Jesus had but his role in heaven after his earthly life.

We then have a rather full retelling of the story of Melchizedek in
Hebrews 7:1-10, after which the author draws some theological conclusions
about Jesus. One of the astounding and interesting and quite Jewish aspects of the retelling of the story is the remark made at Hebrews 7:3 that
Melchizedek was without father or mother, without genealogy, and without beginning or end. This conclusion seems to be based on the fact that
the Genesis narrator does not tell us where the man came from or where
he went. He is unprovenanced except to say that he is King of Salem. The
silences in the story are assumed to be pregnant, and in a culture where genealogy determines identity, absence of genealogy leads to interesting conclusions. It is concluded as well that he was somebody very important
since the great Abraham, the father of the faith, tithed to him.

The author of Hebrews parlays this story into a legitimation of a critique of the levitical and Aaronic priesthoods. Why would there be a need
for another priesthood of the ilk of Melchizedek's if those priesthoods had
been sufficient unto the day? The author then urges that Christ is a better
priest because he was capable of being a priest forever as the Psalmist foresaw. He became the heavenly high priest not because of his earthly genealogy but because of "the power of an indestructible life" (7:16). To say that
this is a creative use of the Old Testament is really to say too little. Notice
that, as with the case of Paul, what drives the rereading of the Old Testament texts is what the author believes about Jesus, in this case what he believes about Jesus' current roles in heaven.

Sometimes Old Testament stories from Genesis, or later stories based
on a Genesis story, are alluded or referred to. For example, even in the brief
letter of Jude we have reference to the story of the destruction of Sodom
and Gomorrah (v. 7), the apocryphal story about the angel Michael dis-
puting with the Devil about Moses' body (v. 9), the story of Cain (v. 11), the
story of Balaam (v. 11), the story of Korah's rebellion (v. 11), and the story
of Enoch, seventh from Adam, amplified by a later quotation from an
early Jewish text. It is interesting how such a short text can be so story-
dependent on the Old Testament, whereas other New Testament texts do
not even mention Old Testament figures, stories, or texts. In the case of
2 Peter we find dependency on Jude for this same material just listed (see
2 Pet. 2:4-16) though the author amplifies it with some additional details
about Balaam, Lot, and others. One thing that one should deduce from all

that we have discussed thus far in this chapter is that the book of Genesis was the storybook that Christians turned to, over and over again, when they were looking for foundational tales that they could relate to Christian stories and Christian experience. There is frankly very little use in the New Testament of the material from about Joshua through 2 Chronicles even though it contains some compelling narratives. There are a few notable exceptions, of course (see, e.g., James 5:17 and the reference to the praying of Elijah, who made it rain), but very few outside of the Gospels and Acts. It will be worthwhile to consider one notable such text, the so-called Hall of Faith found in Hebrews 11.

In Hebrews 11 we have the roll call of faith beginning with how Abel offered a better sacrifice than Cain, how by faith Enoch, the one who pleased God, was taken out of this world without experiencing death, and how by faith Noah built the ark (cf. the retelling of the same Noah story in 1 Peter 3). There is then more extended treatment given to faithful Abraham in regard to his journey by faith to the promised land, in regard to his trusting God and so being able to sire a child in his old age, and how by faith he offered Isaac up in sacrifice. There follows reference to Isaac blessing Jacob and Esau, Jacob blessing Joseph's children, Joseph foreseeing the Exodus, and Moses' parents by faith hiding their infant. Like the story of Abraham, the story of Moses receives more than passing mention. By faith Moses refused to be known as the son of Pharaoh's daughter, left Egypt, and kept Passover, and by faith the people of Israel passed through the Red Sea with Moses. By faith the walls of Jericho fell. By faith the harlot Rahab welcomed the spies. The roll call then briefly lists Gideon, Barak, Samson, Jephthah, David, Samuel, and the prophets, and then follows a long litany of the trials and tribulations of God's people through which they endured and indeed prevailed. But the Hall of Faith does not end there, for in Hebrews 12:1-3 Jesus is listed as the final and climactic example of faith — the Author and Perfecter of faith.[10]

The Reuse of the Old Testament in Revelation

The most complex use of the Old Testament in the New, including the use of Old Testament stories, comes in Revelation. It is necessary then that we

---

10. On which see pp. 211-13 below.

consider this book in a little more depth to understand what was happening when the Old Testament was reappropriated. The fact that Revelation is full of allusions to and partial quotations of the Old Testament is of course well known.[11] The quotations are however rare, and one gets the impression that John simply has an Old Testament–saturated memory, and so images, ideas, and parts of stories have been taken up into a new Christological whole. This is for the most part correct, but it has led to the mistaken notion that John used only the Old Testament and other early Jewish (and Greco-Roman) sources rather like the way a miner goes after gold, digging around for what he is looking for without much regard for the original setting in which the precious material is found. It is also urged that in this reappropriation of earlier material John shows little interest in the original significance or meaning that a verse or an image or an idea originally had. This view has of late been challenged.[12] R. Bauckham and J. Fekkes have both argued that John has engaged in meticulous exegesis of his source material, largely the Old Testament prophetic books.[13] Fekkes, following the earlier conclusions of R. H. Charles, rightly stresses that John the prophet draws his materials directly from the Hebrew or Aramaic prophecies in the Old Testament, not from the LXX.[14] This suggests that while Revelation may not be an example of translation Greek, it may well be an example of second-language Greek, by which I mean the author's primary language is the Semitic one.[15] John is a prophet who uses apocalyptic images and symbols. The apocalyptic symbols and ideas serve the cause of prophetic interpretation of numer-

---

11. For a fuller version of this discussion see my *Revelation*, pp. 10-15.

12. A useful survey of the entire discussion pro and con about these matters can be found in G. K. Beale, *John's Use of the Old Testament in Revelation* (Sheffield: Sheffield Academic Press, 1998), with a helpful critique of those such as J. P. Ruiz and S. Moyise who do not see the author as sensitive to the literary context of the Old Testament material he uses.

13. One should also see R. Bauckham, *The Climax of Prophecy: Studies on the Book of Revelation* (Edinburgh: T. & T. Clark, 1993), esp. pp. 38-91.

14. J. Fekkes, *Isaiah and the Prophetic Traditions in the Book of Revelation: Visionary Antecedents and Their Development* (Sheffield: Sheffield Academic Press, 1994), p. 17.

15. Which places in doubt the suggestion that the author's Greek style is deliberately prolix because of his apocalyptic subject matter. John's interest is in unsealing the seals. His concern is for revelation, not deliberate obfuscation.

ous Old Testament texts, and clearly the Old Testament is John's primary nonvisionary source of material. John believes wholeheartedly that he and his audience live in the age when various prophecies and stories have been and are coming true, and so there is a definite concern on his part about the relationship between promise/prophecy and fulfillment though he approaches the matter somewhat differently than do the First and Third Evangelists.

It is no accident that Revelation is the only book in the New Testament that, like what we often find in Old Testament prophetic works, includes first-person oracles in the name of the deity. John sees himself like many another prophet as God's mouthpiece, and he would repudiate the notion that what he unveils is "his" prophecy. No indeed, it is the revelation of Jesus Christ that this book contains. This is indeed why John stresses the inviolability of these prophecies (Rev. 22:18-19). It is important to recognize then that John is talking about a sort of prophecy which unlike some other New Testament prophecy referred to by Paul (in 1 Corinthians 14; cf. 1 Thess. 5:21) does not require sifting and weighing or testing or evaluating, but rather like the prophecies in the Old Testament is by and large meant to simply be received and applied. "John not only takes up *where* the Prophets left off — he also takes over *what* they left behind. He is not only part of a prophetic circle, but stands in a prophetic continuum which carries on and brings to final revelation the living words of God entrusted to the care of the brotherhood (Rev. 10.7)."[16] It is in this context that one must evaluate John's use of the Old Testament, including especially its prophetic portions.

For example, in the first place, perhaps the main reason John does not quote the Old Testament very frequently is that he approaches that material not as a scribe or sage or apostle but as a prophet. "He does not commend his visions on the basis of apostolic authority conferred by the *earthly* Jesus. Nor is his book a personal word of exhortation which derives its authority from quoting divine revelation. . . . His commission gives birth to a new prophecy — a fresh revelation — which is authorized simultaneously by God, the *risen* Christ, and the divine Spirit."[17] This new revelation can entail quoting the Old Testament, but since John sees himself as on a par with Old Testament prophets, or among their number, he

16. Fekkes, *Isaiah and the Prophetic Traditions in the Book of Revelation*, p. 58.
17. Fekkes, *Isaiah and the Prophetic Traditions in the Book of Revelation*, p. 66.

does not very often feel the need to quote it (but cf., e.g., Rev. 2:26b-27 to Ps. 2:8a, 9). The vast array of allusions and quotes of the Old Testament (at least 278 allusions in the 404 verses in the book) serve a variety of purposes, one of which is to bolster the authority of the entire work, and the *ethos* of the speaker, John.

John speaks like the prophets of old both in the use of prophetic diction and the first-person style, but also by the use of prophetic phrases, images, and ideas. John does not borrow Old Testament material merely for its poetic effect or metaphorical force; he "wants the readers to appreciate the prophetic foundation of his statements."[18] Fekkes shows in great detail how in the vast majority of cases John's use of an Old Testament text goes beyond similarities of language and imagery, to a similar use of themes, and the correspondence even extends "to the setting and purpose of the original biblical passage" when compared to its reuse in Revelation. John seems to choose his texts on the basis of theme and the issue he wishes to address, rather than on the basis of canonical source, though clearly he favors apocalyptic material such as we find in Ezekiel, Daniel, and Zechariah, as well as material from Isaiah, Jeremiah, and Joel. "Special books do not appear to play as important a role as special themes."[19] It is untrue that John "simply uses the Old Testament as a religious thesaurus to pad his visions with conventional symbolism and rhetoric."[20] Fekkes then goes on to demonstrate, using examples from Isaiah, that the way John uses the Hebrew Scriptures is not in an ad hoc manner, but in accord with known early Jewish hermeneutical procedures.[21] As it turns out, John is interested in exegesis and being faithful to the thrust of various Old Testament prophetic texts, and he handles them in conventional ways. "By means of a Revelation of Jesus, John became the 'high priest' and prophet who handled them, interpreted them, and delivered their message to the expectant community."[22]

Fekkes is also helpful in describing how the book of Revelation may have been composed. He recognizes that John had actual visionary experi-

18. Fekkes, *Isaiah and the Prophetic Traditions in the Book of Revelation*, p. 69.
19. Fekkes, *Isaiah and the Prophetic Traditions in the Book of Revelation*, p. 103.
20. Fekkes, *Isaiah and the Prophetic Traditions in the Book of Revelation*, p. 288.
21. Fekkes, *Isaiah and the Prophetic Traditions in the Book of Revelation*, pp. 191-278.
22. Fekkes, *Isaiah and the Prophetic Traditions in the Book of Revelation*, p. 289.

ences but that what we have in this work is not a mere transcript of such experiences but the literary repristinization of them. But then one must also take into account John's previsionary influences, as well as his post-visionary redaction of his source material. It is neither a purely literary product, nor merely an exercise in exegesis of the Old Testament texts, but some combination of revelation, reflection, and literary composition.[23] "For all that Revelation is visionary, it is not *ad hoc*. And for all that its use of Scripture is implicit, it is not superficial."[24]

What I have been saying up to this point leads to the conclusion that John does not much use the Old Testament as story, nor does he much take over Old Testament stories. He concentrates on prophetic portions of the Old Testament, where stories are not told, but rather oracles are given. He does however wish to make clear that his own story is rather like the stories of the apocalyptic prophets of old, and so he does convey visions that are often similar to those of Ezekiel, Daniel, and others. The stories John tells draw on the principle of analogy or the principles of typology. What happened to Babylon of old is going to happen to Rome (and possibly others) in the future; therefore, the demise of the latter can be described using images and ideas related to the former. This is not so much fulfillment of old stories as the telling of a new one that is analogous to the old stories. The fall of Rome is not really predicted in the Old Testament. In short, what we find in the use of the Old Testament in Revelation is not so much a narrative logic as an oracular or prophetic one, which is what we would expect in the one book of prophecy found in the New Testament.

Israel's Stories in the Gospels and Acts

An entire book could certainly be devoted to the study of the use of the Old Testament in the Gospels and Acts, but our focus here is not on just any sort of use of the Old Testament, but rather on the drawing on and reappropriating of Old Testament stories. We are going to begin with the book of Acts and work our way back to the four Gospels.

23. Fekkes, *Isaiah and the Prophetic Traditions in the Book of Revelation*, pp. 289-90.

24. Fekkes, *Isaiah and the Prophetic Traditions in the Book of Revelation*, p. 290.

There is of course a strong stress in Acts on the fulfillment of Old Testament prophecies in Jesus and in the Church which is readily apparent (cf., e.g., Joel 2 in Acts 2 applied to believers and Isaiah 53 in Acts 8:32-33 applied to Jesus). This involves the use of oracles, now seen as fulfilled in the New Testament and the eschatological era, and is not really narratological in character. Luke however is the evangelist interested in recounting salvation history both past and present, and so it is no accident that we find such an accounting in story form in various places in Acts, particularly in Acts 7 in the speech of Stephen, but also in Acts 13:16-41. This does not amount to just a retelling of the story of Jesus in the light of the Old Testament, as we sometimes find in the early chapters of Acts (cf. Acts 2 and 4). We will give some detailed attention to these two speeches to see how the Old Testament stories are being used.

The sermonette found in Acts 13 is characterized as a word of exhortation (or put another way, a piece of deliberative rhetoric meant to change the behavior of the Jewish audience in the near future).[25] This sermon begins the review of salvation history at a different juncture than does Stephen's speech in Acts 7. Here the focus is on Israel's election and the formative events of the Exodus. Yet strikingly there is little real attention paid to Moses. It is by God's uplifted arm that Israel was led out of Egypt. It was God who cared for them in the wilderness. Verse 19 indicates that it was God who cleared the land of Canaan of the seven nations so that Israel could inherit it for about 450 years. The period of the judges up to Samuel is mentioned briefly in verse 20. Salvation history is being divided into epochs. Verse 21 refers to the rise of the monarchy, and it is God who raised up and deposed Saul. Notice the careful language about David with which the Scripture is laced in verse 22. There is first a partial quote from Psalm 89:20, "I have found David," then he is called "a man after my own heart" (1 Sam. 13:14), and then Isaiah 44:28 is quoted: "who will do all I want him to do." David is said to be raised up for Israel, something that will then be said in very similar terms of Jesus in verse 30. The rest of the sermon has to do with Jesus' story and its context.[26] Here it is sufficient to note that the Old Testament is used to stress

---

25. On all of what follows see my *The Acts of the Apostles: A Socio-Rhetorical Commentary* (Grand Rapids: Eerdmans, 1998), pp. 409-13.

26. Which will be treated in the next chapter.

that Israel is what it is, so far as anything good is concerned, because of the work of God. There is an implicit denial of human achievement or earned privilege. Second, the Davidic origins and connections of Jesus are prepared for and stressed by giving more attention to David at the end of the Old Testament portion of the review of salvation history. Jesus is written into the story at the juncture where a clear messianic connection can be made.

The speech of Stephen has been subjected to all sorts of analysis, a good deal of it wrong.[27] Stephen's speech is not a rambling diatribe that only at the end gets to the point; nor is it basically critical of the Law or the Temple. Indeed as Acts 7:38 shows, Stephen calls the Law God's living oracles. This sermon is critical of people; in particular, it is critical of Jews who down through the ages have rejected God's prophets and messengers and therefore God's word. It is also critical about some assumptions regarding the Temple, including the notion that God simply dwells in the Temple. In fact Stephen is very much dependent on the Pentateuch in this sermon, citing mainly Genesis and Exodus to build his case. His most telling indictment of Israel is that they do not keep the Law (v. 53). It seems that Stephen is drawing on the Deuteronomistic vision of the history of Israel — God's repeatedly disobedient Israelites are admonished by God's prophets, whose words are repeatedly rejected, bringing judgment on the disobedient Israelites (cf. 2 Kings 17:7-20; Neh. 9:26; 2 Chron. 36:14-16). False assumptions about the Temple are also rebutted, chiefly that God can be confined to some sort of sacred space. What Luke is arguing for in his use of the Old Testament here is that God transcends human structures, not that God's presence cannot be found in temples.

The speech of Stephen is framed with glory, beginning with the glory of God appearing to Abraham (7:2) and concluding with the glorious vision of the Son of Man (v. 56). The speech will set about to make clear that the early Christians, such as Stephen, stand in a line of continuity with God's chosen leaders such as Abraham, Joseph, Moses, and the prophets. This sermon, prior to verse 52, is not specifically Christian, but the way it plots the trajectory of salvation history and the way it uses Old Testament stories are meant to lead the hearer to a Christian conclusion about Jesus and his followers. It is then a Christian reading of the history, though not overtly Christian in its content up to verse 52. The use of the Old Testa-

27. See my discussion in *Acts of the Apostles*, pp. 259-75.

ment in this speech is basically by way of allusion, with amplification (e.g., angels mediated the Law).

The expansion of the story of Abraham is clear. We are told God appears in glory to Abraham in Ur. The biblical text does not say this, but Genesis 15:7 makes it evident that he was called out of Ur. Verses 3-5 record the process of going to Haran and then on to the promised land. Verse 8 refers to the covenant of circumcision (cf. Gen. 17:10) which was made with Abraham. In some ways what Stephen does not say about Abraham is as significant as what he does say. He does not speak about Abraham's faith, much less about his faith being reckoned as righteousness. Rather the emphasis lies on the promise of offspring and land.

Stephen skips for the most part the story of Isaac and Jacob and chooses to mention the story of Joseph's jealous brothers. Despite their jealousy and Joseph being sold into Egypt, God used the situation for good. It seems clear that one of the principles of selection of material is to establish the pattern of Israel's misbehavior, disobedience, and rejection of the message and messengers of God. But it is also clear that to some degree the story of Joseph is seen as a foreshadowing of the story of Jesus. Joseph experienced an amazing reversal, going from being a slave in Egypt to helping rule Egypt. God is the God of surprising reversals.

In verses 13-14 there is a major Lukan theme, the theme of the second chance, based on the double visit. By this I mean that in salvation history God will visit his people more than once. If he visits them the first time and they do not recognize him, they can claim ignorance; but if he comes a second time in the person of a Joseph or a Moses or a Jesus, ignorance can no longer be used as an excuse.

Verse 17 suggests that the promise of land to Abraham was first fulfilled when Israel first fully occupied the land after the wilderness wandering. Verse 20 turns to the story of Moses, which is divided into three forty-year periods. Moses was born and was seen as beautiful in God's eyes. Stephen (going beyond what the Old Testament says, but cf. similarly Philo *Life of Moses* 1.21-24) speaks of Moses' education in Egyptian ways and wisdom, and how by being brought up by Pharaoh's daughter he became powerful in word and deed. The second forty-year period is presented in verses 23-29, with Moses presented as a ruler and a judge. Verse 25 is especially critical, as it is not found in the Exodus story. It is often possible to tell where the emphasis lies by asking what an author adds to an Old Testament story. This verse portrays Moses as a reconciler who assumes his people will recognize what he is trying to do on their behalf. But Moses is rejected and indeed betrayed by his own people who reveal he had killed an Egyptian, which in turn causes Moses to flee and become a resident alien in Midian.

At verse 30 we are told that an angel appeared to Moses in the wilderness of Sinai in the burning bush (see Exod. 3:2 LXX). Again God manifests his presence outside the temple precincts (one of the major themes of this speech). Moses hears the voice of God from the bush, trembles, and averts his eyes, showing that he is a pious man who knows that a person cannot look at God and live. Moses has been told of the mistreatment of Jews in Egypt and that God has come down to help them, using Moses as his agent and messenger. The tone of the discourse changes at verse 35 where direct address begins to be used and we have five references to "this Moses." Stephen is pointing out a repeated pattern: God sends leaders; Israel rejects them. "This Moses" leads the Israelites out of Egypt, having performed signs and wonders, and he continues to perform such acts and lead God's people for forty years. It is finally at verse 37 that we get a clear clue as to where this discourse is going: Moses prophesied that God would raise up a prophet from among Israel "for you." Deuteronomy 18:15 is being applied to Jesus, just as Acts 3:22 was. Moses is portrayed as the founder of a true religion conveying the living words of God to the people, but unfortunately verse 39 says that he was pushed aside by God's people, who turned to a deity of their own devising, an idol. It seems clear that one of the major points of this telling is to clarify the difference between true and false worship. Stephen says that God turned them over to their own sin and they became a captive of their own choices.

Stephen is not interested in focusing on the royal lineage of kings. David and Solomon's story is mentioned only in passing, and only insofar as worship and places of worship are part of their story. David asked that he might find God a dwelling place, but he was not allowed. Solomon however is not criticized for building God a temple. At this juncture we have a direct quote of Isaiah 66:1-2. The point is not that God's presence can't be found in a temple but that it cannot be confined there, and, furthermore, that God cannot be controlled by building temples and offering sacrifices. What is being critiqued in this lengthy retelling of Israel's story is not only Israel's rejection of God's messengers and message, but a God-in-the-box sort of theology that thinks that God can be

Signs of the Roman presence in the Holy Land were everywhere, even on the beach at Caesarea Maritima where an aqueduct was built. Luke, in his presentation of the story of Jesus and his followers, seems to be most cognizant of the Roman presence in his telling of the story of Jesus and in his retellings of the Old Testament story. This may in part be because he wrote some of his two-volume work in Caesarea in the late 50s while awaiting Paul's release from house arrest there.

confined, controlled, and manipulated through temple and sacrifice. Idolatry is the attempt to fashion and control God with human hands, using human means. All of this leads up to the indictment of Stephen's audience, whom he sees as repeating the negative pattern of various forebears.

Luke uses the Old Testament stories in Acts as a way of helping the audience to remember, and in some cases go and do likewise, but more often go and do otherwise. The stories are often told in embellished or enhanced forms, and always with the end in view, which end is the story of Jesus and its sequel. It is interesting that it is especially the stories of Abraham, Moses, David which come into play repeatedly to one degree or another, but these stories are used in a rather different fashion than Paul uses them. Abraham, for instance, is not used as the paradigm of righteousness by faith.

The Gospel of Luke uses the Old Testament stories in somewhat the same manner as we find in Acts, except that in the Gospel there is a stronger stress of how Jesus is the consummation or fulfillment of prophecies, and so less emphasis is placed on his relationship to Old Testament stories (as opposed to oracles — notice the emphasis on what the prophets have spoken in Luke 24:25-27, though Moses is mentioned, as are all the prophets). Nevertheless, quite a bit can be said.

First, it may be observed that Old Testament stories affect how Luke tells the story of Zechariah and Elizabeth and John in Luke 1. We are meant to hear echoes of the story of Hannah and Samuel of course. This sort of storytelling has as its underlying assumption that there is a pattern to God's dealings with people, as well as a pattern to how they can and should respond.

But notice that Luke has an even more noteworthy prophet in mind when he thinks of John. Luke 1:17 says that John will go on before the Lord in the spirit and power of Elijah. But that is not all. John is also living out the prophecy of Isaiah 40 about a voice crying out in the wilderness, preparing the way of the Lord (see Luke 3:4). Jesus confirms that he is living out that Scripture and fulfilling it (Luke 7:27) just as he confirms in Luke 7:21-22 to John that he himself is living out Isaiah 61. Already in Luke 4:18-19 this text is indicated to be Jesus' life verse: "The Spirit of the Lord is upon me, because he has anointed me to preach good news to the poor . . . to proclaim the year of God's favor" (Isaiah 61). Notice that those not in the know try to apply the story of Elijah to Jesus (due to his raising of a child as Elijah had done [cf. Luke 7:11-17];[28] Herod the tetrarch is confused because he has already beheaded the one he thought was the Elijah figure [Luke 9:7-9]; see also Luke 9:19).

The choice to stick with prophetic texts in the Third Gospel is also reflected at Luke 11:29-32, only this time it is not oracles but rather the story of Jonah that is seen as a parallel to the story of Jesus. Jonah was a sign to the Ninevites of coming judgment if they did not repent. But they did do so. This is coupled with the story of the Queen of Sheba who came from the ends of the earth to listen to Solomon's wisdom. These two wit-

28. The Old Testament text serves only as precursor and subtext, not as part of the story itself here.

nesses, the Ninevites and the Queen, will testify on judgment day against those who refused to listen to Jesus. Here there is comparison by contrast. These earlier pagans listened. Jesus' Jewish audience largely did not.

The Old Testament is used again in Luke 11:50 to stress moral responsibility and judgment coming on Israel for their rejection of Jesus — "this generation" is to be held responsible for the shedding of the blood of all the prophets from Abel to Zechariah! This presupposes knowledge of the stories of how so many of these figures were killed or rejected by God's people. The same complaint or lament is made about Jerusalem as about "this generation" in Luke 13:34. Since there are many stories in the form of parables that Jesus tells in this Gospel, it should be clear that Jesus is more interested in telling his own stories, rather than reusing or reiterating the Old Testament ones. This in part reflects the actual ministry of Jesus, but it also reflects the way Luke periodizes salvation history: "The Law and the Prophets were proclaimed until John. Since that time the Good News of the Kingdom of God is being preached" (Luke 16:16). Now is the time for recognizing the fulfillment of Old Testament prophecies, yes, but for proclaiming not the old stories but the Good News. Again we see this pattern of drawing on Old Testament stories to warn of coming judgment on the unsuspecting and unprepared in Luke 17:26-27: "Just as it was in the days of Noah, so also will it be in the days of the Son of Man. People were eating and drinking and marrying and giving in marriage up to the day Noah entered the ark. Then the flood came and destroyed them all." There follows in 17:28-34 a similar use of the story of Lot and his wife and the judgment that befell Sodom and Gomorrah. Jesus is living in the age of fulfillment, but that meant the fulfillment of foreshadowing stories of judgment as well as the fulfillment of the Good News.

The episode of the cleansing of the Temple as recorded in Luke 19:45-48 includes the quotation of two Old Testament texts, Isaiah 56:7 and Jeremiah 7:11. Jesus in the use of the latter text is alluding to the destruction of the Temple at the hands of the Babylonians, as foretold by Jeremiah (see likewise Mark 11:17 which Luke is following). This was a nightmare that most every Jew knew by heart. It is not surprising that this utterance and the action in the Temple got Jesus in hot water with the high priest and his entourage.

A more surprising use of the story of Moses at the burning bush is found at Luke 20:37-38 (following Mark 12:26), where Moses' reference to the God of Abraham, Isaac, and Jacob is taken to show that these three gentlemen will rise from the dead, since God is God of the living and not of the dead, "for to him all are alive." This could be said to be an example of when a story has a hidden meaning or fuller sense.

In some regards it is not surprising that Luke does not spend a lot of time retelling Old Testament stories. He believes he is writing about the age of the fulfillment of prophecies for a start, not a time of retelling old stories, and he also believes the emphasis must be on the Good News, the new thing that is happening. Thus even when there are allusions to old stories or a partial retelling of them, it is in service of the Good News, and sometimes in service of warning what happens to those who reject the Good News — they become like Lot's wife, or Noah's neighbors. Notice too that Luke the salvation historian does not spend a great deal of time quoting or alluding to Old Testament stories even in the Passion Narrative. He wants the Jesus story to speak for itself, though he is happy to cast the tale from first to last so it has a "biblical" ring to it. Elizabeth is not Hannah, and neither John nor Jesus is really Elijah, but taking the Old Testament story as casting material or as background scenery or as subtext is a technique Luke uses.

Mark is even less interested than Luke in having his central characters retell or draw on Old Testament stories. There is in Mark 2:25-26 Jesus' response to the Pharisees, "Have you never read what David did when he and his companions were hungry and in need? In the days of Abiathar the high priest he entered the house of God and ate the consecrated bread, which is lawful only for priests to eat. And he also gave some to his companions." The story is found in 1 Samuel 21, and there is some confusion as to whether Jesus has told the tale rightly or not. Was it Abiathar or Ahimelech who was high priest on that occasion?[29] For our purposes what is important is that the story is used to provide a precedent which justifies Jesus' disciples' behavior on the Sabbath.

The story of Elijah comes up for discussion, not surprisingly in relationship to John the Baptist and Jesus, at various junctures (see Mark 6:15; 8:28), but Mark 9:11-13 is of special interest. Here it is not the story of the historical Elijah that is in view, but the expected eschatological one who was prophesied in Malachi 4:5. But one must also note the way Isaiah 40 is reused in Malachi 3:1, which prepares for what is said in Malachi 4:5-6. The

---

29. See the discussion in my *The Gospel of Mark: A Socio-Rhetorical Commentary* (Grand Rapids: Eerdmans, 2001), pp. 130-31.

description of John in Mark 1 of course draws on Isaiah 40, but it is clear from the way Mark's narrative ensues that John raises the question about the eschatological Elijah and where he (or Jesus) might be living out that story. Thus, when Jesus says Elijah does come first and restores all things (before the Son of Man must suffer many things and be killed and rise), he is clearly placing the mantle of that story of Elijah on John, not on himself. And he says that the story did not have a happy ending — "and they have done to him everything they wished, just as it is written about him." This last may be an allusion to the death threat made by Jezebel in 1 Kings 19:1-3 against the historical Elijah. But there is something very offensive about this retelling of the story of Elijah. The historical Elijah escaped the clutches of Jezebel and lived until he was taken up into heaven by God. But this latter-day eschatological Elijah suffered a grisly death, beheading at the hands of a latter-day Jezebel-like queen: Herodias.

At Mark 10:6-8 the Genesis story of Adam and Eve is briefly addressed. Genesis 1:27 and 2:24 are quoted. The point of the citations is not just to refer to the first couple but the first coupling, and God's intentions of there being a permanent, one-flesh union. Here we have the notion that in the eschatological age, God's design for the creation order before the Fall should not merely be reviewed but should be enacted. The story is told in a way to make it clear that there should be no more taking into account the hardness of the human heart. Divorce should not happen to those whom God has joined together, though the telling recognizes that some third party could possibly tear them asunder.

The citation of the beginning of Psalm 22 at Mark 15:34 does fall within our purview because in that psalm the author tells his tale of woe and distress, and calls out for God to rescue him. It is not clear that we are meant to think that Jesus is conjuring up the entire psalm, which ends on a happier note than it begins, but it is clear that the quote and partial allusion to the story in that psalm are important. Jesus identifies himself with the unrighteous or unjust suffering of the psalmist. But notice even here an Elijah *traditio* enters the picture. The listeners think Jesus is calling for Elijah to come and rescue him. There was a widespread belief in early Judaism that Elijah would come in a time of need and rescue the righteous and protect the innocent.

The use of Old Testament stories in the Gospel of John is even sparser than in Mark. The Gospel of course starts with an echo of Genesis 1, God's creation of the world. But it filters this story through what is said about the Wisdom of God in places like Proverbs 3 and 8–9, and also in the Wisdom of Solomon. It is in the main the story of Wisdom, rather than the story of the Father, that lies in the background here.[30]

At John 1:51 the story of Jacob at Bethel is alluded to (Genesis 28). Jacob falls asleep at Bethel and has a dream "that there was a ladder set upon the earth, and the top of it reached to heaven, and behold the angels of God were ascending and descending on it" (28:12). But here the angels are ascending from and descending on Jesus! I would suggest that this means that Jesus is the place where heaven and earth, God and humankind, meet. Jesus is the Christian's Bethel. Jesus, not a place, is the gate of heaven — the way. He is also the locus of God's presence on earth — the house of God on earth.

John 3:14 refers to the story of Moses lifting up the snake in the desert and draws an analogy with the lifting up of the Son of Man. The story of the bronze serpent is found in Numbers 21:8-9. It was made to protect God's people from dying when they were bitten by a poisonous snake. The bronze snake was lifted up on a pole so it could be seen, and those who looked on it lived. At a simple level then the use of this story is meant to suggest that those who want to live need to look to the Son of Man who will be lifted up on the cross. But there may be more here. Since a snake is an emblem of Satan, it may be that John is alluding to the notion that through the cross, through the lifting up of the Son of Man, one gains immunity from the venom of the powers of darkness, from eternal death. The Son of Man can convey divine life, and what happened on the second tree reversed the effect of what happened at the first one.[31]

The story about manna from heaven is not only alluded to but quoted in John 6:31 (quoting Ps. 78:24, 25; cf. Exod. 16:4; Neh. 9:15). Jesus in essence says to those quoting the story that they need to get the story straight. Psalm 78:24ff. is especially at issue here. It was not Moses who provided the manna but rather God. The point of this discussion is to make clear that One greater than Moses is present to offer a sort of sustenance that satisfies in a way that manna never could.

30. On what follows see my *John's Wisdom: A Commentary on the Fourth Gospel* (Louisville: Westminster/John Knox, 1995).

31. This reading of the story is possible especially in view of the fact that in John 19 the author goes out of his way to portray the paradigmatic man and woman disciple standing beneath the tree that the Son of Man hangs on, who while still hanging on the tree gives these two new life and bequeaths them to each other. See pp. 188-90 below.

When one gets to the Passion Narrative in John, much like what can be found in Matthew, there are a plethora of Scripture quotations and allusions, but to prophecies and Psalm texts, not to stories. The motif is that of fulfillment, not the retelling or extension of a story or analogy or typology based on an Old Testament story. This is not a great surprise since in this Gospel Jesus is not really portrayed as a storyteller. He is not shown to be the parable giver that the Synoptic writers stress that he was.

As was the case with Mark's Gospel, there is a quotation from Psalm 22 in the Passion Narrative at John 19:24, only in this case it is a different portion of the story of the righteous sufferer. Here Psalm 22:18 is quoted about the dividing of his garments by his adversaries after casting lots for them. The reference to Jesus being thirsty in John 19:28 conjures up yet another story about a righteous sufferer found in Psalm 69 (here alluding particularly to 69:21).

Our last Gospel for consideration is Matthew. We have dealt at length with the sapiential orientation of this Gospel, and, when that orientation is coupled with the fulfillment of prophecy stressed in the First Gospel, and we add how Matthew takes over some 95 percent of Mark, none of this would lead us to expect to find many echoes or quotations of Old Testament stories in this Gospel.[32]

The royalty of Jesus is a big stress in this Gospel, which begins with the Davidic genealogy (even though it is Joseph's, not Mary's) and ends with Jesus portrayed as the King of the Jews even on the cross. There is the story of the royal birth from Isaiah 7:14 of one to be called Immanuel, which is quoted in Matthew 1:23. The context in Isaiah is of a prophetic sign that will be given to the house of David. So, the very beginnings of the story of Jesus are couched in royal Davidic terms.

Things get more interesting in Matthew 2:15 where we have a quotation from Hosea 11:1, the story of how God called his child Israel out of bondage in Egypt. Here the story of Israel is recapitulated in Christ. He is now the son who is being called out of Egypt. The interesting thing about the use of the Exodus story here is that it sets up the motif that Jesus is Israel gone right. This son does not wander back to the land over the course of forty years; he comes right back; he is the one, as he later tells John, who must fulfill all righteousness for Israel (Matt. 3:15).

32. See my *Jesus the Sage: The Pilgrimage of Wisdom* (Minneapolis: Augsburg/Fortress, 1994), pp. 341-70.

Though Jesus definitely speaks in parables in this Gospel, Jesus does not by and large tell or retell Old Testament stories in Matthew. It is interesting, however, how Matthew adds to his Markan source a Scripture quotation from time to time, which does conjure up a story. For example, in Matthew 8:17 there is a quotation of Isaiah 53:4, the ultimate story of the righteous sufferer, but here it is used to refer to Jesus healing people and taking up their infirmities, in the sense of alleviating their diseases. The parallel account in Mark 1:29-34 does not have this Scripture citation that brings into the discussion the story of the righteous Suffering Servant. There is an even fuller quotation of a Servant song story at Matthew 12:18-21 where Isaiah 42:1-4 is quoted at length to illustrate that the Scriptures had pretold the story of the one who would withdraw and yet continue to heal, being very careful not to harm anyone.

There is a brief allusion to the story of the destruction of Sodom and Gomorrah at Matthew 10:15 with Jesus making the application that they will have a more lenient judgment than those cities which reject Jesus' messengers. This same sort of allusion to the Sodom story is replayed at Matthew 11:23-24, only in this case Capernaum is the city which is specified as due for a harsher judgment. There is also an explicit statement at Matthew 11:14 that John the Baptist is the latter-day Elijah of Malachi's prophecy,[33] a story which is reiterated and developed further at Matthew 17:11-12.

In Matthew 12:3-4 the Evangelist takes over Mark's retelling of the story of David taking priestly bread on the Sabbath, only he eliminates the complications by eliminating the reference to Abiathar.[34] Similarly, in Matthew 19 he takes over the Mark 10 material on God's creation-based plan for marriage, but the context in Matthew is the question as to whether one can divorce for any and every cause. At Matthew 22:32 the contextual reference to Moses and the bush is eliminated from the Markan source in the saying about God being the God of the living, not the dead.

An expanded version of the story of Jonah is brought into play at Matthew 12:39-42 compared to what we find in Luke. Here the portion of the story about Jonah being in the belly of the whale is also related, and a parallel is drawn to the death and resurrection of the Son of Man! This is quite a use of the Jonah story, which is not of course literally about death and resurrection, and at Matthew 16:4 it will be reiterated that Israel will

33. See pp. 136-38 above.
34. See pp. 136-37 above.

receive only the sign of Jonah. In the reference to the blood of the righteous from Abel to Zechariah (Matt. 23:35), Matthew adds that Zechariah is the son of Barakiah, who was murdered between the altar and the Temple. Thus, more of the story is given than in the parallel.[35]

It is difficult to know what to make of the Matthean telling of the demise of Judas. Three texts (Jer. 19:1-13; 32:6-9; Zech. 11:12-13) are apparently being drawn on. Only the first of these actually involves a story about a purchasing of a potter's field. It appears that the Evangelist is suggesting that motifs both from a story and from prophecies are fulfilled in the story of Judas's demise.

Conclusions

Even a cursory reading of the material in the New Testament that draws on Old Testament stories shows that there is a great wealth of material being used in the New Testament. The tendency to focus too much on prophetic texts being fulfilled can cause one to overlook how often the New Testament writers grounded, illuminated, amplified, and explicated their proclamation of the gospel by the use of Old Testament stories. It is interesting that the material most frequently used is from the Pentateuch, particularly the foundational stories in Genesis, and to a lesser degree those from Exodus. Notice that large portions of the historical books are never quoted or alluded to at all, and this even includes a lot of interesting material in Joshua and Judges as well. The story of the righteous sufferer, as told either by the psalm writers or by 2 Isaiah, comes up for a good deal of use, not surprisingly. But as rich a cornucopia of material as all this is, it pales by comparison to the new stories that the New Testament tells about its own heroes, whether we think of Jesus, or the disciples, or the holy family, or many others. The Old Testament stories are used far less in comparison to the great wealth of new stories that are told in these twenty-seven books. It is to these new stories that we must turn our attention in the next chapter.

35. See pp. 136-37 above.

Exercises and Questions for Study and Reflection

→ List your favorite Old Testament stories. Then list the stories from the Old Testament that come up with some regularity in the New Testament. Does your list look similar to the New Testament list? If not, what do you make of this fact? Do you think it is possible to tell which Old Testament stories were the favorites of New Testament writers by the ones they choose to use? Why or why not?

→ Reflect on the difference between a literal use of the Old Testament and a homiletical or less precise use of it. Are both legitimate? How do you feel about how flexibly the New Testament writers used Old Testament stories?

→ Write a paragraph about the difference between a quotation, an allusion, and an echo of an Old Testament story. Cite an example of each. What is the difference between quoting and borrowing phrases and ideas for your own purposes?

→ Why do you think it is the Old Testament stories from Genesis and Exodus that are most cited or used in the New Testament? Why do you think more materials from the historical books are not used?

→ Why do you think the story told in Isaiah 53 and in the Psalms about the righteous sufferer was found so helpful in understanding and explaining Christ's death?

7 | Stories of Paul and Peter: The Trials and Tribulations of Apostles

It may seem somewhat odd to begin the discussion of New Testament stories with someone other than Jesus, since he is the dominant character in the New Testament; however, as we have said before, Paul's letters are our earliest witnesses and present us with the earliest Christian stories told, and, as missionaries go, Paul and Peter are our two most important figures. We will deal with members of Jesus' family in a separate chapter, before concluding our study with an examination of the stories of Jesus both outside and within the Gospels.

Paul — Apostle to the Gentiles

You would think that with as many Pauline letters as we have in the canon, we would know a great deal about the apostle to the Gentiles. The truth is, however, that Paul is not writing an autobiography in any of these letters; he does not in the main focus on himself; and in fact his discussions of himself are remarks made largely in passing. We know more about Paul and his life from Acts than we do from Paul's own letters. But we must start with the letters and work our way to Acts. Since Paul, after Jesus, is the only figure for whom we have a rather full portrait, it will be useful to provide first a chronological outline of his life and work.[1]

---

1. See my *The Paul Quest: The Renewed Search for the Jew of Tarsus* (Downers Grove, Ill.: InterVarsity, 1998), pp. 304-31, for a more detailed treatment.

A.D. 5 (± three or four years) — Saul is born in Tarsus in Cilicia of conservative Jewish parents who have Roman citizenship.

A.D. 10 (or a little earlier) — Saul's family moves to Jerusalem, while Saul is still quite young.

A.D. 15-20 — Saul begins his studies in Jerusalem with R. Gamaliel, grandson of R. Gamaliel the Elder.

A.D. 30 — Jesus is crucified by Pontius Pilate.

A.D. 31-33 (or 34) — Saul persecutes the Church in Jerusalem.

A.D. 34 (or 35) — Saul is converted on the road to Damascus, and travels on to Damascus.

A.D. 34-37 — Paul in Arabia and Damascus.

A.D. 37 — Paul's first visit as a Christian to Jerusalem.

A.D. 37-46 — Paul preaches in his home region. Results unknown but possibly a time of great persecutions (see 2 Cor. 11:23-29).

A.D. 41-42 — Paul's visionary experience and thorn in the flesh (2 Cor. 12:1-10).

A.D. 47 (approximately) — Barnabas finds Paul in Tarsus and brings him to Antioch.

A.D. 48 — Paul makes his second visit to Jerusalem (Acts 11 = Galatians 2), the famine visit with Barnabas (and Titus). There is a private agreement between Paul and the "pillars" of the Jerusalem church that he and Barnabas would go to the Gentiles, while Peter and others would go to the Jews. Circumcision is not imposed on Titus, and issues of food and fellowship are apparently not resolved at this meeting.

A.D. 48 — Paul's first missionary journey with Barnabas follows his second visit to Jerusalem (Acts 13–14), including a visit to south Galatia.

A.D. 49 — Paul and Barnabas return to Antioch. The "men who came from James" visit the church there, and the Antioch incident transpires (Gal. 2:11-14).

A.D. 49 — Claudius expels Jews from Rome, leading to the arrival of Priscilla and Aquila in Corinth.

A.D. 49 — Later the same year, Paul discovers that the circumcision party has visited his congregations in Asia Minor and has bewitched some of his converts there. Paul writes Galatians in response to this crisis shortly before going up to Jerusalem for the third time.

A.D. 49 or 50 — The Apostolic Council is held in Jerusalem (Acts 15). Public agreement is reached that Gentile converts do not need to be circumcised but they do need to avoid the basic actions that offend Jews, namely, idolatry and immorality and in particular the sort that transpired in pagan temples. They are not to attend idol feasts in idol temples.

A.D. 50-52 — The second missionary journey takes Paul and Silas not only to Asia Minor but also to Macedonia and Greece. This period of Paul's life is recorded in Acts 15:40–18:23. It is during this period of time that Paul picks up Timothy in Lystra (Acts 16:1) and Luke in Troas (16:10-13).

A.D. 50-52 — Paul stays in Corinth. He writes 1 and 2 Thessalonians.

A.D. 51 — The Gallio incident transpires (Acts 18:12-18).

A.D. 52 — Paul returns to Antioch after a brief visit to Jerusalem (Acts 18:22).

A.D. 53 — The last missionary period for Paul as a free man. He journeys overland from Antioch to Ephesus, which is to be his base at least until A.D. 55, and perhaps until sometime in A.D. 56.

A.D. 53-54 — Paul writes his first (currently extant) letter to the Corinthians.

A.D. 55 — Paul receives news of real trouble in Corinth from one of his coworkers, and this precipitates the so-called painful visit to Corinth from Ephesus, a visit mentioned only in 2 Corinthians 2:1. This visit is a disaster, and it is followed by a stinging letter of rebuke, sometimes identified wrongly with 2 Corinthians 10–13.[2] Titus is the bearer of this stinging letter, and Paul becomes fearful he has overdone it. After some missionary work in Troas, Paul crosses over into Macedonia hoping to meet Titus and hear how his letter has been received. This journey is referred to in both 2 Corinthians 2:12-13 and in Acts 20:1-16.

A.D. 55 (fall, or possibly spring 56) — A relieved Paul writes 2 Corinthians, probably from Philippi or somewhere in Macedonia. Afterward he visits Corinth for three months and then returns to Philippi in time for Passover.

A.D. 56 (late)or early 57 — Paul is again in Corinth where he writes

---

2. See my discussion in *Conflict and Community in Corinth: A Socio-Rhetorical Commentary on 1 and 2 Corinthians* (Grand Rapids: Eerdmans, 1995), pp. 327-30.

Romans (see Rom. 16:1) in preparation for his planned trip to Rome after a visit to Jerusalem (Rom. 15:25).

A.D. 57 — Paul, traveling by boat, sets out for what would be his last trip to Jerusalem. He sails from Philippi to Troas (see Acts 20:6) and then on to Miletus. Paul hurries on in order to be in Jerusalem in time for Pentecost in May of A.D. 57. After arriving in Jerusalem and briefly visiting with the Christians there, Paul is taken into Roman custody after something of a riot in the Temple precincts.

A.D. 57-59 — Paul is in custody in Caesarea Maritima awaiting the resolution of his case.

A.D. 59 (fall) — Journey to Rome.

A.D. 60 (spring) — Arrival in Rome.

A.D. 60-62 — House arrest in Rome. Production of the Captivity Epistles.

A.D. 62 — Release from house arrest.[3]

A.D. 62-64 — Further missionary travels east, and possibly also west.

A.D. 64-65 — Rearrest during the Neronian crackdown after the fire in July of 64.

A.D. 65-68? — Imprisonment in Mamertine prison. The production of the Pastoral Epistles, shortly before or after Paul's execution.

A.D. 66-68? — Execution of Paul in Rome by beheading.[4]

In his earliest letter, Galatians, Paul does make some autobiographical remarks. Besides learning that he converted various Gentiles in Galatia, we also learn that Paul is a Jew (2:15), that he claims to have been commissioned by Jesus Christ and God the Father (1:1), and that he has a gospel that is not of human origin (1:12) — rather it came by way of a revelation from Jesus. As a Jew he practiced the Jewish way of life, and this led to an intense persecution of the Church in an attempt to destroy that community (1:13). Paul is able to say that he had advanced in education and standing in Judaism beyond many his own age, being very zealous for the traditions of the ancestors.

---

3. Though of course it is also possible that Paul was executed at this juncture, in which case he did not write the Pastoral Epistles since they deal with a time subsequent to that of the end of Acts.

4. We owe to 1 Clement 5 the information that Paul was beheaded during the reign of Nero.

Paul's sense of call is a strong one. He believes that God set him apart even from birth (1:15) and revealed his Son Jesus within Paul (i.e., by revelation to the innermost part of his being), for the purpose of preparing Paul to preach to the Gentiles (1:16). Once this event happened in his life, he first went off to Nabatean Arabia[5] and then returned to Damascus, which makes it clear that he had been in or near Damascus at the time of his awakening. Paul did not consult with any human beings during this time, including those who were apostles before him. About three years later, Paul did go up to Jerusalem to get acquainted with Peter, a fact that presupposes he knew who Peter was before then. The only other apostolic figure he saw on that trip was James, the brother of Jesus (1:18-19). After that Paul went to Syria and Cilicia (presumably including Damascus and Antioch). In his first trip to Jerusalem he had only had a private visit with Peter and James. He did not make himself known to the churches in Judea; they only heard by word of mouth about the change in his life.

Then, fourteen years after his conversion, Paul made a second trip up to Jerusalem, this time taking both Barnabas and Titus along. Here again Paul has a private meeting with leaders, presenting his gospel to them lest he be "running in vain." This shows that he felt it critical to have the approval of the leadership in Jerusalem for his missionary work with Gentiles. On this trip, no one compelled Titus to be circumcised. There is the implication that some from Jerusalem had been observing what Paul was doing for some time, and that they had been demanding that Gentiles become Jews in order to be full-fledged followers of Jesus. Paul insisted that those from Jerusalem added nothing to his message, and subtracted nothing from his work. The end result of that meeting was that Peter, James, and John gave Paul and Barnabas the right hand of fellowship and recognized the grace given to Paul, agreeing that the pillar apostles should go to the Jews, while Paul and Barnabas focused on the Gentiles. It is clear from what follows that this did not mean Paul and Peter would go to different regions. Rather, they would focus on different ethnic groups. This is why we find both Peter and Paul in Antioch together in Galatians 2:11.

There was a confrontation in Antioch between Peter and Paul because, prior to coming to Antioch, Peter had been comfortable with eating with Gentiles, but under some pressure from people who came from

---

5. See my *Grace in Galatia: A Commentary on St. Paul's Letter to the Galatians* (Grand Rapids: Eerdmans, 1998), pp. 117-18.

James, he withdrew, and so Paul accused him of hypocrisy. Even Barnabas was led astray by those Paul calls the circumcision party.

This biographical vignette tells us a fair bit about Paul shortly before his conversion, and what ensued after that, but since this is a purposely selective account meant to prove a point to the Galatians (namely, that Paul did not get his message or his ministry from Jerusalem leaders or the Jerusalem church), it is not as revealing as one might like. Paul is not shy about telling his own story, but not for its own sake. He is not really giving his testimony in Galatians 1–2. He is sharing with those who already know him and have experienced his mission. Paul says a little bit more about this in Galatians 4:13-14 where he mentions that it was because of some sort of illness that he first preached the gospel to the Galatians, but despite this he was welcomed by them as a messenger from God. There is a passing remark in Galatians 6:17 to the effect that Paul bears the marks of Christ on his body. Whatever he is specifically referring to, this seems to indicate that he had suffered for the cause of Christ during the course of his missionary work. This impression will only be further confirmed in his subsequent letter. Let us consider the next earliest letters, 1 and 2 Thessalonians and 1 and 2 Corinthians.

Paul gives us precious little biographical information in 1 Thessalonians, and none of any consequence in 2 Thessalonians. He tells us he came to Thessalonike after having suffered and been insulted in Philippi (1 Thess. 2:2). Paul and his coworkers avoid a patronage situation by working for their own living while in Thessalonike (2:9). The response was positive in Thessalonike but the new converts were persecuted and ridiculed by their fellow citizens, and so they suffered much, as the church in Judea had suffered from their fellow Jews (2:14). Paul was in Athens when he heard of the suffering, and he sent Timothy to see how the new converts in Thessalonike were faring. He brought back a good report (3:2, 6) prompting the writing of 1 Thessalonians, which has a strong flavor of thankfulness. Paul's great care and concern for his converts and his pastoral spirit are an important part of his story that is well manifest in this letter.

1 and 2 Corinthians are much more helpful in revealing parts of Paul's story, especially 2 Corinthians, and we will recount some of the data in that letter first. A much neglected text in the study of Paul's conversion is 2 Corinthians 4, particularly 4:6. Here we find a partial citation of Genesis 1 that refers to God making light to shine out of darkness. Paul wishes

to connect the text however with the fact that "Christ has shone in our hearts to give the light of the knowledge of the glory of God in the face of Christ." What Paul is saying is that conversion is the beginning of a whole new world for the convert. He or she becomes a new creature, or part of a new creation. This new world of illumination dawned on Paul on the Damascus road when he saw the risen Lord, or as he puts it here, he saw the very presence, the very glory of God in the shape of the face of Jesus. The new creation then is very much like the first one, a matter of God "calling into being the things that do not exist" (Rom. 4:17b). This implies a radical departure from the past, a truly new and fresh start. The emphasis is on discontinuity with the past. While it may be in part that Paul is envisioning here his story in terms of the story of the first Adam, it is clear enough that he envisions it even more in terms of the story of the last Adam — the one who gave up much and took the form of a servant.

This is very much how Paul sees himself, as is clear from an autobiographical text like Philippians 3:4-10, and it is not an accident that Paul tells his own tale here with echoes of the way he just told the story of Christ in Philippians 2. Paul's status and standing and prerogatives in Judaism were considerable, and he was advancing in it well beyond his peers, as he tells us in Galatians 1. He was on the way up, not on the way to become a servant among human beings. Yet as a Christian, Paul is prepared to count all of that in the loss column in comparison to the surpassing privilege of knowing and being known by Christ, and being conformed to his image.[6] Thus Paul, in a text like Galatians 6:15, is clearly able to distinguish between the things that once mattered greatly to him, such as whether one was circumcised or not (cf. Phil. 3:5), and the things that now matter, namely, the new creation. Paul is not just talking about re-creation, but a new creation with an emphasis on the word new. This comports with the fact that Paul is not simply talking about a renewed covenant either, but rather a new one which eclipses, brings to closure, and in various senses fulfills or completes the old ones and the whole process of God covenanting with his people.

2 Corinthians 5:17 of course describes the fact that when a person is in Christ he or she is a new creature. Among other things, this changed dramatically Paul's view of Jesus. Whereas formerly he evaluated Jesus from a fallen and worldly point of view, he certainly does so no longer. Yet

---

6. We will say more about this text on pp. 152-54 below.

it would be a mistake to think that Paul sees conversion as involving only a transvaluation of values and attitudes about various matters. He believes that conversion also entails a change in one's spiritual makeup. One's life becomes christoform in shape.

It is not an accident that one of Paul's favorite descriptions of himself is "servant" (Phil. 1:1; Rom. 1:1). Paul's story is analogous to that of Christ and is modeled on it. But this is not just a matter of imitating Christ; it is also a matter of being conformed to the image of Christ by God. Thus Paul speaks of suffering the sufferings of Christ in 2 Corinthians 1:5. In Paul's view the trajectory of his own life is much like that of his Master. Paul's hope is to be completely conformed to Christ's image by means of obtaining a resurrection like his.

It appears quite likely in view of 1 Corinthians 15:8-9 that what was being said about Paul is that his transformation from persecutor of the Church to apostle of Christ was something that happened with unnatural haste. Early Jews were used to persons becoming proselytes to Judaism gradually, after first having been inquirers or God-fearers for a period of time. Paul in contrast seemed to have had a sudden change of character. Ancient persons were naturally suspicious of claims about people changing their nature or character, for character was seen as innate, something one was born with, and then manifested over the course of one's life.[7] It is thus not surprising that some were calling Paul an *ektrōma*, and therefore someone unfit to be or be called an apostle of Jesus due to his persecuting activities (15:8-9). An *ektrōma* was a miscarriage, a stillbirth, or an abortion, in short, a child rushed prematurely into the world. The image is connected here by Paul to his being the last one to see the risen Lord. The implication would seem to be that had this not happened quickly, it might not have happened at all.

It is not clear whether Paul means just that people saw his conversion as something that happened too suddenly, with ungodly haste, or whether they also saw his sudden adoption of an apostolic role as also too hasty. It may also be that Paul means that the appearance he received from the Lord happened out of due season, indeed, apparently well after the other appearances to judge from Acts, and so, had it not happened as it did, out of due season, it would not have happened at all. In any case, it is clear that

7. See pp. 73-82 above.

both Paul and his critics saw him as unworthy to be an apostle. But it wasn't a matter of worth; it was a matter of grace.

Being born a new creature in midlife was of course no easy thing, as it meant giving up much that one had worked for and loved. It meant in one sense dying to one's past and being born again. Paul speaks for himself and other Christians when he says in Romans 6:2-4 that conversion means being buried with Christ in baptism, being baptized into his death, and so beginning to be put into the story of Christ. The heart of the creed for Paul was that Christ died for our sins according to the Scriptures, was buried, and was raised on the third day (1 Cor. 15:3-5), and this becomes the heart of his description by means of analogy of what happens and will happen to Christians in Romans 6:2-4. Just as Christ died for sins, so believers die to sin (6:2). Just as Christ was buried, so the believer has been buried with Christ in his death (6:4). And just as Christ has been raised, so too the believer can now walk in the Spirit, walk in newness of life, and look forward to his or her own future bodily resurrection. Of a similar sort is what is said in Colossians 2:6-14. When Paul refers to the circumcision of Christ in 2:11, is he referring just to what happened to him or also to what happens to the believer in Christ? The believer is raised together with Christ "through faith in the effective working of God who raised him from the dead." Christ's story is efficacious for the believer when by analogy it is recapitulated in that believer such that one goes from being dead in trespasses to being made alive in him. What Christ has done for the believer on the cross and in the resurrection is the basis of what he later does in the believer. Christians experience Christlikeness in the Spirit only because Christ himself first experienced death and resurrection.

The story of the Christian lives of Paul and others does not stop at the point of justification by grace through faith, though a text such as Galatians 2:15-21 makes it clear that is the crucial beginning point.[8] One must go on to work out one's salvation with fear and trembling; one must go on to grow in grace and in holiness. One must consciously choose to walk in the Spirit and not indulge the works of the flesh (Galatians 5). One must have a sense of the already, but also of the not yet of one's Christian existence — suspended between new birth and new body, between inner renewal and outer decay. The two crucial things remaining to be said about the Christian's story is that one should not expect to be exempt from suf-

8. See my discussion in *Grace in Galatia,* pp. 169-94.

fering in this life, since Christ and his apostles were not, and, second, one must have a clear vision that Christ's history is the believer's destiny. This is precisely what Paul has in mind when he talks in 1 Corinthians 15 about the believers being the latter fruit of a crop of resurrection persons of which Christ was the first fruit. This is also what he has in mind when he speaks of believers being destined in advance to be conformed to the glorious resurrected image of God's Son (Rom. 8:29). The moral conforming is happening now, the physical conforming later. Thus, Paul himself sees his life as a pilgrimage toward resurrection — "I want to know Christ and the power of his resurrection and the sharing of his sufferings by becoming like him in his death, if somehow I may attain the resurrection of the dead" (Phil. 3:10-11). Paul knows this latter will not happen before the Lord returns. This means that the present is a time for striving and pressing on toward the goal. Every Christian, like Paul, should have the honesty to admit "not that I have already obtained this or have already reached the goal; but I press on to make it my own, because Christ Jesus has made me his own" (Phil. 3:12).

The mark on and of the Christian is the mark of Christ. He belongs to Christ and imitates his Master and is spiritually conformed to the image of that Master. This involves both tragedy and triumph, both sorrow and joy. The words of William Penn would have been heartily endorsed by Paul as a description of the Christ-like life — "no pain, no palm, no gall, no glory, no cross, no crown." And indeed no final resolution until the author of all these stories brings down the curtain himself on the human drama in the person of his Son when he returns. Then the human story, the story of Israel, the story of Christians, will be finally and fully gathered up into the story of Christ, and every knee shall bow and every tongue confess, whether willingly or unwillingly, that Jesus Christ is Lord, and the glory will be to the Father.

There are a few more things to learn from the Corinthian correspondence about Paul. He engages in an exercise in mock boasting in 2 Corinthians 11:21–12:10. The function is to shame the Corinthians into realizing that they have become too enamored with the pseudo-apostles and have valued the wrong things in leaders. Paul insists that he also is Hebrew of Hebrews (he knows the sacred language), he is an Israelite (he embraces the religious heritage), and he is proud to be one of Abraham's descendants. He is a true servant of Christ, the proof of which is how hard he has worked, how many times he has been in prison, been flogged, been beaten with rods, been stoned, and been shipwrecked. Paul offers a long litany of hardships as the things he is prepared to brag about. He even brags about a humiliating escape in a basket from Damascus when King Aretas's agent in that city was after him (11:32). He then, tongue in cheek, brags about a visionary experience he has had although he is not free to recount its substance, but he says that to prevent him from getting too big a head, he was sent a stake in the flesh, which had plagued him ever since that experience. He became a walking demonstration not merely of human frailty but of how God's power is made perfect and often best manifested in weakness. Paul is angry with his converts, and yet he loves them dearly — or better, his anger with them shows precisely how much he cares.

Beyond the outline of things in relationship to the period of the Corinthian correspondence listed above, we learn a few extra things from 1 Corinthians. We learn, for instance, that Paul came to Corinth with some fear and trepidation, and in due course there was an evaluation of him that his personal presentation of the gospel was somewhat weak, but that his letters were weighty. We also learn a good deal about Paul's ability and flexibility in ministering to both Jew and Gentile (1 Corinthians 9) so that he might by all means win some. Paul's passion for evangelism is evident throughout his letters, which is remarkable since they are all written to Christians. We also learn in 1 Corinthians that Paul had baptized a few souls in Corinth but was glad he didn't baptize more because the Corinthians made too much of the initiation and began to act like partisans of one or another apostle, depending on who baptized them (1 Cor. 1:12-17). We also learn that Paul was followed to Corinth by Apollos, whom he sees as a colleague, not a rival (1 Cor. 3:5-23). We also learn that Peter has been to Corinth as well. 1 Corinthians 9:5 is an interesting passing comment. Paul claims the right to travel with a believing spouse, and he tells us that Peter and the brothers of Jesus do so, as well as other apostles. But Paul's story is that he has deliberately remained unmarried, having been given the grace to do so (1 Corinthians 7). This is probably all the more remarkable because Paul came to the Christian faith as an adult Pharisee who was likely married before he ever converted, to judge from the usual age at which Jews married and the usual practices of Pharisees. This means that in addition to other things that Paul gave up, he also lost his family when he found Christ.

Another text of importance that tells us something of Paul's self-understanding is found in Philippians 3:3-10. Paul here goes beyond what he says in 2 Corinthians 11:22. Here we learn that he was named Saul for a reason; he was of the tribe of Benjamin, a tribe noted as being the one that remained faithful to Judah. Paul also says that in regard to the sort of righteousness one could gain through obedience to the Law, he was faultless or blameless. This stunning remark rightly reminds us that Romans 7:7-25 is not meant to be Paul's autobiographical remarks about himself and how he was as Jew. Paul does not manifest a late Western guilt-ridden conscience, unlike the way Augustine and his successors read Paul's story. But what Philippians 3:6 must mean is that Paul could not be charged with violating the Mosaic Law, or put differently, he was not guilty of transgression — a willful violation of the Mosaic Law. This is not to say that he was without sin. Blameless under the Law is not the same as guiltless of sin, or to put it the other way, Paul is not claiming to have been pure and perfect before conversion, just not chargeable under the Law.

Another feature of Paul's story, both before and after his conversion, is his zeal. It is mentioned not only in Galatians 1 but also much later in Philippians 3:6. The zeal for the Law was supplanted in his life by an all-consuming zeal for Christ. Early on Paul speaks of having been crucified with Christ, and of being in the process of being conformed to his image (Gal. 2:20). Indeed Paul says that he died, and that Christ became the Lord and ruler of his life. He seeks full conformity to the image of Christ, wanting Christ's story to be fully recapitulated in his own. "I want to know Christ and the power of his resurrection and the fellowship of sharing in his sufferings, becoming like him in his death, and so, somehow to attain to the resurrection" (Phil. 3:10). Paul is not living out his own life; he is living for and into the life of Christ.

Paul in Romans manifests his constant drive to be moving forward, living out the plot of the story God has unveiled for him. So, he must go to Rome after delivering the collection to Jerusalem, not only to share more of the gospel there, but as a staging ground for going further west (Romans 1 and 15). Paul as he tells his story is never short of desire, and never big on resting on his laurels. He is a man in almost perpetual motion, attempting to set the world on gospel fire. It is not a surprise at all that Luke retells the story of Paul in even more detail than Paul does himself. We must consider the Lukan portrait of Paul at this point.

Luke's Presentation of Paul

Luke, to judge from the "we" passages in Acts, which we find beginning in Acts 16:10-17 and continuing off and on through to the end of Acts,[9] was only a sometime companion of Paul toward the end of Paul's missionary journeys and during his periods of incarceration in Caesarea Maritima and Rome. It was enough time to get to know the man well and hear his own retellings of his own story. But Luke has chosen to focus on Paul the evangelist, not Paul the nurturer of congregations by letters. We do not hear of Paul the pastor and letter writer to any real extent in Acts, but this is not a surprise since it is Luke's task to chronicle the movements of salvation history, in which movements Paul's acts of evangelism and church planting play a major role. Paul's conversion is recounted an amazing three times at length in Acts 9, 22, and 26 precisely because Paul is the apostle to the Gentiles and the spread of the salvation to the Gentiles largely occurs through Paul. The story of the movement heading west is the story of Paul heading west. Thus Luke stresses more than Paul does that Paul was also a miracle worker, like Peter and other early Christians, and he also stresses the considerable social status of Paul: he is a Roman citizen (perhaps seeking to impress Theophilus), though Paul trots out his Roman credentials only in a pinch, when they will aid his continued ministry of spreading the gospel. He does not mention them for merely personal advantage. Luke also leaves out some of the sense of Paul being a controversialist, but then this is because Luke does not portray Paul's internal dialogues with congregations. He also does not place any real stress on Paul being an apostle with a capital A. Why? If one carefully examines where Paul brings up his apostolicity in his own letters, it is where an issue of internal control and authority comes up. In other words, Paul is an apostle in relationship to those who are already Christians. He is simply another missionary in relationship to those he is seeking to reach. Paul is not so much an apostle to the Gentiles as an apostle to those churches that are largely made up of Gentiles. Luke's interests in Paul are historical, not biographical, which is perfectly clear from the fact that Acts ends without recounting Paul's demise. For Luke the paradigmatic story in Paul's life is the story of his conversion. It was a historic event which led to the Gentile mission in a major

9. See my *The Acts of the Apostles: A Socio-Rhetorical Commentary* (Grand Rapids: Eerdmans, 1998), pp. 480-86.

Paul was the apostle assigned to the evangelization of the Gentiles, and Luke is careful to portray his encounter with the center and heart of pagan religion and culture in Athens in Acts 17.

way, also a historic event. Let us consider Luke's three accounts of this crucial episode in Paul's story.

First of all Luke gives the proper background, portraying Saul as a well-educated Pharisee who is so zealous he stands as witness to Stephen's death and then starts his own one-man crusade, walking nearly a hundred miles to Damascus to extradite some Jewish Christians back for trial in Jerusalem (see Acts 8:1-3). In that context Luke presents the three renditions of the paradigmatic Pauline story on the following pages.

Triple Anatomy of a Conversion

Acts 9:1ff. third person	Acts 22:1ff. first person	Acts 26:1ff. first person
Luke's summary from talking with Paul	In Hebrew/Aramaic; Paul's Greek summary given to Luke?	Spoken by Paul to Festus and Agrippa — Luke present
Saul to high priest; letters to synagogues to bring Christians back to Jerusalem (vv. 1-2)	Letters from high priest and council to bring back Christians to Jerusalem for punishment (v. 5)	Authorization from chief priests (v. 10)
Light from heaven flashed about him (v. 3)	At noon, great light from heaven shone about me. (v. 6)	Light from heaven shining around me and those with me (v. 13)
Fell to ground, heard a voice (v. 4)	Fell to ground, heard a voice (v. 7)	We all fell to the ground; I heard a voice saying *in Hebrew* (v. 14)
"Saul, Saul, why do you persecute me?" "Who are you, sir?" "I am Jesus, whom you are persecuting." (vv. 4-5)	Same as Acts 9 Same as Acts 9: "I am Jesus of Nazareth, whom . . ." (vv. 7-8)	Same as Acts 9 except "It hurts you to kick against the goads." The Lord said: "I am Jesus whom you are persecuting." (vv. 14-15)
"Rise, enter the city. You will be told what to do." (v. 6)	"What shall I do, sir?" "Rise, go into Damascus. You'll be told all that is appointed for you to do." (v. 10)	"Rise, stand on your feet. I have appeared to you for this purpose, to appoint you to serve and bear witness to the things in which you have seen me and to those in which I'll appear to you, delivering you from the people and from Gentiles
Men stood speechless, hearing voice, seeing no one. (v. 7)	Men saw the light, did not hear the voice of the one speaking to me. (v. 9)	to whom I send you, to open their eyes, that they might turn from darkness to light." (vv. 16-18)

Saul arises. Can see nothing. Three days without sight and food. Led by hand into Damascus. (vv. 8-9)	Paul can't see due to brightness of light. Companions led him by hand into Damascus. (v. 11)	———
Vision of Ananias (vv. 10-16)	Ananias (no vision mentioned). "Brother Saul, receive your sight." (v. 13)	———
Ananias lays hands on Saul. "Jesus sent me that you may regain sight and be filled with the Holy Spirit." (v. 17)	"The God of our fathers appointed you to know his will, to see the just one, and to hear a voice from his mouth. You'll be a witness to all people of what you've seen and heard." (vv. 14-15)	———
Something like scales fall from Saul's eyes; he regains sight and is baptized. (v. 18)	"Rise and be baptized, and wash away your sins, calling on his name." (v. 16)	——— (No mention of Ananias)
Takes food and is strengthened. (v. 19)	———	The above was a heavenly vision. (v. 19)

What we have here in miniature is a telling of the story of Paul, in so far as it has bearing on the story of the Christian movement recounted in Acts. Various features of this telling call for comment. The first and in some ways most important comment is that the story is meant to be cumulative. That is to say, the second version builds on the first, and the third on the first and second. The first account in Acts 9 is the only third-person account. The difference in audience between the second and third versions explains some of the notable divergences in the accounts. (For example, Ananias is omitted from the third account, and the comment about the goad is added for benefit of the Roman audience. Ananias the good Jew is stressed in the second account because of the Jewish audience.) It needs also to be stressed that apparently Luke was present at the third of these occurrences of the telling of the tale, but note that Acts 26 is also a compressed version of the tale that leaves Ananias out, whereas Acts 22 is an interrupted version of the story. All of these accounts are certainly summaries written up by Luke. The major difference between the portrayal of Paul in Acts 22 and in Acts 26 is that in the former narrative the intent is to portray Paul as a good Jew being obedient to God's guidance, whereas in Acts 26 there is the attempt to impress on Festus and the others that Paul is a prophet.

Among the things we learn about Paul from this tale thrice told is the fact that he was raised and educated in Jerusalem, not Tarsus. We also learn that he had close connections with the high priest and significant differences with his instructor Gamaliel (cf. Acts 22:3 to 5:34-39). Notice that in the second account the story is interrupted: Paul mentions he was sent to the Gentiles (22:21). This second account also presents Paul speaking to his audience in Aramaic and, when a riot breaks out, stressing that he is a Roman citizen to the Roman centurion (v. 25). Notice also at Acts 22:17-18 that Paul is depicted as a visionary, warned in a trance by Jesus himself to flee Jerusalem. This comports not only with the presentation in the conversion accounts of Paul receiving a vision of Christ, but also the portrayal of Paul in Acts 27:23-26. Paul is a spiritually perceptive man, in tune with God and his emissaries.

The account in Acts 9 is in the third person, and among other things it stresses that Paul's conversion is a process that begins on the Damascus road but concludes only in Damascus, when he receives his sight, is filled with the Spirit, and is baptized (9:17-18). Ananias is also portrayed as a visionary at 9:10-16. This is much like the story of Peter found in Acts 10, where both Peter and Cornelius have a vision in order to bring the two together.

The core of the three versions of the story is the same and is as follows: (1) Saul was authorized by some priestly authorities to take action against Christians, and the story indicates this included taking action against them in Damascus. (2) While traveling to Damascus Paul saw a light and heard a voice. (3) The voice said, "Saul, Saul, why do you persecute me?" (4) Saul answered, "Who are you, sir?" (5) The voice said, "I am Jesus whom you are persecuting." All three accounts then emphasize that the encounter on the Damascus road involved a real communication to Saul alone, and that this encounter turned Saul from an anti- to a pro-Christian person. It is quite possible that Paul himself alludes to the nature of this experience and its impact on him in 2 Corinthians 3:18 and 4:6. There is an emphasis in Luke's accounts that this event was an objective event, because others also saw light and heard a sound, though they did not see Jesus or hear an articulate utterance. It should also be stressed that Saul's name does not change at this juncture in the narrative in Acts. It changes when Saul begins to evangelize Gentiles and adopts the Greek name Paul (Acts 13:9), perhaps in order to reach Sergius Paulus who has the Latin form of the name. Luke's interest in this story of a conversion is not mainly biographical; rather, he is interested in the crucial role Paul was to play in the early Christian movement and in salvation history. As should be clear from the speech Peter makes in Acts 15, Paul is not distinguished in Acts from Peter by his theology of grace or even his willingness to reach out to a Gentile, but rather by his historical function as having the ongoing commission to focus on the conversion of the Gentiles. It is to be noted that in regard to the commission, Acts 26 eliminates the middle man, Ananias, whereas in Acts 22 the commission to Saul to go to the Gentiles comes through Ananias, even though in both accounts it ultimately comes from Jesus. Notice that the third-person account in Acts 9 says nothing about Saul becoming a missionary to Gentiles, but in the narrative logic of Acts it was not yet time to mention that.

What these accounts have in common with what Paul says in his letters is that he did not receive his conversion, commission, mission, or message from a human source. There is no Christian instruction of Saul prior to the Damascus road, and Ananias is not presented in Acts 22 as the ultimate source of Saul's commission. Notice that Ananias does not teach Saul about Jesus, which comports with what Galatians 1:7 and 16 say about how God revealed his Son to Paul. By "gospel of Christ" in Galatians Paul means the distinctive and essential insights he received directly from God, not a human source.

There is of course much more that could be said about the story of Paul as it is presented in Acts. He is shown to be an indefatigable missionary to the Gentiles, focusing on Turkey and Greece in his work and heading for Rome, though not by the means he had anticipated. Luke stresses that he continued to reach out to his fellow Jews by going to the synagogue, something that only a passing remark from Paul's letters like that in 2 Corinthians 11:24 would confirm. Luke stresses Paul was a miracle worker more than Paul himself does (but see Rom. 15:19), but then Luke is a salvation historian, while Paul is writing as a pastor and an apostle. Both Luke and Paul stress the trials and tribulations of the apostle to the Gentiles, but neither tells us clearly how Paul met his end in Rome. This is because the message was more important than the messenger, and the mission more important than one solitary life. Though Luke has great admiration for Paul, he is not writing his encomium in Acts, any more than Paul is writing his biography in his letters. Luke has toned down the controversial side of Paul's work in arguing with his converts and other Christian workers, but he does not leave Paul's flaws out of the picture. Paul's persecution of Christians is clearly depicted as wicked, and in Acts 21:10-15 Paul does not take the warning from the prophet Agabus or from other Christians not to go up to Jerusalem. Rather, he is depicted as headstrong or, to put it another way, "determined." While Paul in his letters stresses his Christian status as an apostle from time to time, Luke stresses his Greco-Roman status as a Roman citizen and the child of a Roman citizen from time to time (see Acts 22:26-28). In all sources the zeal, and passion, and hard work, and suffering of Paul are made manifest. It is not a surprise that a later writer in 2 Peter 3:15 was to say that Paul's message in all his letters was that God's patience with us means salvation. The gracious offer of salvation through Jesus was indeed the heart of Paul's message and his own experience. This is the tale both Luke and the apostle himself tell us, and tell us well.

Peter — the Bridge between Jesus and His Church

Astoundingly enough, Peter is the only figure who spans almost the entire story of Jesus and the Early Church as told in Luke-Acts. He is there at the beginning of the ministry of Jesus, and he is still there in Acts 15 when the historic decision is made to allow Gentiles to follow Jesus without being circumcised and being required to keep the Mosaic Law. What happened to him after A.D. 50 is not told in Acts, but we have some clues from 1 Peter and John 21. Let us consider Peter's story as told in the Gospels and elsewhere in the New Testament.

The earliest Gospel, Mark, recounts the calling of Simon Peter in its very first chapter. Indeed Mark 1:16 makes Peter and his brother Andrew, both described as Galilean fishermen, the very first persons Jesus called to be his disciples. We are told at Mark 1:18 that at once they left their nets and followed Jesus. Was this by sheer force of personality that they made such an abrupt change in their life patterns? According to John 1:40-41, however, Andrew had been a follower of the Baptist prior to becoming a disciple of Jesus, and Andrew went and recruited Peter to follow Jesus. Calling Peter "Cephas" is related at the beginning of Peter's story in the Fourth Gospel

(John 1:42), but not until the setting apart of the Twelve at Mark 3:16 in Mark. Perhaps then Mark's story of Peter begins after the beginning, as he does mention the Baptist and his ministry first in Mark 1.

Still in Mark 1, we hear the tale of how Jesus went into Peter's home where Peter's mother-in-law was sick with a fever (1:30-31). Jesus immediately goes and takes her by the hand, and she becomes well, immediately gets up, and begins to wait on them! Peter begins already in Mark 1 to be portrayed as the representative of the disciples to Jesus, speaking and acting for them. For example, he is the one mentioned in Mark 1:36 as leading the disciples in seeking out Jesus, who had gone apart to pray. Simon is mentioned first of those set apart as the Twelve and as apostles in Mark 3:16. The next place his name occurs is at Mark 5:37, where he and the Zebedee brothers are taken into the chamber where the daughter of Jairus is raised from the dead. It will be this same three, the inner circle of the Twelve, who will experience the transfiguration in Mark 9.

Most of the stories about the Twelve in the Synoptics do not mention Peter by name, but we know of his presence since we are told the Twelve were there. Thus, Mark wants us to assume that Peter was present for all or most of the major miracles and teaching and preaching of Jesus. Mark 8:27-30 is however different, for here again Peter is the spokesman for the Twelve, and it is he at Caesarea Philippi who correctly identifies Jesus as the Christ. This story is told in more elaborate form in Matthew, as we shall see. In general, Matthew has a somewhat more fulsome portrait of Peter than our earliest Gospel. The sequel to the great confession is that Jesus makes it clear that the Son of Man must suffer, be killed, and rise again, but Mark 8:32 says that Peter took Jesus aside and began to rebuke him for saying this. Peter in turn is rebuked and even called an agent of Satan (v. 33). This incident and the later threefold denial of Jesus are the low moments in the portrayal of Peter in the Synoptics.

Mark 9:2 says that Jesus deliberately took Peter and the Zebedees up the mountain where the transfiguration transpired. He wanted them to have this experience. Peter once again speaks for the disciples in this tale, saying, "Rabbi, it is good for us to be here. Let us put up three shelters, one for you, one for Moses, one for Elijah." But Mark quickly adds the comment: "He did not know what to say, they were so frightened." This is a very human moment in the story of Peter. We see him excited and eager to do something to help. But he speaks first without really thinking the implications through, a behavior that was to characterize him on other occasions as well, as we shall see. Notice, however, on the positive side that Peter is spiritually perceptive enough to recognize that he was seeing Moses and Elijah in this vision.

We next find a particular reference to Peter at Mark 10:28, where Jesus is speaking about the cost of discipleship and Peter reminds him, "We have left everything to follow you!" Jesus reassures him they will not go unrewarded. Peter is portrayed later in this chapter as being one of ten disciples who were indignant at the Zebedees when they asked for special seats next to Jesus in the kingdom (10:41). It is interesting that though Peter is portrayed as the leader of the Twelve and he has obvious shortcomings and flaws, "ego" does not seem to be his issue in the Gospel writers' portrayals.

In the Passion and Resurrection narratives Peter comes up for special mention at several junctures. For instance, it is Peter who remembers Jesus' cursing of the fig tree and remarks on the fulfillment of the curse when they see the tree again (Mark 11:21). Jesus' response is interesting: "Have faith in God." Apparently Peter is amazed that the tree has withered, and Jesus goes on to suggest that with faith and prayer Peter and others could do mighty miracles as well. The prophetic discourse in Mark 13 is portrayed as a response to a private request from Peter, James, and John to explain what Jesus meant about the destruction of the temple (13:3-4). They are the ones who receive this crucial teaching about the future. Both as witnesses to miracles and as privately instructed disciples, the three stood apart from the Twelve to some degree. This makes Peter's denial of Jesus all the more reprehensible. This reprehensible denial is made all the more so by the episode at the end of the Last Supper where Peter emphatically denies (Mark 14:31) that he will ever disown Jesus, even if he has to die with him. But Jesus tells him that he will deny him three times before the cock crows twice that very night (14:30). So, one can say that there is a double denial by Peter that he will fail in this way (vv. 29, 31), but then later there is a triple denial by Peter just as Jesus had predicted.

Jesus makes one more attempt to train the inner circle of the Twelve by taking them aside in the Garden of Gethsemane to watch with him and pray (Mark 14:33). Notice that Jesus particularly comes to Peter and chides him for not keeping watch (v. 37). Jesus expects Peter, as the leader of the Twelve, to set the example of true discipleship. It is however Peter who follows Jesus at a distance when he is arrested (14:54), and it is this act of courage that puts him in the situation in which paradoxically he denies Jesus. The story as told in Mark 14:66-72 is compelling as a tale of human frailty under pressure. Peter, when confronted about being with Jesus by a female slave, says, "I don't know or understand what you are talking about" (v. 68). This could be Peter claiming that he did not understand the woman's accent since he is a Galilean and the issue of Aramaic accent does come up in this story. But Mark does not indicate that Peter merely did not comprehend. The story is presented as though Peter understood but pretended he did not. Peter in fact denies he was with Jesus again in verse 70, and here his accent is noted. Then in verse 71 Peter invokes curses upon himself and swears to them, "I don't know this man you are talking about." The desire for self-preservation is strong, but once the cock crows Peter realizes the enormity of what he has done, remembering the exact words of Jesus, and so he weeps bitterly (v. 72). This is the last time we hear of Peter in the Passion Narrative. There is however one more reference to him in Mark. In the resurrection story in Mark 16:1-8 the angel tells the women not only that Jesus is risen but to "go tell his disciples and Peter. He is going before you into Galilee. There you will see him just as he told you" (16:7). There seems to be a special concern about the restoration of Jesus' relationship with Peter. The story of that restoration is not told in the Synoptics, but we find it in John 21.

The portrait of Peter in Matthew, who takes over 95 percent of Mark's account, is somewhat fuller, and it will be our task to consider how he adds to or subtracts from the Markan account, leaving a somewhat different effect. We will then turn to John's account, who adds for us the foot-washing and restoration stories, and finally to an examination of Peter in Luke-Acts, the historian's account.

The account of the call of Peter in Matthew 4:18-20 differs little from Mark's. It however comes after Jesus' temptations and initial preaching (4:12-17), and so the story of Peter is more spaced out in Matthew than in Mark. For example, we have the first Matthean discourse in Matthew 5–7 before we have the story of the healing of Peter's mother-in-law, found in Matthew 8:14-15, again with no real difference from the Markan account. Matthew however omits the mention of Peter and the Zebedees going in to witness the raising of Jairus's daughter (Matt. 9:25). The naming and sending out of the Twelve appears in Matthew 10:1-5 without real variation from the Markan account, except that they are not called apostles and are not called to be with Jesus. Peter's name is again mentioned first.

It is in Matthew's Gospel that we get the famous story of Peter walking on water, a story not found in his Markan source. It comes in Matthew 14:22-36 in the pericope about Jesus walking on water. Peter asks at verse 28, "Lord, if it is you, tell me to come to you on the water." Jesus says "Come," and Peter gets out of the boat and walks on water in the direction of Jesus. It is not until he sees the wind that he becomes afraid and begins to sink, and immediately Jesus reaches out to him and rescues him. Jesus then says, "You of little faith . . . why did you doubt?" (v. 31). Peter is characterized by the term (*oligopistoi;* see Matt. 16:8) used in Matthew to chide the disciples when they falter in faith. When we compare this with Mark, Mark's portrait is more severe, accusing them of having no faith at various junctures.[10] On the positive side we may say that Peter certainly exhibited more faith than his fellow disciples by taking the steps outside the boat. He is seen then as exemplary up to a point, but also as flawed and lacking sufficient faith when he gives way to his fears.

The critique of Peter continues in Matthew 15:15 where when Peter requests an explanation of a parable, Jesus replies, "Are you so dull?" Yet the remark is directed to all the disciples. Peter is simply the one speaking for them. There is a bit of a more positive portrayal of Peter in Matthew's account of the Caesarea Philippi episode found in 16:13-20. In this account Jesus says to Peter after his confession, "Blessed are you Simon son of Jonah, for this was not revealed to you by flesh and blood, but by my Father in heaven. And I tell you, you are Peter, and on this shelf of rocks I will build my assembly and the gates of Hades will not overcome it. I will give you the keys to the kingdom of heaven, and whatever you loose on earth will be loosed in heaven." This is all the more striking in view of the fact that Matthew does not leave out the rebuke of Peter as an agent of Satan, which he takes over from Mark and places at Matthew 16:23 when Peter protests that Jesus will never be killed in that way. Matthew even enhances that account, having Peter say "Never, Lord!" to Jesus once the Son of Man's prediction had been spoken, and he also adds in Jesus' response, "You are a stumbling block to me . . ." (v. 23). Thus, the blessing and commissioning of Peter for a special task in Matthew 16:17-20 stands out all the more starkly. Let us consider it briefly.

The naming exercise is in itself important, as it establishes a closer relationship between Jesus and Peter. Simon is a friend who has been given

---

10. See my *The Gospel of Mark: A Socio-Rhetorical Commentary* (Grand Rapids: Eerdmans, 2001), pp. 421-42.

a nickname — Rocky (Cephas/Peter). Second, Jesus declares that he is the sort of person on which he will build his community of followers. The gates of the land of the dead will not prevail against that community, which is to say that the assembly of Jesus' followers will not die out. Notice too the emphasis on Peter being one who has received a revelation from God. The truth about Jesus' identity did not come to him by mere deduction or human logic. Peter is not depicted here as Sherlock Holmes but as one who is open to a fresh word from God. The reference to being given the keys to the kingdom and the power of binding and loosing is an allusion to the prohibiting and permitting of obligations and regulations, and this power is conferred not just on Peter, but on all the leaders among the disciples in general (Matt. 18:18). The imagery of the keys comes from Isaiah 22:20-22 and refers to the role of the official who held the keys to a city, or in this case to a religious sphere such as a temple.[11] This text is not about the ability to declare someone saved or lost, but it does suggest that the one who has the keys has the power to share the Good News and so usher others into the Kingdom of God. However one interprets these verses, they convey the notion that Peter is given a very significant role in the Kingdom by Jesus, and a very high commendation as well. This is presumably in part because of his openness to revelation about Jesus and his faith, however weak at times. It is the faith of Peter that makes him the Rock in a positive sense, and the implication is that Jesus will build his community from persons of like faith.

The transfiguration is told somewhat differently in Matthew 17:1-13 compared to Mark 9. For one thing, Matthew omits Mark's parenthetical remark that Peter did not know what he was saying. For another thing, we are told that when the divine voice spoke and identified Jesus, the three disciples fell to the ground terrified, and Jesus came and comforted them and told them not to be afraid (v. 7). After this the vision disappears, leaving only Jesus and the three together.

The story of the temple tax found in Matthew 17:24-27 tells us that the tax collectors of the two-drachma tax came to Peter and asked if Jesus paid the temple tax. Peter replies in the affirmative. Jesus however wants to

11. One thinks of the amazing and tragic story of the Church of the Holy Sepulchre, where varying competing Christian groups could never decide who had rights to the door and keys to the building, and so for many centuries the keeper of the key has been from various families of Jerusalem Moslems.

correct Peter's thinking about the matter a bit, and he immediately addresses Peter when he comes into the house. He asks if a royal person taxes his own family, or others? Peter readily answers — others. Jesus draws the conclusion that the children are and should be exempt. He seems to be suggesting that he, as the Son of God, should not be taxed for the Temple where God resides. But to avoid offense, Jesus asks Peter to use his fishing skills, take the first fish he catches, and take the four-drachma coin found in its mouth and pay the tax for both Peter and Jesus! Quite a fish tale indeed, and it perhaps shows that Peter was too hasty in suggesting that Jesus regularly paid such a tax. In the days when this Gospel was written the Temple had been destroyed, and Roman tax collectors collected the money and gave it to a pagan temple, thus further shaming the Jews. This story is about a sensitive matter, and Peter has not thought through his response before he speaks to the tax collectors.

In Matthew 18:21-22 as the introduction to the parable of the Unmerciful Servant who should have been forgiving, we have Peter asking Jesus how many times he should forgive someone who has sinned against him. Peter suggests up to seven times, doubtless thinking he is being very merciful. Jesus replies seventy times seven (490 times). Jesus is suggesting that a person should be forgiven as many times as is necessary, not a literal 490 times. Unlimited forgiveness is a posture of grace that goes well beyond mere generosity or being magnanimous. Peter however is shown here to be the disciple who is thinking through the implications of the gospel of forgiveness. Peter is also portrayed in Matthew, as in Mark, as the disciple who stresses the cost of discipleship already paid by himself (Matt. 19:27).

It is interesting that Matthew actually downplays the role of Peter in the Passion Narrative. For example, in Matthew 21:20 it is the disciples, not Peter, who make the remark about the withered fig tree. Similarly, it is the disciples who are given the prophetic discourse, not the inner circle of three in Matthew 24:3. It is also interesting to compare and contrast the end of the Last Supper episode in Matthew and in Mark. Unlike Mark with its vehement protest of Peter to the announcement that he would deny Christ three times, Peter merely declares that even if he has to die he will never disown Christ (Matt. 26:35). Matthew makes it clear that all the other "disciples" said the same thing (Mark simply has "they all" said the same thing). So, Peter's rebuttal is set clearly in the context of the disciples all denying that they would disown Jesus.

The story of the Garden of Gethsemane is told much the same in

Matthew as in Mark. Matthew 26:36-46 is pretty much verbatim taken over from Mark. However, Jesus' stress that Peter should watch and pray for his own good, and not merely to support Jesus, lest Peter himself fall into temptation and sin is highlighted in verse 41, as was also intimated in the Markan account. It may be that Matthew portrays Peter's famous denial scene in the courtyard of the high priest a bit differently than Mark. In Mark 14:66-72 it is one female slave that identifies and confronts Peter; in Matthew it is two different female slaves, and so there is the testimony of two witnesses against him in Matthew. Furthermore the second denial is strengthened in Matthew where it is recorded that Peter denied knowing Jesus with an oath (Matt. 26:72). The third denial of Jesus is more curt in Matthew — "I do not know the man" (cf. Matt. 26:74 to Mark 14:71). Lastly, in Matthew Peter does not break down before his inquisitors, unlike in Mark. Instead, he goes outside the courtyard and weeps bitterly. Peter does not appear again by name in the Gospel of Matthew. At Matthew 28:10 the women are simply told to go tell the disciples Jesus is going before them into Galilee. There is no special mention of Peter.

The Gospel of John simply does not spend the time on the Twelve that the Synoptics do, and so accordingly we do not have much about Peter during the period of the Galilean ministry. We have considered the call narrative in Mark and John already,[12] and we can note that Peter is mentioned purely in passing at John 6:8 as being Andrew's brother. There is certainly no attempt to portray Peter as a prominent disciple during the ministry, before we get to what is a rough equivalent of the Caesarea Philippi episode in John at 6:68-69. Jesus had been teaching in the synagogue in Capernaum, and he had offended many disciples who deserted him at that juncture. He then turns to the Twelve and asks if they want to leave too (one of the rare references to the Twelve in this Gospel). Peter replies: "Lord, to whom should we go? You have the words of eternal life. We believe and know that you are the Holy One of God." Peter then is portrayed as the one who makes the good confession and recognizes that Jesus speaks the words of salvation.

It is not until John 13 that we have any real episodes in this Gospel that give Peter significant amount of play. There is then the famous interchange between Jesus and Peter: "Lord, are you going to wash my feet?" Jesus replied: "You do not realize now what I am doing, but later you will under-

12. See pp. 161-62 above.

stand." "No," said Peter, "you shall never wash my feet." Jesus answered: "Unless I wash you, you have no part in me." "Then Lord," Simon Peter replied, "not just my feet but my hands and my head as well." Jesus answered: "Those who have had a bath need only to wash their feet; their whole body is clean. And you are clean . . ." (vv. 6-10). The interchange reveals once more the spontaneous Peter who can do an about-face on something in the blink of an eye. What Jesus is doing is providing a model of servanthood, but, in addition to that, suggesting that unless a person is cleansed through Jesus one cannot be in fellowship with him. The task of washing feet was of course usually relegated to household slaves who would meet guests at the door, anoint their heads, and wash their feet as they came off the hot, dusty roads. Jesus leads by setting an example of service.[13]

There is not really a presentation in the Fourth Gospel of the Last Supper itself, but the conclusion of that story is found in a different form in John 13:36-38. Peter asks Jesus where he is going. Jesus replies cryptically that where he is going Peter cannot follow. Peter replies, "Why not? I will lay down my life for you" (v. 37). Jesus in effect says, "Oh really," then adds, "before the cock crows you will deny me three times." There is no response recorded by Peter. In fact Peter is completely silent right on through the Farewell Discourses in John 14–17, though we hear from other disciples such as Thomas and Philip and Judas, not Iscariot.

We do however begin the Passion Narrative proper with a revelation about Peter. The Synoptics tell us that someone cut off the ear of the high priest's servant, but only John 18:10 tells us both that it was Peter who did this, and that the servant's name was Malchus. Once again the story reveals an impetuous Peter whose haste tends to get him into trouble. This same chapter tells us as well what we already knew from the Synoptics, namely, that Peter followed Jesus to the high priest's house. Yet in this account he goes with another disciple who was known to the high priest. In this account we hear that the other disciple went into the house, came back out, spoke to the female slave who was at the door, and brought Peter in. It was at this juncture that she asks if Peter is one of the disciples, and he denies it (v. 17). This scenario is basically repeated in verse 25 with an anonymous person asking Peter the same question and again Peter giving the same answer. The third occurrence of this motif brings in a servant who was pres-

13. Is there possibly a connection between the emphasis of this story and the way Jesus is viewed in 1 Peter?

ent with the party that arrested Jesus, and he recognizes Peter as the one who cut off the ear of the servant of the high priest. He asks, "Didn't I see you with him in the olive grove?" Peter denies it and the cock crows. We are not told how Peter responded to this occurrence. Peter does not appear again in the Passion Narrative.

In John's Gospel alone we have the story of Peter and John running to see the empty tomb once Mary Magdalene has reported this fact (John 20:2-9). Often great contrasts are made between the spiritually imperceptive Peter and the insightful Beloved Disciple. Peter sees the burial clothes neatly folded up. He enters the tomb first even though the Beloved Disciple arrived first. We hear about this latter disciple that he saw and believed, but then it is added, "for they still did not understand from Scripture that Jesus had to rise from the dead" (v. 9). Are we to think that the Beloved Disciple believed on the basis of the empty tomb that Jesus was risen, something he did not yet know from Scripture? Probably not since that disciple is not depicted as reacting as Mary does when she encounters the risen Jesus. More likely we are to think that the Beloved Disciple believed that, like Elijah, Jesus had been taken up directly to the Father without resurrection. Had he not said he was returning to the Father? If this is correct, then the contrast between Peter, who apparently deduces little or nothing from the empty tomb, and the Beloved Disciple, who deduces everything, is probably too sharply drawn.

Our final Johannine story about Peter is found in the epilogue in John 21:4-23. It is a powerful story on many levels. The disciples are fishing and catching nothing. Someone on the shore tells them to cast on the other side of the boat. There is a great catch, the Beloved Disciple says it is the Lord, and impetuous Peter wraps his clothes around him and immediately dives overboard and swims to meet him. Peter climbs back on the boat and drags ashore a net full of fish — 153 to be specific. The image of Peter is of a big, strong man.

After breakfast by the sea, Jesus initiates a conversation with Peter. He calls him by his proper name "Simon son of John" and asks him, "Do you love me?" Jesus uses the verbal form of *agapē*, but Peter responds with *phileō*. Jesus then recommissions Peter, saying, "Feed my lambs." Jesus asks again if Peter loves him, again using the verbal form of *agapē*. Peter again responds with *phileō*. Jesus then commissions Peter to shepherd his sheep. Jesus asks a third time about Peter loving him, only this time it is Jesus who uses *phileō*, and Peter responds in kind with the same verb, with the addi-

Peter was a fisherman called from his nets and boats to follow Jesus. He did not have the education or erudition of a man like Paul, but precisely as a fisherman he would need to have known some Greek to sell his goods and to deal with the toll and tax collectors, especially in the somewhat cosmopolitan environment that existed in and near Tiberias on the Sea of Galilee.

tional bit of pathos: "You know everything, you know I love you." Jesus responds, "Feed my sheep."

Should we make much of the change in verbs and the progression here in this story? I think so on several counts. Notice first that Peter, who denied knowing Jesus three times, is reconfirmed and recharged three times. Notice the reference here to the charcoal fire. The only other time we hear of one of those is in the denial story in John 18. Every detail of this story is carefully crafted and significant. There is certainly a progression in the commission. First, Peter is commissioned to deal with the neophytes, the new followers of Jesus, called lambs; he is to feed them. Then he is to shepherd or watch over the sheep. Finally, he is to feed the mature in faith. There is a natural progression here. This leads one to expect the same in regard to the verbs. Thus, the discourse would involve this: (1) Jesus first asks Peter if he loves Jesus with an unconditional God-given kind of love. Peter is only prepared to say he loves him like a brother. Perhaps he does not understand fully what is being asked. (2) Jesus asks again if he loves him with a divine love. Peter says again that he loves Jesus like a brother. (3) Finally Jesus queries Peter at the level to which he is prepared to respond — "Do you love me as/like a brother?" says Jesus. "Yes, you know I do," says Peter. We are meant to see the restoration of one who denied Christ three times, but not without allowing that he still has need to grow in his love and spiritual life. This reality is also made plain in the final Petrine episode in this Gospel, which we will address in a moment. John 21:18 gives us Jesus' word about Peter's future. There was a time when he was young and he had the freedom to go where he wanted, but the day is coming when he will be old, when he will be dressed and led by the hand by someone to the place he would not willingly go. The Evangelist intrudes in the story and adds, "Jesus said this to indicate the death by which Peter would glorify God." Then Jesus reiterates, "Follow me," with the implication to the cross and beyond. This story is obviously written after Peter had died at the hands of others, with a hint that it was by crucifixion, like his Lord.

Peter at John 21:20-21 then asks about the Beloved Disciple. Jesus responds hypothetically — "If I want him to remain until I return, what is that to you? You must follow me." This story is told to indicate how the rumor arose that the Beloved Disciple would live until Jesus returned. It also indicates that the Beloved Disciple must have outlived Peter by a great deal.

The story of Peter in the Fourth Gospel then concludes with a rousing recommissioning, but also with a promise of a denouement like Jesus'.

Peter is present in both Luke-Acts as an important character in the narrative of salvation history. We must concentrate on the special contribution Luke makes to the portrait of Peter, recognizing that he too follows the Markan account. There are no references to Peter prior to Luke 4:38-39 where Luke simply repeats the story of the healing of Simon's mother-in-law. Simon is introduced to the audience only indirectly at this juncture. The call of Simon to the ministry then comes in Luke 5, where we have a story of a great catch, which is similar in some ways to the one we just referred to in John 21. But in Luke's telling of the call of the first disciples we hear that Jesus stepped into Simon's boat, asked him to put out a bit into the water, and then he taught those standing on the shore from the boat. Once he had finished speaking he tells Peter to put out into deeper water and let down the nets for a catch. Simon responds that he will do so since the master asks him to, but they had worked hard all the previous night and had caught nothing. There ensues a huge catch of fish, to which Simon responds, "Go away from me, Master, for I am a sinful man!" (v. 8). Jesus' response is to reassure Simon, telling him not to be afraid and that from henceforth he will be catching even more elusive creatures — human beings (v. 10). The response to this is the pulling of the boats onto shore, leaving everything as it is, and following Jesus. This story shows the concern of the historian to describe the antecedents to the call of the first disciples and their following of Jesus, and to show how they quit their former trade, bringing closure to that part of their lives.

Luke presents the selection of the Twelve in Luke 6:13-16 as a matter of Jesus choosing twelve from among the larger circle of disciples. Simon, as in Mark and Matthew, is once again mentioned first, and is said to have been named Peter by Jesus. Peter does not occur again in the narrative until Luke 8:45 where we are told that it was Peter who said to Jesus that people were crowding and pressing against Jesus. This prepares us for the reference to Peter, James, and John entering the room of Jairus' daughter in Luke 8:51. The Lukan version of the Caesarea Philippi confession does feature Peter (Luke 9:18-20), but notice that Luke entirely leaves out both the rebuking of Jesus by Peter, and the counter-rebuke by Jesus. Peter was introduced to Luke's audience on a note of humility in Luke 5, and he is not portrayed as being arrogant or ignorant or spiritually obtuse here. Luke adds to Mark's account of the transfiguration only the note that Peter and the disciples were sleepy, but they woke up in time to see Christ in glory and the two legendary figures of Moses and Elijah with him. Luke retains Mark's comment that Peter did not know what he was saying when he made the comment about building booths.

Peter is from time to time depicted by Luke as the spokesperson for the Twelve. For example, at Luke 12:41 Peter asks if Jesus has told the parable for the disciples or for everyone. Jesus does not answer directly but tells another parable about watchfulness. Luke does not give the sort of attention to Peter's story in his Gospel that Matthew does.

Peter does not occur by name again until Luke 22:8, where we are told that it is Peter and John who go and make the preparations for the Passover. There is a telling Lukan moment at the end of the meal (Luke 22:31-34) when Jesus says: "Simon, Satan has asked to sift you as wheat. But I have prayed for you, Simon, that your faith may not fail. And when you have turned back, strengthen your brothers." Peter replies, "Lord, I am ready to go with you to prison and to death." There is then the word of Jesus about Peter's threefold denial, to which there is no response or rebuttal. Once again Luke has prepared his audience for what is to come with Peter, but at the same time he has given them hope that Peter will survive the sifting. Peter is like Christ in being sifted by Satan, and this suggests his importance to the ministry of the Good News. Notice that Peter is not singled out for critique in the Garden of Gethsemane (22:39-46).

The presentation of Peter's denials is milder in tone in this Gospel (22:54-62) than in Mark. Peter swears no oaths, but rather simply denies knowing Jesus or knowing what the inquisitors are talking about. But there is a unique and devastating conclusion to Luke's presentation of the story. Immediately after the third denial and the cock's crowing, Jesus, who is in the house of Caiaphas but can see Peter outside in the courtyard, "turned and looked straight at Peter. Then Peter remembered the word the Lord had spoken to him: 'Before the cock crows today, you will disown me three times.' And he went outside and wept bitterly" (vv. 61-62). Peter then is confronted by Jesus about his sin, even before Jesus dies. Luke in Luke 24:1-12 tells the version of the story we find in John 20 with some variation in detail. The crucial verse says that Peter responded to the report of the women about the empty tomb by running to the tomb, bending over, and seeing the linen strips lying there. Then "he went away wondering to himself what had happened" (v. 12). This is not exactly what one would call a response of Easter faith.

It is curious that Luke tells us that after the tomb occurrence Jesus appeared to Simon first before he appeared to others of the Eleven (24:34). But then Luke does not relate the story of that appearance itself. The appearance to Peter is also confirmed in 1 Corinthians 15:5, though that text also does not give us any further details. We must rest content with knowing that Jesus appeared to Peter, and that accounts for the prominent role he plays immediately after Easter both in the upper room, and then in the Jerusalem church. To that story in Acts we must now turn.

It is true to say that the dominant human figure in the first half of Acts is Peter, while the dominant figure in the second half is Paul. Some have even dubbed this work the Acts of Peter and Paul. Peter however disappears without a trace in Acts 15, and Paul is left waiting out his house arrest in Acts 28. Luke is not interested in finishing the stories of Peter and Paul since he is not writing mini-biographies. It is the progress of the movement and of salvation history from Jerusalem to Rome that is of paramount importance to Luke.

Peter is mentioned first among the disciples in the upper room (Acts 1:13), and it is Peter who takes charge and speaks to the believers about the choosing of a new twelfth disciple. In fact Peter gives a brief speech based on the Psalms about Judas and the need for a replacement. Nothing in Luke's Gospel has really prepared us for this, as we are not told what Peter said when he went out on mission ventures with his brother during the ministry. Peter will be presented as a preacher and a healer in Acts, much like his Master. Notice however that Peter does not designate the new member of the Twelve. He is chosen by the casting of lots.

At Acts 2:14 it is again Peter who stands up and rebuts the charge that the disciples are drunk. He then launches into a long quotation from Joel, followed by a sermon about Jesus laced with quotations from the Psalms. He is presented as a very effective preacher, for over 3,000 accepted his message on that day, repented, and were baptized (2:41). This was the real jump-starting of the Christian movement, and Peter is depicted here as the apostle to Jews from all over the world present at Pentecost (2:7-12). Of course it was not just the power of Peter's preaching, for we are told that various disciples miraculously spoke in the various languages of the visitors on this Pentecost occasion. The Spirit came down on the disciples in the upper room, and they spoke in tongues, but the gift of power from on high was not just for their own benefit, it was to equip them for witnessing, which they turn around and do almost instantly. Peter is depicted as only one effective witness among many.

The Pentecost story is followed by the story of Peter and John's trip up to the Temple (Acts 3), on which occasion Peter speaks to a cripple, commands him to stand up and walk, and extends his hand to him; the man does indeed rise up and walk. Peter then again preaches a Christologically focused message in the temple courts (3:12-26). This leads to trouble, and Peter and John are jailed. Yet this does not stop the success of the message, and we are told that the number of the saved grew to about 5,000 (4:4). Peter is depicted as a person full of the Spirit who speaks on the basis of the leading of the Spirit, not on the basis of higher education (cf. 4:8 and 4:13). Peter is depicted also as a brave man (4:13) who now will not deny Christ and will not back down from testifying, though the authorities insist he should (4:18-21).

One of the stranger stories in Acts is told in Acts 5 about how Ananias and Sapphira committed the cardinal sin of lying to the Holy Spirit. Peter's role in this drama is considerable. Peter is depicted as having prophetic insight into what this couple had done wrong, and he confronts them about their sin. They did not have to give all, but they did need to be honest about what they had given. First the husband and then the wife die on the spot when Peter confronts them. The wife even lies to Peter's face, and Peter instantly predicts that she will share her husband's fate (vv. 9-10). Did Peter curse this couple? Is this a negative miracle, like the cursing of the fig tree? Perhaps, but notice the fear that comes over the community when this happens. People begin to see Peter as a great miracle worker of mighty power, and so Acts 5:15 records that people actually laid the sick in the streets, hoping Peter's shadow would fall on them and heal them. Peter is not said to respond to this sort of magic-tainted faith. Between the healings and the other miracles and the preaching, this is too much for the authorities, who then jail the apostles, including Peter, but an angel sets them free. Peter then has another opportunity to address the Sanhedrin briefly, and surprisingly a Pharisee on the council, Gamaliel, diffuses the situation by saying that if this Jesus movement is of God it will prosper, and if not it will die. He gives a brief review of the rise and fall of other messianic movements, which leads to a releasing of the apostles.

We do not hear of Peter again until Acts 8:14, where in passing we learn that he and John came to Samaria to confirm the work of Philip among the Samaritans, which they do, laying hands on the Samaritans so they may receive the Holy Spirit. Notice their role as agents of the Jerusalem church in this story. There is also the famous confrontation between two Simons. Simon Magus wants to purchase the power of the Holy Spirit from Peter and John, but Peter issues a curse, "May you and your money perish." Simon Magus is called upon to repent and pray to the Lord, and then with prophetic insight Peter adds, "for I see that you are full of bitterness and captive to sin." Notice however that all Simon Magus manages to do is ask for a prayer that nothing bad should happen to him. Peter and John are said in verse 25 to return to Jerusalem, preaching their way through various Samaritan villages.

Acts 10–12 provide something of a climax to the Peter chronicles in Acts, for Peter will show up again only in Acts 15 for the council, and then disappear altogether from the story line of Acts. Acts 10 provides us with the remarkable story of two visions, not unlike the story of Paul in Acts 9.[14] First, a centurion named Cornelius, who was a God-fearer, has an afternoon vision in which he sees an angel of God. The angel instructs Cornelius to send men to Joppa to the house of Simon the Tanner where they will find Peter. They are to bring him back to the military headquarters in Caesarea Maritima where Cornelius is stationed. Meanwhile, Peter the following day goes up onto the tanner's roof to pray, becomes hungry, falls into a trance, and not surprisingly considering his condition has a vision about food. He sees a tablecloth with all sorts of four-footed animals, reptiles, and birds on it, which are unclean and therefore inedible animals for observant Jews. Peter is ordered to get up, kill, and eat. Peter protests, saying that he has never eaten anything unclean. In fact Peter has to be confronted three times. The gist of the vision is that God has made these things clean, and so they should no longer be called unclean or impure. Right when the vision reaches its climax, the messengers from Cornelius arrive at the house. Confused by the vision, but prompted by the Holy Spirit, Peter goes down from the roof, meets the men, and invites them to stay overnight; they will travel the next day. There is some irony in the story because the profession of tanning hides made a person unclean, so Peter is probably being inconsistent. He does not have a problem with staying in the house of an unclean Jew or inviting unclean Gentiles into it, but he refuses to eat unclean food! Peter's vision however has implications for the way one relates to people, not just to food. Luke stresses here, as in the story of Paul in Acts 9, how God is engineering all this together for good, even when the human actors in the drama are not clear about what is going on.

14. See pp. 157-58 above.

Peter goes to Cornelius's house, makes introductory remarks, including the remark that it is not appropriate for Jews to enter a Gentile house or associate with them, and rebuffs an attempt by Cornelius at doing obeisance to him (Peter is portrayed as an ordinary man endowed with God's Spirit). Cornelius relates how he came to send for Peter. Peter concludes (v. 34) that God does not now play favorites but rather accepts all those who fear him from any nation. He preaches the story of Jesus,[15] and the Holy Spirit interrupts him, falling upon Cornelius and his family who begin to speak in tongues, which confirms to Peter and the other Jewish visitors who are with him that God has indeed blessed them, giving them the same gift that the Jews had received on Pentecost. Though Peter is not portrayed in Acts as the missionary to Gentiles, any more than he is portrayed as the lead missionary to Samaritans in Acts 8, nonetheless, Peter and the episode with Cornelius are to pave the way for Paul, and so Peter is shown to be a precedent setter, and he is called on the carpet for it. Peter concludes that if Cornelius and kin have the Spirit, there is no good reason to refuse water baptism to them.

Word of what Peter has done spread throughout the believing communities in Judea. Acts 11:1-18 tells the story of the aftermath. The initial shocked response to Peter in Jerusalem is — "You went into the house of Gentiles and ate?" (v. 3). Peter then retells the story of the Cornelius episode. We learn in the retelling that six fellow Jewish Christians went with Peter from Joppa to Caesarea as witnesses, and Peter brings them with him to the Jerusalem church to back up his story. Notice that it is said that it is the circumcised believers in Jerusalem who criticize Peter for his actions. These are probably the same folks called Pharisaic Jewish Christians in Acts 15:1, 5. Peter relates the story in full, stressing how the Spirit fell on the Gentiles as it had on the Jews, and Peter concludes from this fact: "So if God gave them the same gift as he gave us, who believed in the Lord Jesus Christ, who was I to think that I could oppose God?" (11:17). This silences any further objections and indeed leads to God being praised and the comment, "So then God has granted even Gentiles repentance unto life."

One of the interesting facets of the portrayal of Peter in these chapters is that Peter is portrayed as a good Jew who is reluctant to forge out in a new direction, even under the impetus of a vision and the leading of the Holy Spirit. In contrast, Cornelius is immediately obedient to the angel

15. On which see below, pp. 180-81.

who speaks to him, putting up no protest at all. The portrait of Peter then is not of the person who masterminded the initial Gentile mission. Rather, he is portrayed as the reluctant apostle who finally after protest and resistance goes and does what God tells him to do. He does not yet understand the implications of cleansing that come from the cross, but as a result of this episode he has an attitude adjustment, and we will find him preaching like Paul in Acts 15.

Acts 12:1-19 tells the humorous story of the arrest of Peter under the impetus of King Herod during the Feast of the Unleavened Bread in Jerusalem. He is guarded in the jail by no less than four squadrons of soldiers! The greater power however lay in the praying saints. Peter is depicted in 12:6 as sleeping between two soldiers and in chains. It was hardly likely he would escape, humanly speaking, and as we shall see, even the praying church has a hard time believing he did escape. Peter is liberated by the angel of the Lord, who wakes up Peter, releases him from his shackles, and tells him to get dressed. Peter is pictured as dazed and confused. He could not tell whether he was just having a vision of something that would happen, or if it was actually already happening to him (v. 9). Gates miraculously open, and once they get back into the city and have walked a block, the angel leaves Peter. It dawns on Peter that he has been rescued not just from jail but from the execution Herod was planning for him.

Peter then goes to the house of Mary, the mother of John Mark. They are having a prayer meeting. Peter bangs on the gate and the servant Rhoda comes. She immediately recognizes Peter, is overjoyed, and goes and reports his escape. But she is told that she is out of her mind — perhaps the prejudices against the witness of women and servants coming into play. Meanwhile, Peter keeps on banging at the gate because in her haste Rhoda has forgotten to let him in. Finally they open the door and are astonished to see Peter in the flesh. They had been praying, but they did not anticipate such a direct and immediate answer to their prayers. Peter tells the tale of his escape and then says, "Tell James and the believers about this" (v. 17), and then it is said mysteriously that Peter left for another place. We are meant to see the transition of leadership in Jerusalem in this story. James is now in charge, and Peter is now on the road, apparently for a long time to come. This prepares for the way the story of the great Apostolic Council of Acts 15 is portrayed.

The last episode in Acts which mentions Peter is the council in Acts 15, which presents him as the major advocate of Gentile mission. After much discussion Peter gets up and makes a rather Pauline speech. He reminds the audience that God had chosen him to speak to Gentiles about salvation through Christ. God showed that he accepted them by giving them the Holy Spirit, in just the same manner, and with the same gifts, as he had given Jews on Pentecost. Peter then adds that God makes no distinction between Jews and Gentiles; he purifies all their hearts through faith (v. 9). But then Peter says something very surprising: Why would the circumcised believers want to put a legal yoke on the neck of Gentiles which even Jews past and present had been unable to bear? No, they, like the Jews, are saved through the grace of the Lord Jesus Christ. This comment in verse 11 is in direct response to the remark in 15:1 that unless they are circumcised they cannot be saved. Peter denies this altogether. This is Peter's crowning moment in Acts, and it leads to a decision by James to not burden Gentiles with the yoke of the Law.[16] Peter does not appear again in Acts, but he has furthered the cause of the gospel that the apostle to the Gentiles and his coworkers would preach throughout the empire. After this juncture, Paul picks up the mantle of the mission to the Gentiles with the full backing of the Jerusalem church, and continues his missionary travels.

We have already heard from the Pauline material about the argument Peter had with Paul in Antioch prior to the Acts 15 council, and how later Peter went to Corinth, traveling with his Christian wife. We have also heard of the prediction in John 21 that Peter's end would be like that of his Master, and would not be under his own control. Can we learn anything about Peter himself after this time from 1 Peter? Let us see.

We have seen earlier that a reasonable case can be made that this letter goes back to Peter and was written from Rome in the 60s.[17] Notice immediately that at 1 Peter 1:1 Peter labels himself in the same fashion as Paul would — he is an apostle of Jesus Christ. Peter writes to converts in what we would today call Turkey, and to judge from 1:18 and 2:10, it is not Jews he is writing to, but mainly Gentiles.[18] The message of God's impartiality and salvation by grace through faith comes through loud and clear in 1 Peter 1. The message that Peter conveys in this letter is, much like his sermons

16. See pp. 197-98 below on James and this episode.

17. See pp. 67-68 above.

18. It is possible that this letter was written after the death of Paul, and so at a time when Paul was no longer able to address the Gentile converts in these places.

in Acts, profoundly Christological in character in 1 Peter 1–2. Jesus is the stone that the builders rejected but that became under God's construction the capstone of the new community. Peter prepares his audience for suffering, and he does so in part by portraying Christ as the suffering servant (see 1 Peter 4).

There are brief personal remarks at the end of this letter. Peter is in Rome with two Pauline coworkers, Silas, who helped him write this letter (5:12), and Mark. This may provide yet another clue that Paul has gone on to be with the Lord. In any case, we see Peter fervently and faithfully proclaiming the Good News the last time we hear from him in the New Testament. There is a broad and gracious spirit to this letter, one hard-earned through suffering and trusting in the God of all grace and the Lord who suffered and rose again.

Second Peter 1:16-18, which may well go back to Peter, shows that later in life he had occasion to reflect on the transfiguration of Jesus and how it confirmed Jesus' Sonship and glory and obedience. Peter could claim as an eyewitness, "We have seen his glory, the glory of the only begotten Son" (John 1:14).

Conclusions

The stories of Paul and Peter are never completely told in the New Testament. We do not have their biographies or autobiographies. They are told in passing because the real story is not about humans but about God and God's divine salvation work. Both men are portrayed as flawed disciples. We hear of their weaknesses; we see their strengths. We learn from them the repeated and ongoing cost of discipleship. Peter is the only major figure to bridge the time from the life of Jesus to the life of the Church, who was a disciple on both sides of the Easter divide. Paul is seen as the pioneer, rushing into places where even angels fear to tread. They both share in the sufferings of Christ, with a profound desire to be conformed fully to Christ's image. We repeatedly sense their zeal, we note their pride, we see their foibles, and we recognize their love for Christ, his people, and for the world. These are very different men, of different social stations in life: one a fisherman, the other a well-trained Pharisee with considerable rhetorical ability. In the end, Peter, perhaps through Silas, also reflects that ability since the Greek in 1 Peter is some of the best in the New Testament. Both are soldiers of the cross, pressing forward toward the crown, guiding fledgling converts in various ways. Their paths overlap; they even cross paths and are at odds briefly. But in the end they serve the same Master with the same gospel. Both are remarkable stories in their own right of how Christ can transform persons and make them useful for the service of the gospel.

Exercises and Questions for Study and Reflection

→ Draw up a chart of two columns. In the first column list ways in which Paul and Peter are alike. In the second column list ways that they differ. How much of this is a difference of personality and how much a difference of ministry focus? From the evidence we have do these two figures preach the same gospel? What differing aspects of the gospel do they each choose to highlight?

→ What leadership role did Peter actually play in the Early Church? Was he the leader of the church in Jerusalem? Have we any evidence that he was the leader of the church in Rome at some point? What seems to be the nature of the dispute he had with Paul in Antioch? What did it mean for Jesus to give him the keys to the kingdom and the power of binding and loosing?

→ What was the basis of Paul's claim to apostleship, since he was never a disciple of Jesus during his lifetime? Summarize Paul's gospel that he preached. Why would it have been a scandal to Jews and an offense to Greeks?

8 | Tales of the Holy Family

It comes as something of a surprise to the casual reader of the New Testament how very little New Testament material overall is devoted to members of Jesus' family. The only two figures of whom we have reasonably detailed portraits are Mary and James. Joseph comes up for some scrutiny in the birth narratives, but disappears thereafter. The other brothers and sisters of Jesus are mentioned only in passing. We will consider first what can be said about Joseph, and move on to dealing with Mary and James. Unlike the case with Jesus, where so much of the Gospels focuses on his death, the New Testament tells us nothing about the death of Joseph, Mary, or James.

Joseph

Mark tells us nothing about Joseph, and the Fourth Gospel mentions only in passing the opinion of some misinformed souls that Jesus is the son of Joseph (John 6:42). Acts also says nothing about Joseph. It is no wonder that later Christian apocryphal works (e.g., The Proto-Evangelium of James) tried hard to fill in the gaps. So, let us turn first to Luke's portrait of Joseph and then consider the fuller picture found in Matthew.

Joseph is basically brought into Luke's narrative because of his relationship to Mary. In Luke 1:27 we are told that Mary is betrothed to a man named Joseph, who is said to be a descendant of David. Absolutely nothing more is said about Joseph until Luke 2:1-7, where we have the account of Jesus' birth. Verse 4 says that Joseph went up from Nazareth to Bethlehem to register for the census because he belonged to the lineage of David. We are told that Mary came along, even though she was pregnant, and even though they were still not yet married, but only engaged (v. 5). Oddly enough, no Gospel tells the story of the marriage of Joseph and Mary, which perhaps took place in Bethlehem, causing less furor over the premature progeny than would likely have been the case in Nazareth.

At Luke 2:16 the shepherds come to the manger and see Jesus, Mary, and Joseph and spread the word about what they had seen. Mary's reaction to all this is mentioned at 2:19, but we know nothing of what Joseph was thinking or feeling. Luke 2:22 says that Mary and Joseph took the infant Jesus up to Jerusalem after his circumcision and after the time of their purification to present Jesus to the Lord, much as Samuel's parents had done in the Old Testament. They also go to offer a sacrifice of consecration. The picture painted of both Joseph and Mary is that of two very devout Jews trying to carry on as normal despite the irregularity of how they came by this child. In the course of this episode Joseph and Mary encounter Simeon, who says that the child is destined for great things as a light to the Gentiles and the glory of Israel. The proud parents marvel at this word. They also run into Anna, a prophetess, who sees the child and then speaks to all who are looking forward to the redemption of Jerusalem. Verse 39 tells us that when Mary and Joseph had fulfilled all that was required by the Law, they returned to Galilee.

At Luke 2:41-52 we fast forward to the time when Jesus is twelve. In the only canonical story we have about Jesus' boyhood we are told that Jesus, Mary, and Joseph went up to Jerusalem together. The parents head home assuming Jesus is with some extended family member in the crowd, but they discover that this is not the case after a day of travel. They return to Jerusalem and search for Jesus and after three days finally find him in the temple courts, listening to and answering questions. The parents are astonished, and Mary berates Jesus: "Son, why have you treated us like this? Your father and I have been anxiously looking for you" (v. 48). But Jesus responds, "Did you not know I had to be in my Father's house?" We are told they do not understand this response, but what it is clearly meant to imply is that Jesus' father is the Heavenly Father. He is primarily under his authority, not that of his surrogate earthly father. Luke further emphasizes this distinction just before he gives Jesus' genealogy when he says of Jesus, "he was the son, as it was thought, of Joseph" (3:23). Notice how this matter comes up again at Luke 4:22 after Jesus' inaugural sermon when the listeners say, "Isn't this Joseph's son?" Of course the hearers of the story in Luke's Gospel know that strictly speaking the answer to this question is "no." It is always important to note who is making a remark in a story, and in this case it is a remark made by those not in the know. We hear nothing more of the story of Joseph in this Gospel. We know he was a devout Jew who accepted a difficult circumstance in marrying Mary and sought to continue to keep the Law. We know that he is nonplussed by some of the things said about his son. We know that he lived at least until Jesus was twelve. That is all Luke tells us. The absence of Joseph in later stories where his presence would be expected — for instance, in Luke 8:19-21 — would probably have suggested to the audience that Joseph did not live to see the ministry of Jesus begin when Jesus was about thirty (see Luke 3:23), or at least he was not alive when the episode recorded in Luke 8 transpired. Yet the silence could be read in other ways as well.

Sometimes it has been said that Luke tells the birth stories from Mary's point of view, and Matthew from Joseph's viewpoint, and there is some merit in this suggestion. There is certainly more about Joseph the devout Jew in Matthew 1–2. In the first place the Gospel of Matthew starts out with Joseph's genealogy, though it is a very peculiar genealogy in various respects. For our part the important point is that the genealogy takes a left turn at the end, reading "and Jacob the father of Joseph, the husband of Mary, of whom was born Jesus, who was called the Christ" (Matt. 1:16). In a patrilineal genealogy this is a very odd way to bring it to conclusion. It indicates something very irregular happened such that Mary is the human parent connected to Jesus, and Joseph is connected directly only with Mary. It should be added however that in Jewish society of that era, if a man adopted a son, the son was entitled to his father's inheritance, including his genealogy. Thus, the statement at Matthew 1:1 that this is Jesus' genealogy is not a mistake.

Matthew 1:18 begins with the discussion of how Jesus came to be born. It mentions the engagement of Mary and Joseph and says that before they had sexual relationships Mary was found to be pregnant by means of the Holy Spirit. This must at least mean that Joseph discovered that she was pregnant, for the next verse says that because of such a discovery, and because Joseph was a righteous man, but also one who did not want to expose Mary to public disgrace, he had decided to dissolve the betrothal quietly. Betrothal in that Jewish situation had to be formally and legally annulled, and only the male party in the relationship could do it.

There was, however, divine intervention in the form of a dream: an angel of the Lord appears to Joseph and says, "Joseph, son of David, do not be afraid to take Mary home as your wife, because what is conceived in her is from the Holy Spirit" (1:20). When Joseph awoke he did what the angel said. Matthew 1:25 then says, "But he was not knowing her until she gave birth to a son." The normal way to read this sentence is that after the birth of Jesus, he did have sexual intercourse with her.

It is an interesting fact that Joseph is nowhere mentioned in the story about the Magi (Matt. 2:1-12, though Mary is said to be present with Jesus when they appear at the house [v. 11]). However, in Matthew 2:13 we hear of Joseph having another dream, and he is instructed to take his family to Egypt because of wicked King Herod. Again Joseph is obedient, and they remain in Egypt until the death of Herod. There is yet a third visionary dream given to Joseph according to Matthew 2:19, this time informing him of the death of Herod and telling him to take his family to the land of Israel. But that is not all. He was further warned in a dream to go to Galilee since Herod's son Archelaus was ruling in Judea. Thus, Matthew 2:23 tells us that Joseph, Mary, and Jesus went to and lived in the tiny village of Nazareth in Galilee. Joseph does not appear again in Matthew's narrative, except that it is said by someone in the crowd when Jesus preaches in his hometown synagogue, "Is this not the carpenter's son?" (Matt. 13:55).

The portrait of Joseph in Matthew is certainly a fuller one than in the other Gospels. He is portrayed as a righteous person very much open to God's leading him through the form of dream messages involving angels. He is portrayed as one who loves Mary and in no way wants to shame her. Rather he seeks to protect his family by first going to Egypt and then going to Galilee. He is also portrayed as a normal Jewish man who, despite the irregularity of the way Mary's first child came into the world, goes on to marry Mary, have numerous children, and practice the trade of woodworking. Apart from the issue of Jesus, it is a normal early Jewish story.

Mary

There is a good deal more to say about Mary than there ever was about Joseph.[1] There are various interesting stories told about her, and even when a

1. On what follows about Mary see my *Women and the Genesis of Christianity* (Cambridge: Cambridge University Press, 1990).

Gospel such as the Fourth Gospel refers to her only twice (John 2 and 19), the stories are interesting and revealing. The briefest of the portraits of Mary is found in Mark. She occurs in only two stories, one in Mark 3 and one in Mark 6, and only in passing in these stories. The earliest Gospel writer is not concerned about or compelled to spend any time on Mary. This reflects the fact that she probably did not play a major role in Jesus' ministry.

Mark 3:21 is set in the midst of the Beelzebub controversy. It suggests that the family thought Jesus was not in his right mind, probably because he kept dealing with demons, and so they went out to take charge of him with the aim of bringing him home. However, the immediate setting of Mark 3:21 is said to be that Jesus was in a house, and huge crowds were pressing in on him for various sorts of healing, and the crowd was so large his disciples didn't even have room to eat. The sequel to the family's decision to take action is recorded in Mark 3:31-35. There we hear about Jesus' mother and brothers standing outside the crowd that Jesus is teaching. The crowd informs Jesus that his mother and brothers are looking for him. Jesus responds, "Who are my mother and brothers?" Then he looks at those seated in a circle around him and says, "Here are my mother and brothers! Whoever does God's will is my brother and sister and mother" (3:33-35). One could call this story "Jesus Disassociates Himself from His Family." The important point in our analysis is that Jesus does not submit to his mother's authority in this matter, and indeed he suggests that his primary family is the family of faith — not those who try to confine him but those who do God's will and try to confirm him.

The only other story of Mary in Mark is found in Mark 6:3-4, and it is not even clear that Mary is present in Mark's account. Jesus is called Mary's son, his four brothers are listed by name, and it is said that his sisters are present with the congregation. Jesus then says, "Only in his hometown, among his relatives, and in his own house is a prophet without honor." This again strikes a discordant note. Jesus' family, including his mother, does not understand him or honor him. This comports with John 7:5, which says that the brothers did not believe in Jesus during his ministry. There may also be a polemical edge to calling Jesus "the son of Mary," for in a patriarchal culture one was normally called the son of one's father, even if the father was deceased. This may in fact be a way of suggesting that Jesus was of dubious origins, which would explain why they do not warmly receive Jesus' message. In any case, the portrait of Mary is both limited and hardly flattering in this Gospel. Like other characters in an ancient biography, Mary is mentioned only insofar as she has contact and dealings with the main character in the story.

The Gospel of John does not mention Mary because of an independent interest in her. In fact, she is never called Mary in that Gospel. She is called the mother of Jesus, being defined on the basis of her relationship with Jesus. The story of the wedding feast at Cana (John 2:1-12) and the story of Mary at the cross (John 19:25-27) frame the ministry portion of this Gospel. It is interesting that while the Fourth Evangelist is usually very particular about revealing persons' names, there are two exceptions — the mother of Jesus and the Beloved Disciple whom we find at the cross.

The Cana story begins with the word that there was a wedding in Cana and Jesus' mother was there. Jesus and some disciples were also guests at the wedding. Cana is not far from Nazareth. Jesus' mother tries to involve Jesus in solving a problem: the wedding has run out of wine. Jesus' response to her is, however, abrupt: "Woman, what is that to me and to you?" This Greek phrase always conveys a note of antagonism. Jesus appears to be disengaging from his mother's authority. In this Gospel, Jesus takes orders only from the Heavenly Father. Only the Father can determine when Jesus' "hour" has come. Jesus does not reject the need to help; it is a question of authority. It may be that the implication here of "my hour has not come" is that Jesus realizes he will have an obligation to his mother in that hour. In the Fourth Gospel it is only at the cross that Mary is ushered into the family of faith. But this story suggests that Mary had some knowledge not only of Jesus' compassionate nature, but also of his ability to do miracles. She was, unlike the brothers, not without some faith in Jesus and what he could do. Notice that she leaves the matter in Jesus' hands when she says, "Do whatever he asks you to do," and she assumes Jesus will act without further prodding. In a Gospel full of deep symbolism it may well be that the reason Jesus' mother is called "woman" by Jesus is that she must work out her role in the Kingdom not by claiming her relationship to Jesus but as a woman. It will be as woman that she enters the community of faith in John 19.

Like the story of the Cana wedding, the story of Mary and the Beloved Disciple at the cross has no parallel in the Synoptic Gospels. Only in John's Gospel do we hear of Jesus' mother being at the cross. The Evangelist is once again going for the deeper significance of the story by presenting the paradigmatic man and the paradigmatic woman beneath the cross.

Notice the order of events in the story in John 19:25-27. Jesus first says, "Woman, behold your son," and then turns around and says, "Behold your mother." Jesus is integrating his mother into the community of faith, and as a sort of last will and testament he is making sure she is taken care of once he is gone. Whereas in John 2 we see disengagement, in John 19 we see unification and engagement. Here Jesus takes the initiative to do something for his mother, but also for the disciple whom Jesus loved. Jesus resolves the tension for Mary between her role as mother and her role as disciple. She can now play a mothering role to a fellow disciple. Jesus calls her "mother" not because he wishes to renew the filial bond, but because he wants his mother to take her place in the community of faith, something that Acts 1:14 shows did in fact happen. Jesus unites his own family with the family of faith and gives them a home in the home of the faithful disciple.

Both Mary and the Beloved Disciple are addressed by Jesus, and both are given a spiritual task. It is interesting though that only the man is called disciple here. Of course his faith and discipleship antedate his relationship with Mary. Mary is not depicted here as mother of the Church, but rather as a spiritual mother in the Church. The Evangelist is however focusing on these two persons as types or models. They are like Adam and Eve beneath the tree, only in this case things go right and the result is life and community with rather than death and alienation from God and humankind. The scene beneath the cross is perhaps also about the new equality in grace of male and female. The new community is served rather than severed by traditional roles and relationships. In Christ the dignity of woman is restored and her equality affirmed, as is shown in the case of Mary. Mary is presented as both woman and mother, as both relative and disciple. Having achieved the reconciliation of the physical family and the family of faith, Jesus was truly able to say, "It is finished" (19:30).

In Matthew Mary first appears in the genealogy (1:16). Jesus is legally in the line of David through Joseph, but Mary is his only human parent. Both Matthew and Luke tell us that a miracle happened to and in Mary that led to the conception of Jesus. The story is not depicted as pagan stories, where a god mates with a human woman, for there is no mating involved. Jesus is a gift given to Mary through a miracle. Luke explicates this more clearly by saying this transpired by means of the Holy Spirit overshadowing Mary. Mary is revealed to be an agent of God's providential provision of salvation.

Matthew 1:18 is meant to make it clear that God is responsible for the child, even though Joseph has his doubts. It also makes evident that Mary is part of a system that involved young teenagers pledged to others in an arranged marriage. Mary is then depicted as fulfilling the role that would be a Jewess's greatest honor, being the mother of a firstborn son who is the Messiah. Through Mary, Israel's national destiny is fulfilled. Matthew 1:20 makes it evident that Mary and her child are to be respected, as gifts from God. And since the child is a gift from God, it is God who gives the name to the child — Jesus. Matthew 1:25 is as direct a statement as one could want that once Jesus was born, Joseph did "know" his wife in the biblical sense.

It is interesting that in the Magi story only Mary is mentioned at 2:11, and this is presumably because of the assumed close connection of a mother with her infant, who was presumably still nursing. The story as it is told suggests that she got to see the first attempt at worshipping Jesus in human history, and she received the gifts the Magi had to give on behalf of Jesus.

It should be noticed that the commands given to Joseph in these birth stories assume the patriarchal nature of the situation and assume his role as head of the family: he is to take Mary as his wife (1:20); he is take the mother and child into Egypt and stay there until he is informed he can leave (2:13); and then finally he is to take them back to Israel (2:21). Mary is depicted as silent and complicit in all of this.

Mary does not appear again in Matthew's narrative until Matthew 12:46-49. Matthew spares Mary by omitting the Markan verse about how she and the brothers thought Jesus was a bit out of his mind and they went out to take charge of him. He does however tell the story of the encounter, saying they came to speak with Jesus (no mention of the subject matter). Matthew is more explicit in making it clear as well that Jesus pointed not just to anyone but to his disciples when he said, "Who is my mother, and who are my brothers?" It is also interesting that in Matthew as in Mark there is no statement about what the Holy Family did after Jesus made this remark. There is however the statement Jesus makes that his disciples are not only his mother or brother, but also his sister.

The last story that mentions Mary in Matthew is the story of the hometown preaching, as was the case in Mark. Matthew 13:53-57 however has slightly less edge to it in the way to which Mary is referred. The question the crowd raises is, "Isn't his mother's name Mary?" which is potentially less offensive than "Isn't this the son of Mary?" As in the Markan account, Mary completely disappears from the story at this juncture. She is not portrayed as a significant figure during the ministry of Jesus, but unlike the Markan account at least her crucial role at the beginning of Jesus' life is related.

We come now to the presentation of Mary in Luke-Acts. There is only one reference to Mary in Acts (1:14), but it is an important one as it confirms she is part of the inner circle of disciples or believers in Jerusalem awaiting the Holy Spirit after the death of Jesus. This provides some indirect confirmation that she was in Jerusalem when Jesus died.

In the Gospel of Luke, it is Elizabeth and Mary, not Zechariah and Joseph, who are first to receive the message that Christ is coming. It is these women who are praised and blessed by God's angels, and who first sing and prophesy about Jesus. Luke presents these women in Luke 1–2 as active participants in God's salvific purposes, not mere observers. They are the first examples of how the lowly will be exalted when the Messiah comes.

Mary is introduced in Luke as a virgin engaged to Joseph. But it is also important to note that Luke has introduced first her relatives Elizabeth and Zechariah, and so the impression left is that Mary is part of the salvation-historical process that also involves others. At Luke 1:28 the angel Gabriel greets Mary with the words, "Hail, Favored One, the Lord is with you." This is an unusual greeting for a woman, and Gabriel, it must be remembered, is one of the most exalted angels by Jewish reckoning. That he would appear in tiny Nazareth to Mary is a shock, and what he says is even more shocking. Mary should rejoice because she is highly favored. She will be blessed with the privilege of giving birth to the Messiah, and in addition being the first human person to call his name. Luke seems to give Mary the same status that Matthew gave Joseph in this regard (Matt. 1:21).

The query that Mary puts to this angelic announcement, found in Luke 1:34, needs to be contrasted with the doubting questions of Zechariah. Mary merely asks *how* this shall transpire since she has no husband, whereas Zechariah, who is struck dumb, asked whether such a thing could happen. Zechariah wanted proof; Mary sought clarification. The angel in turn tells her that she will conceive by means of the aid of the Holy Spirit. There is a striking similarity between the angel's response at Luke 1:35 and Acts 1:8 — both texts speak of the coming of the Holy Spirit. Mary is then depicted as present at the birth of Jesus, and also at the birth of his community. Luke then is presenting Mary as a key link between the life of Jesus and the life of the Church, even though Peter is presented as even more of a bridge figure.[2]

Mary's response to the angel's explanation is the classic expression of what submission to God's will and word should look like: "Behold, I am the handmaid of the Lord; let it happen to me according to your word" (1:38). Actually the Greek text calls her the slave of the Lord, and so Luke portrays Mary as binding herself totally to God's will. She gives up her own plans and desires for the future. Her response is all the more remarkable as it reflects her knowledge of what effect this could have on her reputation in her community and her relationship with Joseph. It could destroy both. Mary is shown to be a person prepared to give up betrothal and reputation for God's purposes, the very kind of sacrifice Luke depicts as characterizing the true disciple. But as we shall see, she is a disciple in training. She makes mistakes and misunderstands at times, all the while storing up in her heart the things she needs to ponder and puzzle out.

Mary goes and visits her relative Elizabeth who gives her a twofold blessing. Luke 1:42 reads: "Blessed are you among women, and blessed is the fruit of your womb." She is blessed because she is the mother of the Messiah, and in addition she has derived honor because her Son is the most blessed person on earth. Obviously part of the message of this story is that motherhood is a blessed and hallowed role, because God has chosen this means to bring Jesus into the world. Neither of these blessings would have ensued, had Mary not first submitted to God's will and plan. There is in fact a third blessing spoken by Elizabeth, found at 1:45: "And blessed is she who believed that there would be fulfillment of what was spoken to her from the Lord." The blessedness of believing can lead to physical blessings, but Mary must wrestle with obtaining a proper perspective on both her biological and spiritual roles. Though Mary has declared herself to be the Lord's servant, she must still learn that that entails being Jesus' disciple first and his mother second. She must also learn that for Jesus the priorities must be to do his Father's will first, and his parents' bidding thereafter if possible.

Next in what we call the Magnificat (Luke 1:46-55), Mary is portrayed as a Jewish prophetess who sings the future and God's praise. This is a song of promise, but also of protest and prophecy. It speaks of the powerful deliverance of the poor and oppressed by the Lord. It bears resemblance to

2. See pp. 173-80 above.

the Psalms and also to the Song of Hannah (1 Sam. 2:1-10). Mary then herself stands in the line of salvation history and plays a prophetic role in salvation history. There is however a difference between her and some other prophetic figures in that she actually helps bring in the salvation she proclaims. She is not merely a symbol of Israel's poverty and need for liberation. She as an individual fulfills her people's hopes by being the willing and submissive vehicle through which the Messiah enters and changes the world. Notice however that Mary recognizes that she is lowly and that her blessedness comes not from her being a perfect person but because of God's favor on her life. The text calls her highly favored, not full of grace. She is a model of discipleship and God's undeserved benefits. She is not portrayed by Luke as a venerable and venerated saint or a sinless and angelic figure. It is however true that Luke goes out of his way to cast Elizabeth in Mary's shadow. There are minor and there are major models of discipleship in this story.

Elizabeth is portrayed as the forerunner of Mary. Her miraculous conception out of due season in life is a reassurance to Mary that the angel's words to her are true. In fact, Elizabeth relates to Mary in a similar way to Luke's portrayal of John relating to Jesus. Notice the deferential tone in both Luke 1:42-43 and 3:16. Just as Elizabeth is given more prominence than Zechariah and is cast in a more favorable light as a model of faith, so is Mary in relationship to Joseph. There is little mention of Joseph until after the major prophecies and songs have been given concerning Jesus. It is Joseph who is silent, like Zechariah in Luke's Gospel, in contrast to Mary's utter silence in Matthew 1–2. It is through the prominence of Mary's forerunner, Elizabeth, and the absence of Joseph that the portrait of Mary is cast into dramatic relief. Her central role continues in the stories about Simeon and Anna.

Anna and Simeon are representatives of the old Jewish order of piety, the old hopes and dreams. But it is to Mary that Simeon turns with the words "Behold, this child is set for the fall and rising of many in Israel, and for a sign that is spoken against (and a sword will pierce through your own heart as well), so that the thoughts of many hearts may be revealed" (2:34-35). Since Luke makes no mention of Mary being at the cross, it is unlikely that this saying has anything to do with that occurrence. The sword is probably symbolic of the piercing anguish of Mary seeing her Son spoken against and rejected by her own people. She is part of Israel, and yet she is being divided between Israel and her Son. There may also be something to the suggestion that this refers to Mary being rebuffed by Jesus (cf. Luke 2:49-50; Luke 8:19-21). Anna is portrayed as a prophetess, much like Mary, and she goes forth witnessing about Jesus once she has seen him. If Simeon is simply prepared as a tired old man to depart in peace having seen Jesus, Anna like Mary represents the new eschatological order of things with women going forth and witnessing about Jesus. It is also true that with Anna's and Elizabeth's portrayals Mary is set in a context where she is seen as one believing woman among a variety of such believing women, and she does not always have the clearest insight among those who are "true" Israel.

The lack of understanding on Mary's part comes out at several junctures in the narrative (1:29, 34; 2:33, 50). Luke 2:50 states explicitly that she and Joseph did not understand the things Jesus told them. In this they are very much like Jesus' disciples (18:34). Luke then does not paint an idealized picture of Mary, and her story is not told as one only full of sunshine and flowers. He is willing to reveal both her joy and her pain, both her insight and her lack of understanding. But notice there is also the reminder that even though she does not understand what she ought to do, she stores Jesus' words in her mind and ponders them (2:19, 51). She is portrayed as a woman growing toward full understanding. It will take considerable time for Mary to understand all these things. Luke apparently, like the Fourth Evangelist, does not believe that full understanding is possible prior to the cross.

In the story of Jesus in the Temple, which concludes the infancy narrative in Luke (2:41-52), the tensions between the claims of the physical and spiritual family responsibilities on Jesus are evident. It is interesting that one can draw a parallel between Mary and Jesus in this story because they both grow in wisdom and stature and in favor with God and humankind as the story goes on. Thoughtful learning characterizes disciples (8:15, 18-21; 10:39). Mary is an approachable model of faith for Luke's audience for she both lacks and seeks understanding, and she both has faith and yet has anxieties.

Luke's story of Jesus preaching in Nazareth, found in Luke 4, does not include any remarks about Mary, nor are the brothers and sisters referred to at this juncture. The mothers and brothers are briefly mentioned when Luke takes over Mark 3:31-35 in Luke 8:19-21. Luke however presents the least offensive version of this story. Mary and the brothers simply come to see Jesus, and Jesus' final word is: "My mother and brothers are those who hear God's word and put it into practice." This leaves room for Jesus' physical family to be included within that description. Mary does not re-appear in Luke's Gospel, but we do find her and the brothers (where are the sisters in Luke?).[3] Acts 1:14 completes the story of Mary by showing that she made the transition into the circle of Jesus' followers in Jerusalem, and was praying and awaiting Pentecost like the rest of the disciples. Luke then presents us with the fullest, and fairest, and most winsome, portrait of Mary in the four Gospels.

James[4]

There are only very brief references to James in the Gospels, and in fact he is not mentioned by name in Luke's or John's Gospel. Consider first the Johannine material. John 7:1-5 says bluntly that the brothers did not believe in Jesus during the ministry. James was certainly not among Jesus' disciples. We do find him briefly mentioned at John 2:12 traveling down to Capernaum with Mary and Jesus and his disciples. Notice in this text how the brothers are mentioned separately from the disciples. In Luke's Gospel we hear of the siblings of Jesus, without naming them, being with Mary when she comes to speak to Jesus in Luke 8:19-21, and the door is left open in this account for them to be included among the family of faith if they will do God's will as Mary had done before Jesus was conceived.

Matthew and Mark are a little more forthcoming about James, and we will consider what Mark has first. Both of these Gospels always portray James with his mother Mary during the ministry of Jesus, as is the case in Luke 8:19-21. There are exactly two episodes when the brothers are mentioned: once anonymously at Mark 3:31-35 where they are a part of the mission to rescue Jesus that fails to achieve its intended aim.[5] They hear Jesus' remark and see his gesture which indicate that it is the family of faith that is his true family. More importantly, in Mark 6:3 we actually have a list of Jesus' brothers, and James is mentioned first. This would normally mean,

3. Unlike Matthew and Mark, Luke does not tell us the names of Jesus' siblings, and of course Matthew and Mark tell us only the brothers' names, and that there was more than one sister.

4. For a fuller presentation of James see H. Shanks and B. Witherington, *The Brother of Jesus: The Dramatic Story and Meaning of the First Archaeological Link to Jesus and His Family* (San Francisco: HarperCollins, 2003), pp. 93-209.

5. See pp. 187-88 above.

and probably does mean here, that he is the next eldest child of Mary. The text says that James is the brother of Jesus; it only implies that he is the child of Mary. The way the narrative ends, however, suggests that Jesus does not find the presence of his siblings in the synagogue (or at least his sisters) to be compelling evidence that they believe in or honor him by their presence (see 6:4).

Matthew's passing reference to James is made somewhat less negative by the omission of Mark 3:21, but, on the other hand, Matthew includes the saying of Jesus about how Jesus will cause division of family members in a home (including presumably his own — Matt. 10:34-36), and since this precedes the account of the family coming out to speak with Jesus (Matt. 12:46-50) and of the family hearing Jesus in the synagogue (Matt. 13:53-57), it sets these accounts in a kind of negative context. It is said in the Matthew 12 account that the brothers as well as Mary wanted to speak to him, and Jesus pointedly asks not only who is his mother but who are his brothers, and then points to his disciples, not his family. The account of the synagogue episode in Matthew 13 sheds a different light on things than the Markan account in one respect. As in Mark, the brothers are listed by name with James first, but the term "relatives" is left out of the list of those who Jesus says do not honor him. The text simply says Jesus is without honor in his hometown and in his own home. This in turn means that the brothers must be seen here as members of Jesus' own home, not merely relatives. This favors the view that the brothers are seen by the First Evangelist as blood brothers, not cousins, as the children of Mary, since they are associated with her in this discussion. In none of the Gospels do we hear anything about James in the Passion or resurrection stories, and so we must turn to Acts and to Paul's letters to continue the story of James.

In Acts 1:14 we find the mother of Jesus and the brothers of Jesus, including James, in the upper room, awaiting Pentecost with the disciples. How did this come about? 1 Corinthians 15:7 tells us that Jesus personally appeared to James. The list also makes it clear that Jesus appeared to quite a lot of other folks before he appeared to James. Indeed we are told Jesus appeared to five hundred persons at one time before appearing to James. It is possible that this appearance followed the one to the disciples in Galilee, which is depicted at the end of Matthew 28. In any case, it was a resurrection appearance of Jesus that seems to have turned James into a disciple of his brother. But can we say more? If we look again carefully at the list in 1 Corinthians 15:5-8, it will be noted that only three individuals are mentioned by name as having received an appearance of Jesus: Peter, James, and Paul. Is it an accident that these three became the three major figures in early Christianity? Surely not. Paul indicates in 1 Corinthians 9 that the criterion for being an apostle is to have seen the risen Lord. It is then not a surprise that we also find in Paul's earliest letter, Galatians, the remarks that by or before A.D. 49 James had become one of the three pillar apostles of the new eschatological community in Jerusalem. Indeed, to judge from Galatians 2, he had become the head of the Jerusalem church by the time of Paul's second visit up to Jerusalem, for we hear about "men sent from James," but also in Galatians 2:9 about James being listed before Peter and John as the ones who gave Paul the right hand of fellowship. This means surely that by the mid-40s at least James is the leader in Jerusalem.[6] Let us consider what Acts suggests about James.

There is no other reference to James after Acts 1:14 until we get to Acts 12. There we have in Acts 12:17 a passing reference to Peter wanting James and the brothers informed that he is free and moving on. This suggests James would be the natural leader once Peter moved on. This in turn brings us to Acts 15, the crucial chapter in the matter.

Acts 15 establishes, beyond cavil, the crucial role James played in the Early Church. He is depicted here as the great mediator standing between the Pharisaic Jewish Christians on his right who wanted to demand that all Christians including Gentiles be circumcised and follow the Mosaic Law to be true followers of Jesus, and Paul on his left who believed not only that Gentiles did not need to keep the Law, but also that even Jewish Christians could view it as a blessed option, not an obligation. Acts 15 reveals several dimensions to the character of James, as well as indicating that, since he is the one who concluded the matter, he must be viewed as the chief authority figure in Jerusalem among the apostles and elders. In the first place the text reveals a James who is concerned about the Gentile mission. Indeed, he is depicted as supporting what has already been advocated about a Gentile mission by finding a Scripture in Amos 9:11-12 that says that the reason Israel is to be rebuilt and restored is so that Gentiles may seek the Lord.

James then issues a minimalist edict requiring that Gentiles stay away from the idolatry and immorality by forsaking pagan temples where one finds meat sacrificed to and eaten in the presence of idols, as well as things strangled, blood, and the immorality that often also transpired at such din-

6. And is probably married as well. See 1 Corinthians 9:5.

ner parties in temples. In other words, James is asking for a clean break with the pagan past, not for the imposition on Gentiles of a modified set of Old Testament Jewish food rules. This ruling is then formed into a letter sent by James and the other elders and apostles in Jerusalem to the Gentile Christians in the Diaspora to instruct them about their future behavior. It is interesting that the other letter we have from James in the New Testament, the canonical letter known as James, is also written to persons in the Diaspora, in this case Jewish Christians, and it also does not impose any kosher food rules on anyone. Both letters are written from Jerusalem, and one thing that seems clear about the story of James is that he is always based in Jerusalem. We have no evidence he was ever an itinerant missionary.

The last passage of interest for the story of the life of James that is in the canon is Acts 21:17-26. James is in fact mentioned only in passing in this text as greeting Paul and receiving his mission report, but he is part of the group who then advises Paul about performing a Jewish ritual of purification in the Temple. The fact that James is mentioned first as the one to whom Paul and the rest report shows his authority and stature as the major leader of the Mother Church. It appears likely that James was a Torah-true Jew throughout his life. He differed from Paul in his belief that this was necessary for a Jewish Christian. We have no record in the New Testament of how he died, in part because Acts 28 ends at about A.D. 60, and James died in A.D. 62 according to Josephus, but Josephus (*Ant.* 20.199-203) does tell us he was martyred, dying a violent death at the hands of the same family of high priests, descendants of Caiaphas, that took Jesus into custody and tried him. Various of these aspects of James' life and leadership are confirmed by a close reading of Galatians 1-2.

Conclusions

The New Testament is full of unfinished and unvarnished tales. Even when it talks about major figures like Paul or Peter or Mary or James, or more minor figures like Joseph, in none of these cases is their demise actually narrated in the New Testament. This may surprise us until we remember that the New Testament is not an attempt at hagiography (a biography of saints); it is a book about the Good News and the progress of the Word in the world. It is about God's activity among Jews and Gentiles through and because of the work of Jesus Christ. The glimpses and small vignettes we do have, however, of these figures depict them as truly human and flawed, but at the same time as people of growing and sometimes strong and courageous faith. In the case of James we see one who overcame a disbelief to become a follower of his brother, or, better said, had his doubts overcome by a personal appearance of the risen Jesus.

Especially compelling is the portrait of Mary in both Luke's and John's Gospel. She is portrayed as a disciple under construction in Luke's Gospel, but in John she is portrayed as one who is integrated into the family of faith at the cross. She, like her husband Joseph and their son James, is portrayed as a very devout Jew wrestling with the meaning of Jesus and his ministry. It is to the meaning of Jesus, as brought out by what can be called narrative Christology, that we must turn in our last two chapters. We turn then to the stories of Jesus himself.

....

Exercises and Questions for Study and Reflection

→ Write a one-page imaginative description of what it would have been like to have Jesus as your older brother. Include in that description what it would have been like to be James, and become the head of the family because Joseph was dead and Jesus was on the road. Would this have made it easier or harder for Jesus' siblings to believe in him?

→ Describe the depiction of Mary in the Gospels of Luke and Mark. How do these pictures differ? How would you explain the differences to someone puzzled about the various accounts? Do you think Mary should be considered a disciple of Jesus prior to his death and resurrection?

→ What does Matthew mean when he says that Joseph was a righteous man and resolved to divorce Mary quietly? Why is the term "divorce" used when they are engaged? What do you think happened to Joseph by the time Jesus' ministry began?

→ Why do the Gospel writers seem unconcerned about telling us the end of the stories of Joseph, Mary, or James?

→ What was it that turned James into a disciple? Describe his role in the Early Church in the light of Galatians 1–2 and Acts 15 and 21. How important do you think James was to the early Christian movement, in comparison to Peter or Paul?

9 | Stories of Jesus outside the Gospels

"Tell me the stories of Jesus . . ." is the text of the hymn, and in the last two chapters of this study we intend to do so. These are stories that have been etched in stone, carved into altars, forged into steel, stained into glass, written into oratorios, and imprinted on our memories. Hearing them again is rather like standing in St. Chapelle in Paris and staring in amazement at the story of the Bible played out in full detail in one room in gorgeous stained-glass windows. We want to consider both the little and large ways these stories have been told. Accordingly, in this chapter we will examine several of the non-Gospel tellings of this story, beginning with Paul.

Jesus in Paul

As is often remarked, Paul spends very little time talking about the earthly ministry of Jesus. Galatians 4:4 says that God sent his Son, born of woman, born under the Law. Paul then affirms the Jewishness of Jesus as well as his humanness. Romans 8:3 says that Christ was sent in the likeness of sinful flesh to be a sin offering. This description makes it clear that he appeared no different than any of us, but in fact he was without blemish and sinless and so could be the perfect atonement. Romans 1:3-4 says Jesus is of Davidic origin, and Romans 9:5 places him in the line of the patriarchs. Paul also retells for us in brief the story of the Last Supper in 1 Corinthians 11:23, indicating he knows of the betrayal of Jesus as well as the new covenant he announced at the Last Supper. But none of this material is nearly so revealing as what Paul says when he draws on Christological hymn material about Jesus, as we shall see in a moment. Paul views the story of Christ from the long perspective not only of salvation history, but also of the story of the divine Son of God who preexisted the creation of all things.

In Paul's letters the stories of Christ and Christians are in various ways closely knit together such that they begin to tell the tale of how the world is being set right again. Christ's story is the fulcrum, the crucial turning point, bringing to a climax the previous stories and determining how the rest of the story will play out and turn out. The story of God's own people in effect contracts to that of the Christ, the seed of Abraham, when he comes, but expands again to include Christ's followers. Thus, once again, as was true when Moses came on the scene, the story of humankind takes a decisive new turn when Christ comes on the scene. Yet when Moses came down from the mountain, he was trailing clouds of glory. Ironically enough, Christ chose to leave his glory behind in order to fully take on the human form, indeed the form of a servant among human beings. The story of the Christ, the plot of his career, is most ably and nobly summed up in the Christological hymn material found in Philippians 2:5-11.[1]

Perhaps we would do well to say first what this hymn fragment is not about. It is not about a contrast between Christ's story and Adam's story. Unlike for instance 1 Corinthians 15:45-49, the language of the last or eschatological Adam who founds a new race of persons is entirely missing here. A monotheistic Jewish Christian like Paul could have never thought it appropriate for a mere human like Adam to be worshipped as exalted Lord, as we find at the end of this hymn. One must also give account of what glory or status Christ had and gave up that other humans did not have. Furthermore, the Genesis story says nothing about Adam and Eve desiring absolute equality with God, only that they wished to be like God. Lastly, verses 5-7 speak of Christ making choices that affected his earthly form and condition. Christ chooses to set aside one form in order to take on the form of a human, indeed a servant among humans. The phrase "being found in form a human being" is inexplicable if he had never been anything else other than a human being. What we are dealing with then in this synopsis of the

---

1. This material appears in a somewhat different form in my *Paul's Narrative Thought World: The Tapestry of Tragedy and Triumph* (Louisville: Westminster/John Knox, 1994).

Christ story is a tale about a person who existed prior to taking on a human form, and furthermore continued to exist beyond death in heaven.

Philippians 2:6-11 is a story divided into two parts. In the first half of the hymn, which has a V pattern (with preexistence, earthly existence, and existence in heaven after life on earth being the three nodal points making up the V), Christ is the actor who thinks and chooses and lives out a planned earthly existence. In the second half of the hymn, however, the story is about what God did for Christ as a result of his attitude and actions leading up to and including his death. We have in this hymn an interesting juxtaposition of the imagery of preexistence, suffering servant, wisdom, and humility and exaltation.

It is important to stress that verse 5 deliberately draws a parallel between the frame of mind and decision making of the preexistent Son of God, and that of Christians. This exalted piece of theological discourse has interestingly enough a ethical function meant to produce the imitation of Christ in and by believers. Christ deliberately stepped down, he deliberately did not draw on his divine prerogatives, he deliberately took a lower place, and he deliberately submitted even to death on the cross. Of course the analogy drawn here between the behavior of Christ and that of Christians is just that — an analogy. But it is a potent one. The essence of the analogy is that we ought to follow Christ's self-sacrificial lifestyle so others may benefit. The first half of the hymn has a parenetic thrust. It may also be that the second half hints that God will do for the believer what he has already done for Christ: provide a resurrection, saying "come up higher, brother or sister," and the like. The crucified conqueror's story is to be recapitulated in the life of his followers, as Paul himself was in various ways experiencing. It is in this same letter Paul says, "I want to know Christ and the power of his resurrection and the sharing in common of his sufferings by becoming like him in his death, if somehow I might attain the resurrection of the dead" (Phil. 3:10-11). Paul mentions this not least because he sees himself as modeling Christ so that his converts will do likewise. This is made very clear in 3:14-17, where Paul pleads directly, "Brothers and sisters, join in imitating me" (cf. 1 Cor. 11:1). The context must be remembered however. This is not hubris; it is the modeling that a good teacher was expected to do. Paul is not claiming to be *the* pattern, only a good example of how one follows the pattern.[2]

2. See pp. 151-54 above.

We may object that Paul believed that the Christian obtained from God an alien righteousness through faith in Christ and apart from works (Phil. 3:9). This is true enough, but it negates none of the ethical thrust of this telling of the Christ story. Indeed Paul assumes that the gift of right-standing with God is the platform or basis for exhorting his charges to Christlikeness and promising them the completion of the process if they remain faithful to the end. To "gain Christ" (3:8) is not merely to gain right-standing with God; it is to gain full Christlikeness at the resurrection (3:10-11).

Some of the details of the story are most revealing of what Paul thinks about the central figure in the story. For example, the word *morphē*, from which we get a word such as metamorphosis, always signifies an outward form that truly and accurately expresses the real being which underlies it. This must mean that Christ manifested a form that indicated he truly had the nature and being of God. This is after all why Paul adds the further phrase, "the being equal to God." This hymn indicates that this status and condition was something the preexistent Son of God actually had. Christ by rights and by nature had what God had. The much disputed term *harpagmos* in all likelihood means taking advantage of something which one rightfully has. Christ did not take advantage of his divine prerogatives and glorious status, but rather set them aside and took on the form of a human being. This probably does not mean that he set aside his divine nature; rather, he set aside the right to draw on his divine attributes (omnipotence, omniscience, omnipresence) while on earth. In short, the incarnation meant the deliberate self-limiting of a divine being in order to be truly and fully human. He lived among humans as one of us, drawing on the power of the Spirit and the Word of God and prayer, just as we must do, to live out his earthly existence. It is thus the human career of Christ, beginning with his taking on the form of a servant and continuing on through his death and resurrection, which is said to be analogous to the plot of the story of Christians.

Christ not only stripped himself but also shunned any rightful human accolades or dignity, taking on the form of a servant or slave. How very differently he lived than most ancient persons, caught up in honor challenges and striving for more public recognition. Yet in the end he was honored. God in fact gave him the divine name, the Old Testament name for God in the LXX: *kyrios*. Here Isaiah 45:21-25 lies in the background. In this hymn then we see, as was the case in 1 Corinthians 8:6, that Paul is affirming a transformed definition of Jewish monotheism. Christ is not given a purely honorific name of which he is unworthy or to which he is ill suited by nature. Paul believes to the contrary that the name matches the nature, and this is why worship is appropriate. Christ's story is the crucial hinge story in the whole human drama that indicates how the story will end. Paul is able to retell this story in many other creative forms (see, e.g., Col. 1:15-20), but the essence of the story is the same in each case. It is about a preexistent divine Son of God who stooped to conquer. The means of triumph was not just taking on the form of a servant, but also dying a slave's death on the cross, and then being vindicated by God through the resurrection (cf. Rom. 1:3-4). This story has in fact a sequel, involving the return of Christ to earth once more. This in turn means that the follower of Christ during the Church age must live between the advents, keeping one eye on each horizon. There is an already-and-not-yet character to the story of Christ, and so to the story of his followers.

Paul is interested in the entire story of humankind from beginning to end. When he reaches the climax of the story, in the story of Christ, it is notable that he focuses overwhelmingly on the end of the Christ story: the death and resurrection, though the coming and true humanity are also emphasized. Paul's gospel about Christ is a passion-and-resurrection narrative with a short introduction. Yet he also does not neglect the cosmic origins and ends of the story, not least because the latter has a direct effect on the believer's story now. If it is true that Christ has led supernatural captivity captive (Eph. 4:8), and believers are no longer in the thrall of demons (though they may still be pestered or persecuted by such foes), then Christians need to know this and not live as those without hope or help.[3] The story of humankind was narrowed down to the story of Israel, in the persons of Abraham and Moses and their successors, which in turn was further narrowed down to the story of the Jewish Messiah, the Christ, and thereafter the story widens again to embrace the story of those who are in the Christ.

3. See pp. 143-55 above.

The Story of Christ in the Sermon Summaries in Acts

There is more than one way of examining the story of Christ in Acts, and in fact the matter is so complex and so bound up with the narrative of salvation history that it will be useful to consider briefly the constitutive parts of the Christ story and the way Luke names the Christ, before considering a few of the summaries themselves.[4] The salvation-history way of telling the story and framing the Christological material is evident by contrasting what goes on before and after Easter. For example, in the Gospel Son of Man and glory are discussed purely in future terms, unlike the case here in Acts. Second, in Acts 7 the Son of Man is standing, not merely seated, at the right hand of God. Clearly both here and in Luke's future Son of Man sayings in his Gospel, Daniel 7 lies in the background. What we see here is the way the time frame affects the Christological expression. Stephen speaks, believing that Jesus has already ascended and is at God's right hand, for the Church exists in the era after Jesus' resurrection and ascension. In other words, the image we find in Acts 7:56 would be out of place in the Gospel unless Jesus was speaking of someone other than himself when he referred to the future coming of the Son of Man. This is but one example of Luke using Christological terms and titles with a clear historical perspective on the differences between the pre- and postresurrection situation and the pre- and postresurrection community of Jesus' followers. From a historian's point of view, the resurrection has decisively changed things for and about Jesus, and so too for and about the community that spoke of him.

It is in fact an integral part of Luke's very spatial and temporal approach to things including Christology that we find at the end of Luke's Gospel (Luke 24) and throughout Acts what can be called an exaltation Christology: a Christology that Jesus is up there in heaven, exalted to the right hand of God. It is not an accident that both the Gospel and Acts include the ascension, an event that makes Christ's bodily absence certain. This too is a reflection of Luke's attempt to think historically about what happened to Jesus and his body. Jesus then, in Luke's view, left nothing behind but his followers. This is also why the sending of the Spirit is so cru-

---

4. What follows in the next few paragraphs can be found in a much fuller form in my *The Many Faces of the Christ: The Christologies of the New Testament and Beyond* (New York: Crossroads, 1998).

cial in the Lukan scheme of things. If Jesus is absent, the Church must have some source of divine power and direction, and the Spirit provides both.

Probably too much has been made of the fact that only Luke tells the story of the ascension, for it may well be alluded to in the Fourth Gospel when we are told that Jesus must return to the Father, and texts like John 20:17 suggest that this has some bearing on Mary and others clinging to Jesus' body. The notion may also be implied in the Christological hymns that refer to Christ's exaltation to God's right hand, and, more to the point, texts like 1 Corinthians 15 not only assert a bodily resurrection of Jesus but also a definite limited period of time after Easter when Jesus appeared in the body to his followers, after which Jesus' bodily presence on earth ceased. In other words, while only Luke articulates the story of the ascension, it seems to be presupposed in other New Testament sources. To the contrary, the Christological hymns which are early assume a descending and ascending Christ, a notion found in Ephesians 4:8 as well when Paul applies Psalm 68:18 to Christ. For a Gentile audience, the ascension of Jesus would have reminded them of ancient heroic figures that were approved by the gods and taken up into heaven. In other words, Luke is telling the story of Christ in a way his audience would find compelling.

It is right to stress that for Luke, the ascension implies a sort of absentee role for Christ in heaven, with the Spirit now acting on earth as Christ's agent. Texts such as Acts 2:33; 3:21; 9:3; 22:6 and 26:13 stress that Christ is in heaven, even if he appears to some on earth such as to Stephen or Paul (cf., e.g., Acts 7, 9 and 23:11). In almost all instances in Acts it is by the Spirit or an angel that God acts on earth (cf. 8:26, 29, 39; 11:28; 12:7; 13:4; 15:28; 16:6; 20:23; 21:11; 27:23). Notice as a corollary of this that we do not really find the "in Christ" or corporate Christ theology in Luke-Acts as we do in Paul's letters. Nor is there any ongoing Immanuel sort of Christology in Acts such as we find at the beginning and end of Matthew's Gospel. In other words, Luke's Christology seems simpler and more primitive than what we find in Paul's letters or in the incorporation theology in the Fourth Gospel, a fact which is confirmed by considering a few of the Christological sermon summaries in Acts (see below).

The historical perspective of Luke is in full evidence if we compare and contrast the use of the term "Lord" in Acts and in Luke's Gospel. Luke calls Jesus "Lord" in the narrative portions of both his volumes (cf. Luke 7:13 to Acts 23:11), in a way the other Synoptic writers refrain from doing in the narrative sections of their Gospels. It would also appear that Jesus even calls himself Lord obliquely once in Luke 19:31-34, but this usage is found in the other Synoptics as well and may mean little more than "master" or "owner." However no other being calls Jesus Lord in Luke's Gospel unless a person is under inspiration (Luke 1:43, 76) or the term is found on the lips of an angel (2:11). Once we get past the resurrection of Jesus, various people can and do call Jesus Lord in the ordinary course of things (cf. Luke 24:34 to Acts 10:36-38).

The same sort of phenomenon can be found in the use of Sonship language. In the Gospel, Jesus is called Son by other than human voices (Luke 1:32, 35; 3:22; 4:3ff.; 8:28), but in Acts at both 9:20 and 13:33 Paul clearly calls him this openly. Then too, words about Jesus as Savior or as one who saves are found only on superhuman lips in the Gospel (2:11, 30; 3:6), but after the resurrection and ascension we find such talk an essential part of the Church's confession (Acts 4:12; 5:31; 13:23). Luke is supremely conscious of the difference the resurrection made in terms of what Jesus did and what he could become for his followers. He could not have truly fulfilled his Christological role, nor could his followers have confessed him as Christ if he had not risen from the dead. The resurrection is for Luke the watershed event for both Christology and ecclesiology.

It is not entirely surprising that in these two volumes, which are so firmly grounded in historical considerations, there is no clear preexistence language applied to Christ, though some texts might imply the notion. It is interesting however that Acts 2:31 implies that David saw Jesus' resurrection coming in the future, but says nothing about David seeing or foreseeing Jesus himself. In any event, Christ's preexistence (which does not deal with his historical manifestation) is not a subject Luke chooses to debate or even really to address. Luke's concern as a historian is to tell the story of Jesus from his birth to his present and ongoing exaltation in and reigning from heaven as Lord over all. He also refers to Christ as the coming judge (Acts 3:20ff.; Acts 17:31) though this is also not a central concern of his in either of his volumes. Notice the focus of Peter's description in Acts 2:22-36, where the whole scope of Jesus' ministry is chronicled from birth as a man (2:22) to his exaltation and coronation in verses 33-36.

The humanness of Jesus is stressed in Acts by the repeated reference to Jesus as "of Nazareth" (3:6; 4:10; and others), just as it was stressed in the Gospel as well. Notice this is often stressed in conjunction with the name Jesus Christ, not just Jesus. Acts 10:36ff. is in various ways one of the more important texts in Acts for Christological discussion for here we not only see the exalted Christ, the one who is Lord over all, but in the same text we find the so-called low Christological notion of God being with Jesus and anointing him with Spirit and power while he was on earth. The point is that Luke wishes to stress Jesus' humanness but at the same time reveal his divine roles as well.

Acts 2:30 and 13:33 bring to the fore God's Son of Davidic descent who reigns over Israel in the latter days. This is not a major image in Acts, but it is significant in that it makes it clear that Luke has no desire to portray Jesus as simply a man or a generic savior, but rather as a Jew, and indeed the Jewish Messiah. This comports with the use of the Isaianic material in Acts (Acts 3:13; 4:27-30), which reveals that Jesus is the Servant of whom the prophet spoke.

It has often been asserted on the basis of texts like Acts 2:36 (where it is said that God has made Jesus Lord and Christ) that Luke tells the story of Christ in a fashion which suggests that at the resurrection Jesus became something he was not previously. This overlooks that Luke is operating in a historical and narratological mode and discusses such things from a functional perspective. The issue for Luke is not who is Jesus before and after the resurrection, for it is "this same Jesus" in both cases, but rather what roles or functions he assumes after Easter that he could not, or could not fully, assume before Easter. Luke's point is that only as the exalted One could Jesus truly assume the tasks of Lord over all and be Messiah and Savior for all. In other words, Luke is not given to ontological speculation; such texts are about roles and functions and what tasks Jesus did when. He is simply telling the story in a historical way and within a historical framework.

While it is true that there is not a great deal of reflection on the atoning nature of Christ's death in Luke-Acts, there is certainly some. One form this takes is found in the problematic text of Acts 20:28 on the lips of Paul. The text probably reads "the blood of His own" referring to Christ's blood. Another form this takes is in the discussion about Christ suffering in order to release people from their sins, or provide forgiveness (cf. Acts 13:38 to Acts 2:38).

Let us look a bit more closely at two of the key titles in Acts: *kyrios* (Lord) and *christos* (Christ). The former is by far the most frequently used title in all of Luke-Acts, occurring almost twice as often as *christos*. In fact the majority of all references to Christ as *kyrios* occur in either Luke-Acts (210 times) or in the Pauline letters (275 times) out of a total of 717 instances in the New Testament. The basic concept Luke has of *kyrios* seems to be "one who exercises dominion over the world," and particularly over human lives and events. In other words the term is always used relationally, for if one is to be a lord, one must have subjects.

The term *kyrios* occurs in Acts 104 times, of which only 18 are references to God the Father and 47 definitely refer to Jesus, with most of the rest referring either to Jesus or God, though it is not always clear which is meant in some of these texts. A clear reference to Jesus is evident in some texts because *kyrios* is combined with the name Jesus (1:21; 4:33; 8:16; 15:11; 16:31; 19:5, 13, 17; 20:24, 25; 21:13), or the name Jesus Christ (11:17; 15:26; 28:31). It is also clear that where we have *theos* and *kyrios* combined, it is not Jesus that is being discussed (2:39; 3:22). In Acts 2:34, which draws on Psalm 110:1, both God and Jesus are called Lord. It would be wrong to conclude from such a text that Luke sees Christ as only the believer's Lord, for Acts 10:36 makes such an assertion impossible.

Luke, even within Acts, seems conscious that as time went on "Lord" terminology was used of Christ more and more frequently. It is striking that the vast majority of references where God and not Jesus is called Lord are found in Acts 1–10 (2:39; 3:19, 22; 4:26; 7:31; 10:4, 33) or on the lips of Jews or proselytes to Judaism. The further one gets into Acts the more Christians speak for themselves, and when they do, "Lord" almost always means Christ. After the council in Acts 15 only one text seems clearly to use *kyrios* of God rather than Christ: 17:24. Luke does not shy away from the paradox of speaking of a risen Lord (Luke 24:34); indeed, it is said to be the resurrection that makes him Lord in some sense (Acts 2:36). What this suggests is that Luke uses the term sometimes to indicate when Jesus began to function as Lord, sometimes as simply the Christian way of referring to Christ in Luke's Gentile environment.

More univocal is Luke's use of *christos* in Acts. The term occurs some twenty-six times, and in every case, not surprisingly, it refers to Jesus. Texts such as Acts 3:18 or 4:26 which have the qualifier "his" make it clear that Luke knows the root meaning of the term *christos* and also understands the term's relational character. If one is "the Christ" one must have been anointed by someone else, namely, God. Hence in Acts Jesus is God's Christ or anointed one, but the believer's (and all other creatures') Lord. The full phrase "our Lord Jesus Christ" (15:26) implies both of these relationships. Luke makes explicit in two places that being a Christian involves confessing Jesus as "the Christ" (9:22; 17:3). It is in the witness to the synagogue that this issue is pressed. By way of generalization we may say that "Christ" mainly functions as a name when the audience is Gentile, but can serve as a title when the audience is Jewish (though texts like 2:38; 4:10; 8:12; 10:48; and 15:26 make it evident that this is not always so). What was critical for Jews to confess is that Jesus is the Christ, the Jewish Messiah (5:42; 17:3), while for Gentiles what was paramount was confessing Jesus as Lord (15:23-26). Luke can also stress that it was God's plan for the Christ to suffer (17:2-3) and be raised (2:31 citing Ps. 16:10). Finally, baptism in the name of Jesus Christ is seen as the characteristic entrance ritual for Christians (cf. Acts 2:38; 10:48).

These are the elements of the story of Christ that are scattered in short phrases and brief remarks in Acts. The pieces of the story are put together however in some of the sermon summaries, three of which we will now consider. For the most part the Christological sermons focus on the end of Jesus' earthly life. In Acts 2 the story is begun with the fact that Jesus was a man accredited by God, as was shown by the miracles he did. We then hear that God was the one who handed Jesus over to Jewish officials, who turned him over to Gentiles for judgment, "putting him to death by nailing him to the cross" (2:23). God, however, reversed that situation by raising him from the dead. A considerable time is spent explaining how death could not hold Jesus and David foresaw his resurrection (2:24-32). Then at verse 32 we hear of Jesus being exalted to the right hand of God, receiving the promised Holy Spirit, which he then poured out on his followers. At the point of exaltation Jesus assumed the role of both Lord and Christ. Before that juncture he could not save anyone because he could not pour out the Spirit, who is the change agent. Notice how Luke tells the story so that it climaxes with where Jesus is now, in heaven, exalted and actively pouring out the Spirit on various people. Christ is not seen as the absentee landlord of the Church but as actively involved in the salvation-historical process.

The sermon in Acts 3:13-16 also concentrates on the end of the life of Jesus, but with differing details. Again Jews are told they handed Jesus over; this time Pilate is specifically mentioned, but it is said that Pilate had decided to let him go. "You disowned the Holy and Righteous One and asked that a murderer be released to you. You killed the Author of life, but God raised him from the dead." The paradoxes in the story are played up in this telling, and the tone is more accusatory though the sermon goes on to say that the Jews acted in ignorance (3:17).

The synagogue sermon in Acts 13:16-41 is much longer and involves a rather long salvation-historical review, not unlike the speech of Stephen in Acts 7. In verse 24 we hear that John preached baptism and repentance to Israel. John denied he was the One who was to come, saying that he was unworthy to untie his sandals (v. 25). It is said that the people and rulers of Jerusalem did not recognize Jesus, but in fact in condemning Jesus they were simply fulfilling Scripture. They found no proper ground for execution, but they handed him over to Pilate. Notice that verse 29 says that when they had carried out all that Scripture had written about the matter, they then laid him in a tomb, but God raised him from the dead and he was seen for many days by those who traveled with him from Galilee to Jerusalem. There follows in verses 33-37 a demonstration from the Psalms that Jesus would be raised and that his body would not be allowed to decay, in a very similar manner to what is found in the sermon of Peter in Acts 2. Verse 39 conveys the notion that through Jesus whoever believes can be justified, even of sins that the Mosaic Law could never exonerate. It will be seen in all these summaries of speeches that the focus is on telling the portion of the story that is of most importance to salvation effected by Jesus Christ. These are evangelistic sermons, and so the focus must be on the death and resurrection and how those events were part of God's plan to save the world, both Jew and Gentile. There are various titles used, and occasional references to Jesus' miracles or teaching, but basically the focus is on the Passion and resurrection. When there is a salvation-historical introduction, it goes back before the time of Jesus' ministry rather than expanding the story to include more of the ministry. A somewhat different way of telling the story is found in Hebrews, but, as we shall see, there too the focus is on the exalted Jesus and what he can and does do for his people while he is in heaven.

The Story of Christ in the Homily to the Hebrews

The contribution of Hebrews to the story of Christ is the discussion about Christ being the believer's heavenly high priest. Yet this homily actually tells more of the story of the end of Jesus' life than we usually have in Paul's letters. There are also brief summaries of the story of Jesus in Hebrews. For example, in Hebrews 12:2 we hear about Jesus the pioneer and perfecter of faith who endured the shame of the cross and sat down at the right hand of

God's throne in heaven. Or again in Hebrews 13:12 we hear, "And so Jesus also suffered outside the city gate to make people holy through his own blood." There is a strong tendency in this homily to read the end of the story of Jesus through the discussions in the Pentateuch about priests and sacrifices. Though our author focuses more on the exaltation of Christ, he certainly also speaks of his resurrection from the dead (13:20). But our author also has a hymnic prologue to his homily not unlike the one we find in John, where he mentions the preexistence of the Son through whom the universe was made (1:2). It also says that the Son, who is the very image and radiance of God, now is sustaining all things by his word and is the heir of all things. It adds that after making purification for sin, he sat down at the right-hand side of God, becoming God's right-hand man. This same sort of hymnic V pattern which we saw in Philippians 2 we find again briefly at Hebrews 2:9, which speaks of Jesus who was made a little lower than the angels, made Son of Man, but is now crowned with glory and honor because he suffered death.

The full humanity of Jesus is stressed. Hebrews 2:17 says he was made like his fellow humans in every way so that he might become both faithful high priest and also atoning sacrifice. He is said to have suffered when he was tempted (2:18). In fact 4:15 says he was tempted in every way that we are, yet was without sin. There is a powerful presentation of the Gethsemane experience of Jesus in Hebrews 5:7-9: "During the days of Jesus' life on earth, he offered up prayers and petitions with loud cries and tears to the one who could save him from death, and he was heard because of his reverent submission. Although he was a son, he learned obedience from what he suffered, and once made perfect he became the source of eternal salvation."

The author of Hebrews has reflected deeply on the meaning of Jesus' death as part of the ongoing story and has some unique insights. He sees heaven as the perfect realm, and therefore suffering and death as a process of perfecting that leads one into the perfect realm. Jesus' death is a perfect sacrifice that makes all further such sacrifices superfluous. Once through the veil, Jesus enters the heavenly sanctuary as a high priest and not only offers the results of the sacrifice to God, making atonement in the process, but also on the basis of the sacrifice intercedes with the Father for his charges (cf. Hebrews 4–10). Not only so, but the story is told in Hebrews 11 so that Christ becomes the climax of the hall of faith. The pioneer and exemplar of how to be faithful even unto death (Heb. 12:1-2).

The story is not told straightforwardly in Hebrews. The author, like a good preacher, repeats himself, but the presentation is powerful and profound and it sheds more light on Christ's role in heaven than does any other New Testament book. It also says more about the atoning sacrifice of Christ on the cross than does any other New Testament presentation. We find then in this book the preexistent divine Son, the truly human Son of Man, the suffering servant and priest, the obedient praying child, the completely atoning sacrifice, the heavenly high priest who intercedes, and the heir of all things. In some ways this telling of Jesus' story has the most scope and depth of all the presentations.

But there is one presentation equally impressive but in a totally different mode and vein that is offered in the last book of the New Testament.

The Story of Christ in the Visions of John of Patmos

John tells the story of Christ in apocalyptic and to some degree mythological form. We will consider the story as it is told in Revelation 12 as a flashback, and then look at Revelation 5, which speaks of Christ's present role in heaven, and finally consider what is said in Revelation 19 about the Rider of the White Horse, which refers to the future role of Christ when he comes to judge the world.

Revelation 12:1 begins by telling us that the author saw a great sign[5] or portent appearing in the *ouranos*. The question arises as to whether we should translate *ouranos* as "sky" or "heaven." Either rendering is possible, but, as the story unfolds, "heaven" seems the more likely translation. We hear of a woman clothed with the sun, with the moon under her feet and a crown *(stephanos)* with twelve stars. Much conjecture has been offered as to whether this crown might represent the constellations or, more specifically, the twelve signs of the zodiac. The point is that in this woman the destiny of the whole race lies, drawing on the notion that stars control one's future or fate. But the question is, Who is this woman?

The conjecture still favored by most Roman Catholic scholars is that this is Mary. This is not impossible, but two factors are usually thought to count against this conclusion: (1) At verse 17 we hear about "the rest of her

---

5. For a fuller discussion of these three texts from Revelation see my *Revelation* (Cambridge: Cambridge University Press, 2003). This material appears in a more detailed form there.

offspring" (*sperma,* seed here). This is surely unlikely to be a reference to Jesus' other physical kin. Rather, it is more likely to refer to believers, perhaps in particular persecuted believers, or those about to be persecuted. (2) The parallels to our text in Isaiah 66:6-9 strongly suggest mother Zion is in view or, as Paul would put it, the new Jerusalem which is our mother (Gal. 4:26). In short, what is in view is the community of God's people, and here there is seen a certain continuity between the Old Testament and New Testament people of God. Jesus was born a Jew into the Jewish believing community. Gentiles are the community of God's other children. Jesus is in a sense a special child of God, as we shall see.

The woman is depicted as being in anguish to give birth. The red or fiery (or bloody) dragon is said to be a second portent in the sky or in heaven. That he has ten horns suggests awesome strength and draws on the apocalyptic imagery in Daniel 7–8 where it refers to nations. Notice the deliberate contrast between the dragon and the woman. The dragon has seven crowns, perhaps indicating his attempt to usurp all power; but his crowns are called *diademata,* whereas mother Zion's crown is the *stephanos,* the laurel wreath for victors. It is possible that the reference to "twelve" refers to the twelve tribes of Israel rather than to the zodiac, and so would be a symbol for the whole people of God. This dragon's tail is said to have dragged a third of the stars from the sky. Notice that the stars are cast to earth, not into hell or the abyss or some other destination. Stars were seen as gods by pagans and as angels by Jews.

One may ask when we are meant to think of these events happening. Certainly there does not appear to be anything here about a primordial fall of Satan and his angels from heaven. Rather, we have here a depiction of either what happened as a result of the triumphant death, resurrection, ascension, and assumption of power by the male child, in which case the whole Church age is seen as a time of being *in extremis,* or the events at the end of human history. This then would refer to a final tribulation before the end, since the Devil knows his time is exceedingly short. Some of course would say that this is a false dilemma. John never pictured a long Church age, and thus he could depict the final tribulation as potentially near at hand.

Verse 4b depicts the dragon almost hovering in front of the woman who is about to give birth so that it can devour the child as soon as it is born. This child is a male child destined to shepherd all the nations with an iron rod. Psalm 2 is clearly in the background here, and the imagery conveys the child's absolute power over the nations, and possibly even his power to judge. John is drawing on the traditions in regard to the birth of Apollo, which were also appropriated by Domitian to suggest that he was a divine being and the conqueror of evil, but John is challenging such arrogance by the emperor in his telling of the Christ story. Christ was the only God who ever walked on the earth in John's view.

The text says that the male child was seized and carried off to God and to his throne. There are various ways this might be understood. Some commentators think that Jesus' birth and death, resurrection, and ascension are in view here. Others think that the only focus here is the death, resurrection and ascension, for it is at this point that Jesus becomes Son of God in power, properly speaking. Against this last view, not only does it require that we interpret this text through a text with which it likely has no relationship (Rom. 1:3-4), but also we are in fact told explicitly that the woman bore a son. The only reference to Sonship is connected with birth, not the being seized or carried off. I thus conclude that the birth and death, resurrection, and ascension are in view here, which is a sort of merism (parts symbolizing the whole) circumscribing the whole earthly career of Jesus. The passive voice "was seized and carried off" implies that God did this. This means John sees God's hand in Jesus' death. What the forces of darkness thought would mean the end of the male child, God used to give him a promotion and further power and authority even over the dark powers.

Where Revelation 12 leaves Christ is exactly where we find Christ in the vision in Revelation 5. Revelation 5 is not about God's work in creation but rather his work in redemption. It is not then a surprise that it starts by talking about a book or a scroll, one written on both the front and the back. The terminology here may suggest that *biblion* should be translated "scroll" here. Possibly lying in the background is Ezekiel 2:9. If so, we see that what is on the scroll is a group of sealed-up prophecies, a hidden revelation which no human being has the power to unveil. The inability of all parties, except the Lamb, to open it indicates that we are indeed dealing with a very special revelation that only one can give and interpret. Nonetheless, some have insisted here that rather than prophecies what is in view is some sort of legal document or even a covenant treaty sealed with seven seals for protection. The fact that there are seven seals simply indicates the importance of this revelation and the need to keep it hidden until the appropriate time.

This is certainly a very strange scroll, for each seal seals only a part of the revelation. A strong angel proclaims in a loud voice, "Who is worthy to open the scroll?" But there is no creature on earth worthy, and so John weeps. Some have suggested that this is the angel Gabriel, but if it was important to know his name, John would likely have told us. In these oracles what is revealed is God's plan of redemptive judgment which spans human history and involves not only the future, which is sometimes referred to, but also the past and the present.

John is consoled by one of the elders (which gives a further clue that the elders are representatives of humankind) for there is one who is worthy to open the scroll and look inside: the Lion of the tribe of Judah who is also called the root of David. What is striking about all this is that in verse 6 when John looks, he sees not a lion but a lamb. Indeed, he sees the slain Lamb of God. Both the lion and lamb images are appropriate to what follows, which speaks of both judgment and redemption, both justice and mercy, both punitive action and sacrifice by the one reading the scroll. The means by which God achieves his purpose of overthrowing the powers of evil is through the slain Lamb and his death on the cross.

Standing, not sitting, right in the middle of the throne and of the four creatures and twenty-four elders is a Lamb, and it looks as though it has been slain. And it has seven horns, symbols of strength, and seven eyes, symbols of omniscience. This last feature of the Lamb has suggested to various commentators that the proper translation of *arnion* here should be "ram" (see, e.g., 1 Enoch 90:9, 38; Dan. 8:3). In fact, the word *arnion* is a diminutive of *arēn* (sheep), and so it literally means "little sheep." Though rams were used in Old Testament sacrifices, it was normally lambs that were offered, and lambs that were eaten as part of the Passover sacrifice. The term that was chosen, coupled with the emphasis on this being the *slain* lamb, favors the translation "lamb" rather than "ram." But this lamb has horns, and so we actually have a fusion of sacrificial lamb and ram features here, which are meant to convey a deliberate paradox. The lamb is vulnerable, and is slain, but the lamb is strong like a ram as well. The enemy may have thought they conquered him, but they did not. He overcame death, though he bears its scars. This is at the heart of John's message of hope to his congregations who face and no doubt fear persecution and even execution.

The angels/spirits of the churches are the eyes of the Lamb in the churches, and in all the earth. Just as God was worshipped in Revelation 4, here the Lamb is worshipped for he is worthy to take the scroll and read it. The implication is clear that the Lamb is divine. The elders (and the creatures?) are each said to have harps and bowls full of incense. The former are used to sing the Lamb's praises, while the latter represent the prayers of the "holy ones." This is probably not a reference to angels, but rather to human saints. If the elders are the heavenly representatives or archetypes of God's people, then it is appropriate that they convey the Church's prayers to the Lamb. These elders are singing a new tune, for no one has been worthy or able to open the scroll and unseal its seals. At verse 9b we find a doctrine of the atonement reflected. The Lamb is worthy because he was slain and by his blood bought for God some from every tribe and tongue and people and nation.

The image of the exalted Christ here who is a proper object of worship and who alone has the authority to read the scroll is an image of not only a glorified Christ, but a divine one reigning from heaven and ruling over the course of future human history. In our next and final Revelation text (ch. 19), John pushes the story even further forward to the time of Christ's return when he will in person execute judgment on the earth.

At the beginning of this section of the book, we hear of heaven itself being opened, and more comes forth than a mere vision. Not merely a door in heaven opens, but heaven itself bursts forth on the scene. We must hark back to the material in Revelation 16:12ff., the judgment of the sixth cup. There we hear of the armies assembling for Armageddon (cf. 17:14). Revelation 16:15 refers to the coming of the Son like a thief in the night. Here then we have the expansion of that comment, and the battle described here should not be distinguished from the one mentioned in Revelation 16 and 17:14.

The figure on the white horse is identified for us almost immediately by the allusion back to the beginning of this book, where we heard of the witness who was faithful and true (3:14; cf. 1:5). To understand this image, several pieces of background information are important. First, in early Jewish literature like 2 Baruch 72, we hear of a warrior Messiah who slays some of the nations and spares others. But more crucial is the material in Psalm of Solomon 17:23-27, and Psalm of Solomon 19.[6] In the former text we hear of one with an iron rod who will break in pieces the nations' sub-

---

6. There are of course Jewish texts that depict God as the warrior; cf. Isaiah 42:13; Habakkuk 3:11-14; Zephaniah 3:17; 1QMelchizedek 18:1-3.

stance and with the word of his mouth will destroy the nations. Psalm of Solomon 19 describes this more fully. Second, the image of Christ with accompanying horde coming forth from heaven is found in 2 Thessalonians 1:7-8. Notice also in that text the use of the image of flaming fire. In addition, one must compare the portrait of the royal figure in Isaiah 11:3ff. As usual, John has drawn on a variety of resources for his images.

When we hear about the eyes of this rider flaming like fire, we are meant to recall Revelation 1:14 and 2:18, and this identifies for us this figure as the Son of Man, not the figure on the white horse mentioned in Revelation 6:2. Notice that this figure has many diadems, in contrast to the seven the dragon had and the ten shared by the ten kings. This rider is King of kings and Lord of lords. None can approach his royalty, royal power, or righteous judgment. Yet, even in this striking vision of disclosure, we hear that the figure has a name that no one knows but himself. Only the Son can understand the full mystery of his own being (cf. Matt. 11:27). More to the point, it was widely believed in antiquity that gods had secret names. If you knew the name of the god, you had some power or control over him.

Verse 13 says that the rider's garment is dipped in blood. The echo here is of Isaiah 63:1-6 where very clearly there is the image of a garment dipped in blood. The two dominant interpretations are that the blood is that of Christ's enemies, or the blood is Jesus' own blood. The combination of the warrior image, which echoes Isaiah, and the Word image, as we shall see, does not favor the interpretation of the blood being Christ's own.

We are told that the name of this figure is the *Logos* (Word) of God. This is reminiscent of John 1, and yet in Revelation this phrase seems to have a different field of focus. The phrase refers to God's decisive oral judging of the nations. Various scholars have noticed the striking parallel to our text in Wisdom of Solomon 18:15-16, where we hear of the all-powerful Word of God leaping from the royal throne in heaven to execute judgment on Egypt. This echo suggests again that the subject matter of these verses is not the redemptive work of Christ (through his shed blood) but rather his work as final judge of all the earth.[7]

At verse 14 we hear of an army on white horses that follow the initial rider. Notice that the army is said to be in heaven. Who then composes this army? It could be the angelic hosts, which would comport with what we find in 2 Thessalonians 1:7ff. and Mark 13:27. Alternatively, it could refer to

---

7. On the Word of God as a two-edged sword, see Hebrews 4:12.

the saints as in Revelation 17:14. There are several other parallels between our text and 17:14 that may favor the latter interpretation. In any event, we are told they wear fine, gleaming, pure white linen, a description applied to the bride of Christ earlier in Revelation 19. It is crucial to note, however, that this army is never said to fight. In fact, they are wearing ceremonial garments, not armor or battle gear. Christ does whatever fighting is required, and that by his word.

Verse 15 is quite clearly a statement about judgment, the sharp sword of the Word issuing from the mouth of the rider and falling upon the nations. There are echoes here of Psalm 2:8-9 and perhaps Isaiah 11:3-4. He will rule with an iron hand. This suggests strong control, not annihilation, and, in view of the fact that various of those he will rule must appear later for final judgment, this seems the correct interpretation here.[8] In verse 15b we hear that the rider treads the winepress of the wine of the fury of the wrath of the almighty God. This is just a further or alternative image to the one already conjured up in this chapter. Isaiah 63:1-4 stands behind this presentation. The army is but a witness, for only the Son treads the winepress. Only he has the power and authority to execute judgment. He alone is King of kings and Lord of lords. Notice that we read that the rider also has his name inscribed on his robe, and on his thigh, or perhaps what is meant is on the part of his garment where the bare thigh can be seen. The inscription is surely King of kings and Lord of lords. Not only does this title express Jesus' universal sovereignty, but also, when it is put back into Aramaic (leaving out the word "and") and its number is reckoned, the result is 777, the victorious counterpart and antidote to 666.

At verse 17 we have a different image — that of an angel standing in the sun, and thus blindingly brilliant in appearance. Here we are told of a gruesome parallel to the marriage feast of the Lamb, namely, the dinner of God served up for birds of prey such as vultures. The description progresses to indicate what happens after the rider smites the nations. There is a great slaughter, and so the carrion birds are seen circling high overhead. Here too we have an invitation to dinner, but of a grizzlier sort. It will entail eating the flesh of kings, tribunes, slaves, free, the little and the large, the great and the small. Here Ezekiel 39:17 lies in the background. The sac-

---

8. It is possible that John sees the millennium rather like the description in 1 Corinthians 15 about Christ gradually putting all things under his feet until the last enemy is conquered.

rificial feast, normally an occasion when humans feast on animals, has been reversed. The triumph of God's kingdom involves a nightmare feast for the wicked and a joyful marriage feast for the saints.[9]

The great battle of Armageddon proves to be a one-sided affair. The rider simply seizes the beast and the false prophet and casts them into the lake of fire. Though the armies had assembled for a battle, it turned out to be an execution. The rhetoric here is clearly judicial in character, and what we see here is a symbolic depiction of a judicial process. Christ merely speaks the judgment against these opponents. The reason there is no real struggle here is perhaps that the victory has already been won through the death and resurrection of Jesus, and perhaps also John is emphasizing the power and sovereignty of Christ. What follows from this scene is both blessing and then bliss, both millennium and then new heaven and earth, but not without final judgment for Satan, his minions, and his human followers. The story here is about a Jesus who is both final redeemer and the final judge of the world. For John the ultimate end and aim is the marriage feast of the Lamb when Christ and his people will dwell together in unity forever in the New Jerusalem.

Conclusions

The story of Jesus can take many different forms: it can be preached, it can be sung, it can be summarized, it can be told in a historical review, it can be related in the context of theological reflection, and it can be cast in the light of Old Testament institutions. The humanness of Jesus can be stressed. The divinity of Jesus can be emphasized. The story fits no one formula, and various genres of literature can be brought into service to present these truths. What these presentations do share in common is placing the heaviest weight on the end of Jesus' human story: the death and resurrection. Both Acts and Hebrews also place considerable weight on the heavenly sequel to the resurrection and the role of Christ in heaven. The book of Revelation not only emphasizes Christ in glory but goes on to stress the connection of Christ in glory to the coming judgments and tribulations which Christ himself will consummate in person on earth at the

---

9. G. R. Beasley-Murray, *Revelation: Three Viewpoints* (Nashville: Broadman, 1977), pp. 283-84.

second coming. But none of these tellings do what the Gospels proper do. None of them really tell us the story of Jesus' ministry as well as focusing on the last week of his life, which was the climax of the earthly portion of the ministry. To these four stories we turn now as we complete our study of the New Testament story.

Exercises and Questions for Study and Reflection

→ On the basis of the Christological hymn in Philippians 2 write a detailed description of Jesus' whole career from his role in creation all the way to his role in heaven after Easter. What do you make of the fact that the Christological hymns do not mention the second coming? Since the term *theos* is not used in the New Testament to refer to the Trinity, always only to either God the Father or Jesus the Son, what do you think Paul and others mean when they call Jesus God? What does it mean that the divine Son was equal with God but did not take advantage of his divine privileges?

→ Describe the role Jesus is said to play as heavenly high priest. Why do you think the author of Hebrews is the only one in the New Testament to describe Jesus that way? What is the connection between the author's view of Jesus' death and the assertion that Jesus was sinless?

→ If you had to describe the various roles Christ is said to play in the speeches in Acts, what tasks would you focus on?

→ What do you find most striking about the visions of Christ in Revelation? Are there aspects of these descriptions that frighten you? Why? What is the difference between fearing God and revering and respecting God?

10 | Stories of Jesus inside the Gospels

The title of this final chapter, like the title of the book itself, is ambiguous. In this case the chapter title could refer to stories Jesus told, or stories about Jesus. However, Jesus did not tell many stories about himself. There are perhaps a few exceptions to this rule. These stories are of course parables, and we will consider them first before looking at what the Evangelists said about Jesus. We will then turn to the four Gospel stories about Jesus.

The Stories Jesus Told about Himself

Most of the parables Jesus told are parables about the coming of the Kingdom, rather than specifically Christological stories. This is probably why the most Christologically explicit and focused Gospel, the Fourth Gospel, does not really include any parables. There are however four stories that reveal something of how Jesus viewed his own ministry, character, purpose, and how his life would end.

The parable of the Sower, the longest parable found in Mark (Mark 4 and parallels), is not directly a commentary on Jesus. It is a commentary on the spread of the Word, the message Jesus and his disciples were offering, and more particularly how that Word is received. The gist of the parable is that it is the condition of the soil that determines the reception or rejection of the seed. In each case the seed and the sower are the same, but the soils and their conditions differ. Would this only have been a commentary by Jesus to encourage his disciples when they shared the Word and it met with rejection or partial or lukewarm reception? Probably not. Probably this is also Jesus' candid comment on how his own ministry was being received. Jesus was not like the preacher who boasted of going from success to success without any failure. Jesus very candidly admitted that there were rejection and lukewarm reception of the Kingdom message in many places. But the story is Good News because when the Word does take deep root, it produces a miraculous harvest in that life. Jesus presents a sober but positive reading of his own ministry, as well as those of his followers.

The second parable of relevance is the all too familiar story of the Lost Sheep (Matthew 18/Luke 15). Again, the story is not directly an allegory about the life or ministry of Jesus. One of the keys to recognizing the point of a parable is to notice when it offers up a statement which is generally speaking not true to life. Hardly any shepherd in his right mind would leave ninety-nine sheep to go and look for one stray. The parable does not say he left the ninety-nine in the capable hands of his assistants or even his sheepdog. It simply says that he left them to find the one lost sheep, "and if he finds it, I tell you the truth, he is happier about that one sheep than about the ninety-nine that did not wander off" (Matt. 18:13 and parallels). This is a very peculiar shepherd indeed, but it is certainly true to the character and ministry of Jesus. He did see himself having as his mission seeking and saving the lost sheep of Israel. He did intentionally banquet with the bad and the wicked. Jesus viewed his ministry as a reclamation project in progress. This parable is however about seeking the lost. The next one we must speak about briefly is about accepting them with open arms when they come back.

The all too familiar parable of the Prodigal Son (Luke 15) is again about those who go astray. And, yes, the central figure in the parable is probably meant to be God the Father, rather than Jesus. But Jesus believed he was God's emissary in such matters. The story is revealing about how God, as well as God in Christ, relates to his own children. He gives them room to make mistakes, to wander off, even to reject him. But when they return repentant and ready to renew the relationship, he welcomes them with open arms. And, of course, those who have never strayed may become indignant with the character of the reception of such sinners. As in the parable of the Lost Sheep, there is much rejoicing, more than in celebrating those who have always been faithful. Why? Because the lost have been found and saved. Because the sinner has come to his senses. Because someone who was in danger of missing the Kingdom altogether has been reclaimed. The compassion and joy of the Father in this story can equally be said of Jesus, for instance, in the story of Zacchaeus (Luke 19:1-10).

Our last parable to consider is found in Mark 12:1-9, and it is in some ways our most important parable. The parable is grounded in the real life hostility of Galilean peasant farmers who worked hard for absentee landlords who cared nothing for them and only demanded the fruit of their labor. Notice too that the parable does not have a happy ending. It ends with the son of the owner being killed and thrown outside of the vineyard. This parable is believable on the lips of Jesus especially toward the end of his ministry when it did not take even a prophet to recognize that Jesus was likely to meet his demise in a violent and untimely fashion in view of the nature of his ministry.

A vineyard was, of course, since time immemorial a symbol of Israel, God's people (see Isaiah 5). And the vineyard workers were of course the leaders who were supposed to be tending the vineyard. In theory, everyone recognized that the vineyard belonged to God. This parable is a salvation-historical litany in some ways like the speech of Stephen in Acts 7.[1] It chronicles how with great regularity Israel had rejected and sometimes even killed the messengers God sent to them. This particular parable comes to a climax with the sending of the owner's son as the one final and last messenger telling the vineyard workers to give the owner his due. The issue however is more complex because, as the parable itself states, the son was the heir and had a right to claim the vineyard and its produce. Jesus seems to be seeing a clash between himself and the Jewish leaders in Jerusalem over Israel, a clash that would lead to his violent death. Jesus seems to have believed that his authority and commission was such that he could come to Israel and not merely proclaim the truth, but claim or reclaim God's people for God.

How then did Jesus tell his own story? Occasionally he gave clues in parables about how he viewed his ministry character, life, and future demise. These parables cumulatively support the view that Jesus did indeed experience rejection during the ministry and expect final rejection. Jesus in contrast practiced acceptance and compassion, even fellowshipping with the lost. This got him in hot water quite regularly with the pious and Law-observant. But perhaps the best summary of how he viewed his purpose on earth and his future is not merely the Passion predictions, such as

1. See pp. 129-31 above.

we find in Mark 8–10, but especially the one we find at Mark 10:45: "The Son of Man did not come to be served, but rather to serve, and to give his life a ransom in place of the many." Jesus saw even his violent end as part of his service and reclamation project for lost people. It was Jesus, then, who transfigured his own violent end into a triumph that would go beyond the tragedy, as a service that would outstrip the suffering, as a ransom that would reclaim and restore those needing redemption.

The Stories Told about Jesus

It is an interesting fact that almost all the stories of any length in the New Testament which speak in detail of the demise of someone who was at some point positively connected to Jesus are found in the Gospels, and these are the stories of John the Baptist, the stories about Judas, and of course all the stories about Jesus himself.[2] We do not actually hear of the end of Paul's story, or James' story, or Mary's story in the New Testament. We only hear what would be the end of Peter's story (John 21). We do not hear about the end of the story of many second-tier characters in the New Testament: Apollos, Aquila and Priscilla, Mark, Timothy, Titus, Philip, Barnabas, John of Patmos, Joseph, the other brothers and sisters of Jesus, Mary Magdalene, the women at the cross, John the son of Zebedee, and many others. The New Testament does not attempt to tell the story of individual Christians in full, but it is very concerned about telling the end of Jesus' story.

We should conclude from this fact that the New Testament in general is *not* a book of martyrs, even though the book of Revelation and other New Testament books encourage preparation for such a fate. This makes the real preoccupation with the death of Jesus and its sequel, especially in the Gospels, stand out. One of the great concerns in the New Testament is to tell how the story of Jesus turned out positively, and this is as true of creedal statements, hymn fragments, sermon summaries, and other shorter forms of the story, as it is of the telling of the story proper in the

---

2. There are two minor and one major exceptions to this: James, the son of Zebedee, whose death is mentioned in one verse in Acts 12; Antipas, who is mentioned in Revelation 2:13; and Stephen, the prototypical martyr, who is mentioned at great length in Acts 7.

Gospels. In part this is because of two things: (1) Jesus' death required some detailed explaining if he was to continue to be an admired figure in antiquity at all. (2) Since the character of the Gospels is supposed to be *euangelion,* Good News, in view of the horrible death Jesus endured it was of paramount importance to tell the very end of the story.

If Jesus' story ended at the cross, without any positive sequel, it could not be called Good News. The Gospels would not be Gospels if they ended that way. In other words, the integrity of the telling of the whole story as Good News was at stake in how one conveyed the end of the story. If there is triumph beyond tragedy, the story as a whole can be presented as Good News. If the story just ends in shocking tragedy, it casts a pall over all the previous episodes in the story. Thus, it is poignant that, though the pre-Passion Narrative material in the Gospels is sometimes cast in the light of the cross, and foreshadows that event (see, e.g., John 11 and the story about the miracle of the raising of Lazarus), nonetheless the story remains Good News because of its ending: "and after three days he arose. . . ." Let us now consider the four portraits, the four tellings of Jesus' story known as Mark, Matthew, Luke, and finally John, bearing in mind that it was important to all these writers that what they were conveying was good news.

Mark

There are no birth stories in Mark, nor in the text of Mark that we currently have is there a recounting of a resurrection appearance.[3] The focus in Mark is all about the ministry all the time. In other words, Mark is concerned to relate the story of only a very few years of Jesus' adult life, years that in his mind reveal Jesus to be the Christ, the Son of God, which is very Good News indeed (Mark 1:1). Mark's telling of the story is dark and abrupt and full of mystery and secrets. It is in fact an apocalyptic reading of the story of Jesus with key visionary or disclosure moments at the bap-

3. The earliest and best text we have today of Mark ends at Mark 16:8. This however is very unlikely to have been the original ending of Mark as I have shown in *The Gospel of Mark: A Socio-Rhetorical Commentary* (Grand Rapids: Eerdmans, 2001), pp. 44-49. Ancient biographies do not leave you hanging as Mark 16:8 does, nor do they end with an incomplete thought "for they were afraid. . . ." Faith, not fear, is the point of this Gospel, and Good News is meant to have the last word, not fright and flight.

tism in Mark 1, at Caesarea Philippi in Mark 8, at the transfiguration in Mark 9, and finally at the cross itself where one hears a proclamation that matches the word of Mark 1:1: "surely this is the Son of God." The disclosure of Jesus' identity to even the disciples is a slow process that comes to a climax in Mark 8. Indeed one can say that the whole first half of this Gospel is meant to raise the who and how questions about Jesus and answer them.

I would suggest that the structure of Mark's Gospel divides rather neatly into several parts. The first part emphasizes the raising of questions about Jesus, such as the following:

Mark's Questions
Mark 1:27 — What is this — a new teaching with authority? Crowd
Mark 2:7 — Why does this fellow speak this way? Who can forgive sins but God? Scribes
Mark 2:16 — Why does he eat with sinners? Scribes
Mark 2:24 — Why are they doing what is not lawful? Pharisees
Mark 4:41 — Who then is this that even wind and water obey him? Disciples
Mark 6:2 — Where did this man get this Wisdom? Hometown folks
Mark 7:5 — Why do your disciples not live by tradition? Pharisees

In Mark's outline he has structured his Gospel so that once the who question has been answered, Jesus is able to reveal what his mission is. All of the questions cited above are ultimately ways of questioning Jesus and trying to figure out who he is. These questions lead to the answering of the major question, Who is Jesus? at Mark 8:27-30. This is a climax in the narrative and a major turning point in the story. It is only after this identification that we then have the explication of what Jesus' real mission is, and this point is reiterated three times in the space of three chapters (Mark 8:31; 9:31; 10:32-34). The essence of these mission statements is that the Son of Man must suffer and be rejected, and on the third day rise. Thus, we may present Mark's outline as follows:

The questions — Who? and Why? 1:1–8:27
The who question answered — 8:28-30 — Peter's confession of faith that Jesus is the Christ
What is the mission? — A mission of suffering — 8:31; 9:31; 10:32-34

Mission accomplished — The Passion and Resurrection Narrative —
Mark 11–16

This is the skeleton of the story, but how does Mark tell the story, and how does he tell it so that it is, and can be, seen to be Good News? In terms of pace, of course, Mark is the shortest Gospel, and there is a rather strong contrast between the material before the Passion Narrative, in which the word *euthys* (immediately) seems to be the adverb of choice, giving the sense that Jesus is running hither and yon preaching, teaching, and healing, and then almost as if the film has been turned down to slow motion, the Passion Narrative, a blow by blow account of the last week of Jesus' life in detail, taking up some 30 percent of the whole narrative. The Gospels are indeed Passion narratives with a long introduction, and the view of all these authors is that the last week of Jesus' life is the most crucial part of the story. It is prime time.

Mark has chosen to tell the story indirectly by presenting Jesus' words and deeds, and one of the strong impressions left in Mark is that Jesus came to preach and teach the Good News about the Kingdom, but he stayed to heal. In other words his focus was not on deed but on word, not on miracle but on proclamation. Jesus responds to requests for healing; he does not set out to heal. Right in Mark 1 we hear these words when the crowds are seeking Jesus for more healings: "Let us go somewhere else — to the nearby villages — so that I can preach there also. *That is why I have come*" (1:38). Then Mark characterizes Jesus' ministry: "So he traveled throughout Galilee, preaching in their synagogues and driving out demons" (1:39). The most frequent sort of miracle account in Mark is exorcism, which stands in stunning contrast to John's Gospel where there are no exorcisms. Jesus is in a pitched battle with the Devil and his minions in this Gospel, and Jesus wins over and over again.

Despite the stated focus of Jesus' ministry, the truth is that Mark does not give us anywhere near the amount of teaching or preaching material from Jesus that the other Gospels do. Mark 4 and 13, a block of parables and a block of prophetic teaching, are two major blocks of teaching by Jesus. Otherwise, it is mainly an action narrative that Mark presents. He wants us to realize that in a world full of lost and even sometimes demon-possessed persons, light breaks through only by the grace and revelation of God. Who Jesus is is not evident to mere mortals unless God reveals it to them. It is interesting however that the demons seem quite readily to rec-

RICK Danielson

Mark's Gospel was likely written from Rome and with awareness of the suffering of Christians which had already transpired, including the violent deaths of Peter and Paul. Despite what many have come to believe, the Colosseum had not yet been built in the 60s when Peter and Paul were martyred. Peter, however, may have lost his life, with other Christians, in the Circus Maximus.

ognize who Jesus is (see Mark 5:7). The disciples, in contrast, are more often the DUH-sciples, jockeying for position in the Kingdom, rather than the illuminated ones who take up their crosses and follow Jesus in this Gospel. Mark is telling us that it is not enough to know the truth about Jesus; one must be transformed by that truth into a posture of discipleship, reverence, worship.

Thus, the story of Jesus in Mark presents confrontation with the powers of darkness and various authority figures (Pharisees, officials in Jerusalem), frustration with the slow-on-the-uptake disciples, and alienation from his own family (Mark 3:21, 31-35; Mark 6). He is an exorcist seen as a threat, a prophet without honor on his own home turf, a teacher apparently without proper credentials, a healer in much demand, and a radical that associates with the unclean and even says that only that which comes out of the heart makes someone unclean. Not only is Jesus in the spotlight in this Gospel, he is pretty much alone in the spotlight, though he keeps trying to drag the disciples and especially the inner circle of the disciples into the light about who he is and what his mission is (e.g., at the house of Jairus's daughter or at the transfiguration or in the Garden of Gethsemane). Like a Rembrandt painting, there are shadows all around Jesus, but this only highlights the radiance of the Christ himself.

One can speak of this Gospel as being about the gradual revelation of the messianic secret of Jesus' identity, but once one gets to Easter, the time for keeping the messianic secret is over. The time for proclaiming from the rooftops "He is risen" has arrived. And the need for Jesus to do what he promised in Mark 14, going before them into Galilee and appearing to them, is imperative if even the disciples are to be ransomed, healed, forgiven, restored, and recommissioned. The commissioning in Mark 3:13-18 required repetition because at the end of the tale the Twelve had betrayed, denied, or completely deserted Jesus. Jesus hangs alone on the cross, and he is buried by neither his family nor any member of the Twelve, nor the women who followed Jesus. Jesus dies and is buried a forsaken, abandoned, shamed man. This seems so unfitting for such a compassionate person who healed others, served others, and lifted the status of women and children, and willingly helped non-Jews like the Gerasene demoniac (Mark 5). It seems so unlikely when one remembers that the disciples saw and experienced so many miracles.

Mark's is a Gospel that is about suffering. It is about rejection. It is about misunderstanding and willful unbelief. It is about evil abroad in the human sphere. And it is about how all that came to be transformed and transfigured paradoxically enough through the ransoming death of Jesus and his subsequent resurrection. The attempt to snuff out the Light and the Life led oddly enough to its wider diffusion. Revelation became an open secret, rather than a matter of a few disclosure moments. Fear is pitted against faith (see Mark 4:39-41), and faith in the end wins out because of the resurrection of Jesus, not because of the earlier teaching or miracles.

Most of all Mark's story is about the suffering Son of Man, the Son of Man in Daniel 7. The one who came before the Ancient of Days and was granted an eternal Kingdom. It is no accident that the only place in the Old Testament where we find the two most dominant phrases that Jesus used is in Daniel 7. Jesus is the Son of Man given the Kingdom and who came once for redemption and who will come again at an unknown hour (13:32) to judge (14:62).

The Son of Man is oh so mortal, but he is also divine. He has no human habitation, but he can dwell with his disciples forever after the resurrection. As Mark 8–10 says, he is destined to suffer many things, be killed, and on the third day rise. Yet this is not just a story about his fate; it is about how his fate changes the destiny of others, for he is the ransom for many (10:45). And in the end Mark would have us know that God's "yes" to life in Jesus is louder than the Devil's or death's or diseases' or decay's "no." Truth is not only revealed; it transforms through the power of the Gospel. This is why Reynolds Price once said that Mark is the most original storyteller of all time, and his Gospel the most influential of all narratives. Mark begins with a voice crying in the wilderness, but it ends with the confident assertion of the divine messenger, "He has risen! He is not here."

Matthew

It is not an accident that in the First and Fourth Gospels Jesus is especially presented as a teacher. Both of these Gospels come at the story of Jesus from a sapiential point of view, viewing Jesus through the lens of Jewish Wisdom literature and Jewish Wisdom thinking about the Messiah. In both these Gospels, Jesus is Wisdom in the flesh, but the presentations could hardly be more different. In Matthew's Gospel Jesus is Immanuel, the Jewish vision of God's presence with his people, but he is the universal Word or Logos who speaks to all persons in the Fourth Gospel. Matthew begins with a Jewish story of virginal conception based on Isaiah, John with a prologue about incarnation, grounded in the things said about Wisdom in Proverbs 8–9 and elsewhere. Matthew presents a Jesus who offers something old and something new, something fulfilling of the Old Testament, and something that goes beyond it. John presents a Jesus who offers Socratic dialogues and miraculous signs and is happy to say, "Before Abraham was, I am." As one New Testament scholar once said, in John Jesus bestrides the stage of history like a God who in the beginning and in the end of the Gospel is said to be Lord and God. In Matthew he appears to be like but greater than Moses or Solomon, implying he is a sage and indeed Wisdom come in person. But there is much more to be said, and so let us probe a bit more deeply.

On first blush, the First and Fourth Gospels seem to be distinctively different from each other. There is no *logos* prologue, "I am" discourses, or sign narratives in Matthew, nor any birth narrative, human genealogy, Sermon on the Mount, or parable collections in John. Matthew follows Mark very carefully and takes over 90 percent of Mark's substance into his own Gospel. John could never be accused of doing that.[4]

On closer inspection, however, these two Gospels share much in common. Both begin with a statement about the origins of their central character Jesus. Both of these Gospels have a notable stress on Jesus as teacher, which in both cases takes the form of several discourses. Both Gospels conclude with not only a full presentation of the Passion events and the resurrection appearances, but with a recommissioning and regathering of some of the inner circle of disciples. Furthermore, I would argue that both Gospels are written by Jewish Christians in the last quarter of the first century to communities that have had ongoing controversies with the synagogue but are clearly separate from it, at least at this point. Thus, in both Gospels the Jewish disciples of Jesus can be separated from "the Jews" (Matt. 28:15; John 10:19-24), which seems to mean primarily those Jews and Jewish authorities opposed to the Jesus movement. Both Gospels seem to have arisen out of a context of conflict and controversy and are shaped not only by whom they are written for but also whom they are written against.

It is also very arguable that both of these Gospels arose out of, or at

---

4. The following few paragraphs appear in another form in my *The Many Faces of the Christ: The Christologies of the New Testament and Beyond* (New York: Crossroads, 1998), pp. 138-50.

least for, a school setting, and were meant to be used in Matthew's case as a teaching aid for Jewish Christian teachers to use with their flock, and in John's case as a tool for Johannine evangelists and teachers to use in presenting the Gospel to outsiders. It is no accident that Jesus is most clearly presented as a teacher with learners (the meaning of *mathētēs*, which we translate as "disciple") in these two Gospels. For example, the term *mathētēs*, which occurs only in the first five books of the New Testament, we find some 73 times in Matthew, some 78 times in John, but only 46 times in Mark, and 37 times in Luke (with 28 more instances in Acts). It is also not a chance happening that in both Matthew and John discipleship is defined as keeping Jesus' commands or words (cf. Matt. 28:18-20 to John 14:15-26; 15:10). It is obvious enough that Matthew's Gospel focuses on instructions for disciples, but there is clearly an interest in portraying Jesus' followers in John also as disciples in a general sense (and not particularly as the Twelve, which hardly receives notice in the Fourth Gospel). Thus, we find Jesus' followers doing the things that disciples of early Jewish teachers did: spending time with the Master (3:22), calling him rabbi (or some variant thereof, 1:38, 49; 4:31; 9:2; 11:8; 20:16), buying food for him (4:8, 31), and baptizing others for him (4:2). Notice too how both Gospels end with stories about how the disciples both doubt and believe even after Jesus is raised from the dead.

The First and Fourth Evangelists, both deeply steeped in Jewish Wisdom literature and lore, adopt different sapiential strategies in their presentation of Christ. Matthew focuses on Jesus as a Jewish sage and concentrates on his public forms of wisdom teaching — parables, aphorisms, riddles, and beatitudes. John follows the discourse form we find in Proverbs 8 or Sirach 24, where one subject is treated and developed at some length, and so portrays Jesus as Wisdom in person.

Matthew and John are also similar in the sapiential way they highlight the use of Father language for God or Father-Son language. In Matthew "Father" is used of God some 42 times, but in John we find a remarkable 115 instances. This is compared to only 5 times in Mark (none of which occur before Mark 8:38) and only 15 times in Luke, some of which come from Q. This usage is closely tied in both these Gospels with an understanding not only of Jesus as *the* Son of God, but also of disciples as sons and daughters of God. Furthermore, a close study of the way both the First and Fourth Evangelists qualify the use of "Father" by the possessive modifier "my" when Jesus is speaking reveals that the authors are trying to stress that Jesus had a unique relationship with God. Theology, Christology, and discipleship are linked in both these Gospels through the use of Father language. When one believes Jesus is God's Son, one can come to relate to God as Father, as Jesus did. Matthew stresses this in a text like Matthew 11:27b where it is made clear that one can truly come to know the Father only through the Son. An adequate comparison of the Christologies of Matthew and John would show that Matthew 11:27-28 is no anomalous meteorite fallen from a Johannine sky but rather evidence that both Gospel writers are deeply steeped in Jewish Wisdom, which affects how they present Christological matters. We must turn more exclusively to Matthew's presentation at this point.

The First Evangelist carefully constructs his Gospel as a word to the wise (or at least to some Jewish Christians, who probably were already teachers), using three primary sources: Mark, Q, and M. Matthew 13:52 should probably be seen as a clue to how Matthew views both himself and his audience. He is a scribe trained for the Kingdom who brings forth both old and new treasures from the Jesus tradition for other Jewish Christian teachers to use. Matthew does not see himself being like later rabbinic scribes, but rather as standing in the mold of the sapiential scribes described in Sirach 39:1-3: "He seeks out the wisdom of all the ancients, and is concerned with prophecies; he preserves the sayings of the famous and penetrates the subtleties of parables; he seeks out the hidden meanings of proverbs. . . ."

The Evangelist does not allude to himself as a sage but rather as a scribe, as is the case with his audience, probably. This distinction is important to the First Evangelist because he wants to portray Jesus as the great sage and master teacher, but himself and his audience as only recorders and transmitters of the tradition. Scribes are not the originators of the tradition but rather the transmitters, interpreters, and appliers of it. It is not an accident that Peter, the first key disciple of Jesus, is portrayed in Matthew 16:17ff. as the one given the authority to bind and loose in the sense of making decisions and giving certain commandments about what one is bound to do and what one is free to do. In other words, Peter is portrayed as the disciple who is given the task of interpreting the Jesus tradition for the Church. There is a deliberate contrast between his teaching and that of the Pharisees who, instead of using (hermeneutical) keys to open the gate to the Kingdom as Peter does, do not allow people to go into the Kingdom (Matt. 23:13, 15). The commissioning of Peter in this role provides the climax of the first main part of Matthew's narrative. Of course the climax of the whole work may be compared to Matthew 16 in this matter, for Matthew 28:18-20 indicates that it is the duty of disciples to make other disciples, and this involves teaching them. In Matthew, but not in Mark, Jesus instructs his disciples on the do's and don'ts of being teachers (5:19). The whole point of mentioning the scribes' and Pharisees' righteousness in 5:20 is that they are rival teachers. Again in Matthew 10:24-25a, a passage not paralleled elsewhere, a disciple is said not to be above his master and teacher (Jesus), but rather is called to be like his teacher.

Thus Matthew edits and arranges his material in careful fashion to present a certain kind of portrait of the central character in the narrative, Jesus. The story is told in a very Jewish way. In general, as was common in ancient biographies, the method of portraiture is indirect, allowing words and deeds and relationships to reveal the identity and character of the main character. A close examination of the editorial work shows the type of pedagogy the author has in mind. Strikingly, in Matthew's Gospel while the disciples repeatedly address Jesus as Lord (cf., e.g., 8:21, 25; 14:28; 16:22), when a stranger or a Jewish leader addresses Jesus, it is as rabbi or teacher (cf. 8:19; 12:38; 19:16; 22:16, 24, 36). Notice that it is only the betrayer Judas among the disciples who calls Jesus rabbi (26:25, 49). What this tells us immediately is that the First Evangelist does not see titles or terms of respect like rabbi or teacher as adequate to describe Jesus. This is not to say that such titles are inaccurate, for indeed texts like Matthew 23:8-10 make it plain that Matthew does want to call Jesus a sage or teacher, indeed *the* teacher of the disciples. Thus, the disciples, who will in turn disciple others, should not seek to label themselves as rabbi or use the customary term of endearment (*abba* or "Father") sometimes used of Jewish teachers or wise men. Note, too, that in Matthew 26:17-19 near the end of Jesus' earthly ministry Jesus calls himself "the teacher" with the assumption that the audience will know immediately who this is. Setting Jesus apart from other potential teachers as sage, and more than sage, is also seen in the contrast found at the end of the Sermon on the Mount in Matthew 7 where Jesus, who teaches with independent authority, is contrasted with *their* scribes. The point here is twofold: Jesus is no mere scribe, and the problem is not with scribes in general but with *their* scribes.

The image of Jesus as sage or teacher is so crucial for Matthew that in editorial summary passages he cites teaching ahead of preaching and healing as Jesus' chief task (cf. 4:23; 9:35; 11:1). This is all the more striking when

Matthew's Gospel presents Jesus as a sage. One way of demonstrating his wisdom is to show how the sage gets out of difficult quandaries, such as whether one should pay the tax to Caesar or not.

one compares the parallel Markan summary at Mark 1:39, where there is no mention of teaching, and when one compares Matthew 11:1 to Luke 7:1, where in the Lukan passage the term "teaching" does not appear. The content of this teaching is seen repeatedly to be parables, aphorisms, and wisdom discourses. This image of Jesus as sage or teacher, and his disciples as scribes or teachers, is crucial and gets at the heart of some of the things that make Matthew's contribution to the Christological discussion distinctive.

Of course much has been made of the idea that Matthew's central idea is that Christ is the new Moses, offering five great discourses, the first even from a mount. Without discounting this idea, probably too much has been made of it. For one thing, it is not clear whether there are five or six discourses (depending on what one does with Matthew 23 in relationship to Matthew 24–25), and for another in the famous antitheses the Evangelist seems as interested in contrasting Jesus with Moses as comparing the two. After all, Moses did not ban oath taking, all killing, or adultery of the heart! Even in the birth narratives where a Moses motif has sometimes been detected, it is surely a secondary motif because Matthew 1 is by and large about how Jesus can be called Son of David and Matthew 2 about how he can be called Son of God (cf. below). Moses is not a Son of David or of God, and he is certainly not a Son of Man figure, and these are the three primary titles Matthew applies to Jesus. We must conclude that the "new Moses" idea, if it exists at all in Matthew, is at most a minor theme, and so one must look elsewhere to discern Matthew's distinctive contribution to the Christological discussion. I would argue: (1) He makes his most distinctive contribution by showing how Jesus is a messianic Son of David, like but greater than *Solomon,* offering even greater wisdom. (2) He is Wisdom come in person and so embodying and conveying the very presence of God to God's people (Immanuel). (3) He is Son of God whose characteristic intimacy with the Father is modeled in part on the relationship of Wisdom to God in Jewish sapiential literature. (4) He is the great eschatological sage, offering God's final teaching for salvation.

What then happens when an early Jewish Christian wishes to tell the story of Jesus as being a person like Solomon but even greater, being the very embodiment of Wisdom on earth? I would suggest that for a largely Jewish audience such as he has, he would stress that Jesus is *the* Son of David in a way his source did not (note the phrase is found eleven times in Matthew but only four in Mark and Luke and *none* in John).[5] The Jewish tone of this Gospel is set right from the very beginning where Matthew expands on his Markan source by adding the birth narratives, which stress that Jesus is the Son of David, the seventh son of the seventh son.

It was also the case however that in Jewish tradition, ultimately Wisdom was *the* teacher of God's people (cf. Prov. 1:20-30; 8:10-16; Sir. 4:24; Wisd. Of Sol. 6:14; 8:4). This role of Wisdom as *the* teacher is assigned by Matthew to Jesus himself, which explains how Matthew can portray Jesus as both sage and Wisdom. In calling Jesus *the* Teacher, a sapiential Christology would be implied to those steeped in Jewish wisdom material (cf., e.g., Wisdom of Solomon, where the teacher is ultimately Wisdom who inspires Solomon but also Solomon as great sage).

The Gospel of Matthew begins with the announcement that it will

5. I would suggest that here we have a salient difference between Matthew and John. The latter's primary target audience may well have been Gentiles (by which I mean Gentiles were the ones with whom the Christian teachers were to share these Johannine traditions), unlike Matthew; hence there is the more universal and less Jewish approach to a host of matters, including the Jewishness of Jesus in John. Jesus is seen in John as the universal Wisdom that made the world, in Matthew as the embodiment of God's revelation to God's people Israel, as *the* Son of David.

present Jesus the Messiah, the Son of David, in other words, Jesus the King, and so it begins where one ought to start with a story about a king, with his royal pedigree. Jesus' genealogy has some surprises in it, but then so did Solomon's, and it is the desire of the Evangelist to show that Jesus is indeed a Solomonic figure, only greater than Solomon: *the* archetypal Son of David.

Kings were often said to have miraculous births in antiquity and Jesus is no different. Not only is Jesus born of a virgin, but he is to be called Immanuel, one of the throne names for the King mentioned in Isaiah 9:6. It must be kept steadily in view that the precise title Son of David is not really attested before the time Psalms of Solomon was written. In other words, our author's frequent use of this title throughout his Gospel reflects a late sapiential perspective, not an Old Testament one. The term Immanuel at the least implies that God is present with his people through Jesus, but the discussion of the form this presence takes is held back until Matthew 11:19, where Jesus is specifically called Wisdom, in other words, God's presence come in the flesh. Again at Matthew 13:42 we will be reminded that the old categories, the old titles, do not fully capture Jesus — one greater than Solomon is present, one who is more aptly described as Wisdom, who is divine and yet who can be distinguished from the Father.

But if Jesus is the great king, *the* Son of David long looked for, one would expect signs in the heavens to announce his coming, and would expect king's counselors and seers to announce his coming and visit him, and that he would be in power struggles with other great kings. This is of course precisely how things are portrayed in Matthew 2. The birth of Jesus is signaled by a great star, he is visited by Magi, he is presented with gifts fit for a king, and he is the subject of a plot by King Herod and forced to flee the country.

Great kings are foretold by prophets, and, when kings travel anywhere, they have heralds going before them announcing their approach and arrival. This is clearly the role John the Baptist plays in the first Gospel. He is said to fulfill Isaiah 40:3, he speaks of the greater one coming after him in a way that downplays his own status (Matt. 3:11), and later in the story he sends his own disciples to find out about the royal or messianic deeds of Jesus (11:2-3). Jesus at that point recites his deeds and in a statement paralleling 11:2 says that Wisdom is vindicated by her deeds (v. 19).

Of course Jewish kings, like most ancient kings, had to be anointed before they could act or speak as royal ones, and so Matthew 3:13-17 records the anointing ceremony and the public pronouncement, "This is my

Beloved Son with whom I am well pleased." Here our Evangelist is drawing carefully not only on his Q source but also, representing it with a sapiential twist, on material from Wisdom of Solomon. It was expected of kings that they "fulfill all righteousness" (cf. Wisd. of Sol. 1:1ff.), and that the endowment of God's Spirit poured out on the king would also include the endowment of divine wisdom to make decisions and help the people. Matthew has added the phrase "with whom I am well pleased" at 17:5 to make clear the parallels between the baptismal and transfiguration scenes. At the Matthean transfiguration we hear that Jesus' face shone like the sun and his clothes became dazzling white, a description extremely reminiscent of the description of Wisdom in Wisdom of Solomon 7:26-29. The point of all this is that Jesus is being portrayed early and late in this Gospel as the royal one, the Son of David, as the one who manifests the very properties of Wisdom precisely because he is Wisdom come to earth.

In the Wisdom of Solomon, what follows the discussion of the investiture of the king with spirit and wisdom is the discussion of the testing of the king (Wisd. of Sol. 2:12ff.). This passage in fact illuminates the two major testing scenes in Matthew 4 and 26–27 and deserves to have a portion of it quoted: "Let us lie in wait for the righteous man, because he is inconvenient to us and opposes our actions. . . . He professes to have a knowledge of God and calls himself a child of God . . . he calls the last end of the righteous happy, and boasts that God is his father." This portion informs our reading of Matthew 4, but notice how what follows it informs Matthew 26–27: "Let us see if his words are true, and let us test what will happen at the end of his life; for if the righteous man is God's child, he will help him, and will deliver him from his adversaries. Let us test him with insult and torture him, so that we may find out how gentle he is [cf. also Matt. 11:29], and make trial of his forbearance. Let us condemn him to a shameful death. . . ." Jesus thus is being tested first and last as the righteous King, the true Son of David, like Solomon. He resists by relying on God's Word or wisdom to resist temptations.

At the beginning of the account of Jesus' ministry at Matthew 4:12ff. another quote from Isaiah, this one from 9:1-2, is offered. Those who knew the context of this quote would know that it is part of a longer passage lauding the coming great Davidic King with numerous throne names, and then it is added in Isaiah 9:6-7, "his authority will grow continually, and there will be endless peace for the throne of David and his kingdom." When Jesus goes forth preaching and healing and teaching, he is meant to be seen as a king going forth bringing righteousness and healing and proper rule to the land.

It is not necessary to go over in detail the sapiential material in Matthew 5–7, which would be better called the Teaching on the Mount. What is striking is that when one examines the topics broached in this so-called sermon, it reads like Proverbs 2–6, which deals with the standing topics the narrow path, beatitudes, warning against sexual impurity, acknowledgement of God's wisdom revealed in nature, and exhortations to guard one's speech, after the introduction of Wisdom herself at the outset of Proverbs. It is also not an accident that the discourse in Matthew 5–7 ends in 7:24ff. with the parable of the Wise Man. The one who hears and heeds this discourse will become such a person.[6] Matthew is portraying Jesus as the king greater than Solomon and, beyond that, even as Wisdom offering her teaching. Thus, the reader will not be jolted when shortly after this Jesus is simply identified as Wisdom.

The miracle stories in Matthew 8–9 also fit into this sapiential presentation of Jesus as one greater than Solomon/Wisdom because Jesus heals as the Son of David, as a Solomonic figure, and Josephus reminds us in *Antiquities* 8.45-47 that God granted Solomon the knowledge of the arts to use against demons and the wisdom to cure illnesses. In every instance after the birth narratives, the phrase Son of David arises in Matthew in a healing context. Jesus is a healer like Solomon; therefore, he should be appealed to using the Solomonic title. We have offered a more detailed analysis along these lines of all Matthew's material elsewhere, but what we have said above should suffice to show that all the different kinds of ministry teachings and narratives are read through a sapiential filter by this Evangelist in the service of his presentation of Jesus as both royal Son of David like Solomon and so as the ultimate Jewish sage, and also as the one greater than Solomon: namely, Wisdom come in the flesh.[7]

This presentation is not partial and piecemeal; it is systematically approached and presented, and cannot be limited to the passages more obvi-

---

6. Note however that Matthew is careful not to call such a person a *sophos* but rather uses the phrase *andri phronimō* lest it be thought that Jesus' disciples could be sages just like Jesus. No, their wisdom is of a derivative sort, depending on the teaching of the Master.

7. See my *Jesus the Sage: The Pilgrimage of Wisdom* (Minneapolis: Fortress, 1994), pp. 349-68.

ously indebted to Wisdom material such as Matthew 23:37ff. where Jesus is seen as Wisdom trying to gather her Jewish children in Jerusalem, or Wisdom offering her yoke in Matthew 11:28-29, which draws on Sirach 6:19-31 and 51:26. The matrix of the whole presentation of Christ in this Gospel is sapiential, and the other titles and terms are fitted into this wider context. This is why focusing on the traditional titles is inadequate, even when it includes the title King.

For Matthew there is one great sage, one great teacher, one final Son of David, one Wisdom of God, one person who can be called Immanuel. This person is Jesus. He was a nonpareil who could be both David's Son and yet also David's Lord, both Son of Man and yet also Son of God. It is indeed hard to imagine a much higher Christology than is conveyed in this Gospel, which begins with a person who is Immanuel and ends with his being given all authority in heaven and earth to empower and send out disciples for the task of replication. The yoke to which Matthew beckons his listeners is at once the yoke of Jesus' wisdom, and yet also the yoke of Jesus as Wisdom who says "take up your cross and follow me" as well as "take my yoke upon you."

We have reached the apex of canonical Christological development with these sorts of statements for it is clear that Jesus is seen as both human and divine, both sage and Wisdom, even if Matthew nowhere directly uses the term *theos* of Jesus. For this Evangelist, the one who was Wisdom and Immanuel was of course not less than divine and yet fully human. In his view it was wise to say this much, but perhaps unwise to try to say more.

With such an impressive run up to the Passion Narrative in Matthew one might have thought that it would be anticlimactic, but this is clearly not the case. The story is told using the Markan skeleton for organization, but there is a good deal of new meat put on those bones. Matthew also spends a third or more of his verbiage on the last week of Jesus' life. How does the story unfold?

For one thing, the Jesus who comes to town in Matthew is a Jesus who sets out to do more than a prophetic sign act in the Temple and some private eschatological teaching to the disciples. Jesus is vividly depicted in Matthew as teaching in the temple courts and elsewhere at length (Matt. 21:23–Matt. 25 is almost entirely teaching material). There are fresh parables, like the uniquely Matthean parable of the Wise and Foolish Virgins; there are seven woe sayings; there is a modified version of Mark 13; and much more. Jesus will teach right up to the time he is arrested.

There is also the peculiar doubling tendency that we find elsewhere in Matthew. Jesus will ride on two animals going into Jerusalem (Matt. 21:1-9)! This is like the story of the two blind men receiving their sight instead of just blind Bartimaeus (cf. Matt. 20:29-34 to Mark 10:46-52 and also Matt. 9:27-34). Matthew seems to assume that if one is good, two is better. But this sort of amplification is typical of Jewish wisdom stories. Throughout his Passion Narrative, as in his birth narrative, Matthew will stress the fulfillment of Scripture repeatedly to a degree that we do not find in Mark.

The upshot of all the parables, the dialogues, the woe sayings, and the apocalyptic discourse is that the discussion gets progressively more ominous the closer one gets to the Passion itself. Preparation for the cataclysm is urged, and alertness. The identity of Jesus as David's Son and David's Lord is stressed (22:41-46). Jesus then is prematurely anointed for burial, seeing that his disciples would not do the task later (26:6-13). The trial before the Sanhedrin becomes a matter of legal words, officials' words. Unlike in Mark, the chief priest says to Jesus in Matthew: "I charge you under oath by the living God: Tell us if you are the Christ, the Son of God" (26:63). Jesus responds, interestingly enough somewhat more indirectly in Matthew than in Mark. In Matthew it reads, "It is as you say," or it could actually be translated "So YOU say" with Jesus in essence having his interrogators be the ones who have confirmed his identity (cf. Mark 14:62 — "I am"). Jesus as sage is portrayed as more subtle at this juncture than Jesus as Son of Man. It is the interrogators who are in fact condemned for unbelief out of their own mouths, rather than Jesus'.

The role of Judas in the story of Jesus is given much greater prominence in Matthew than in Mark. We hear about Judas agreeing to betray Jesus (Matt. 26:14-16), and after the Last Supper we have a detailed account of Judas hanging himself (Matt. 27:1-10), something that is entirely missing in the Gospel of Mark. The enormity of the betrayal is then emphasized. By words the great Master of words is betrayed. The Sage and Wisdom, who has done his job as Sage and Wisdom to the bitter end, is done in by his own form of discourse. By a seeming act of love and compassion, a kiss, the Master of Compassion is betrayed. The paradox is meant to be palpable.

The story of the death in Matthew has some additional features as well. There is the infamous Matthew 27:25: "All the people answered, 'Let the blood be on us and on our children.'" There is some real animus in this Gospel between the Jews who support Jesus against the Jews, particularly the Jewish officials, who opposed and condemned him. This is an intra-

Jewish heated debate, and therefore cannot be seen as an example of anti-Semitism. The innocence of Jesus is also stressed in this same passage. Pilate's wife sends Pilate a message while he is interrogating Jesus, saying, "Don't have anything to do with that innocent man . . ." (Matt. 27:19), and Pilate himself declares his own innocence in these proceedings (27:24).

There is also the story of the miracle that transpires at the moment when Jesus died and the temple veil was rent. "The tombs broke open and the bodies of many holy people who had died were raised to life. They came out of the tombs and after Jesus' resurrection they went into the holy city and appeared to many people" (27:52-53). The story presents Jesus' death as the turn of aeons, and the trigger that sets in motion eschatological events, including the resurrection of others. The centurion at the cross is not just responding to the majesty of Jesus, and how he did not curse from the cross, but to the earthquake and "all that had happened" when he says, "Surely, he was the Son of God" (27:54). Matthew also adds the guard at the tomb story, before and after the report of the resurrection of Jesus (27:62-66 and 28:11-15), showing that there was extra and impartial confirmation that the tomb was empty. It also provides the answer to where the story came from that the body was stolen by the disciples. The guards were bribed to say so. "And this story has been widely circulated among the Jews to this very day" (28:15). Here we have a clue about why Matthew tells the story of Jesus' demise as he does. He wishes to rebut counter readings of the story, and amplify what he takes to be the true reading of the story. Matthew's presentation of Jesus' story is an example of Jewish Christian apologetics done in narrative form and as part of the ongoing debate with the synagogue.

Finally, Matthew insists that the story ended largely on a happy note. The female disciples may have fled from the tomb afraid, but they also fled with joy (28:8; cf. Mark 16:8). Jesus met them along the road; they clasped his feet and were the first to worship the risen Lord (28:9). They are then commissioned to go and tell the brothers to go to Galilee where they will see Jesus. This sets up the grand finale in Matthew 28:16-20 where Jesus is presented as Immanuel, one who will be with them always. But notice that, unlike the women, some of the Eleven in Galilee doubted when they saw the risen Lord, though many believed (28:17). The shadow of Thomas seems to have even crept into Matthew's positive story telling. Then Jesus the plenipotentiary and divine One commissions his disciples to go and make disciples of all nations through baptism in the threefold name, "teaching them to obey all I have commanded you" (28:20). The great Sage and Wisdom insists that his Wisdom must be passed on and obeyed, and he promises to be Immanuel, God's presence with them from then on. This form of the story of Jesus is equally impressive as Mark's, not in spite of its differences from Mark, but precisely because of them.

Luke

The Gospel of Luke is not a story in isolation. It is presented as part of the ongoing story of salvation history. It begins with the story of John the Baptist's family and his birth, and it ends with the disciples waiting in Jerusalem for power from on high. Rather than the final words of the resurrected Jesus bringing final closure, as in Matthew 28, they in fact prepare for the next chapter in the story, which is to be continued in Acts. In Matthew 28 the disciples are told to go. In Luke they are told to stay.

Luke has structured his Gospel so that the story of Jesus, while seen as the crucial episode, the turning point in the story of salvation history, is nonetheless to be seen as part of God's larger and ongoing dealings with humankind. Jesus is the Savior of the world and in that regard is unique;[8] but as a prophet, teacher, and healer he has predecessors and successors.

Luke is writing for a Gentile audience, and it is part of his agenda to stress the universal scope of the Good News, both up and down the social scale, and across geographical and ethnic lines, as well as across gender lines. Worship of Jesus was not to be a cultic act for some one particular group in the Greco-Roman world. His Gospel quite deliberately has an orientation toward Jerusalem, so that salvation is shown to come in Jerusalem, from the Jews, and through Jesus, and his Acts moves from Jerusalem to the world. Though Jesus and following him are for everyone, this does not cause Luke to lower the cost of discipleship. He is the one who insists that one must take up one's cross "daily" and follow Jesus. He will show

---

8. Luke alone among the Synoptic writers calls Jesus Savior (Luke 1:47; 2:11; Acts 5:31; 13:23). Surprisingly, this title is found elsewhere in the Gospels only at John 4:42. It was a term common in the Greco-Roman world, often used of the emperors, and before that even of Julius Caesar, who was once called "God manifest and the common savior of the world." Luke is in fact attempting to say something similar of Jesus in his two-volume work.

how various different sorts of people, male and female, young and old, Jew and Gentile, elite and ordinary, meet this challenge. How does the story of Jesus fit into this salvation history?

Luke's strategy is to bring Jesus into the picture in relationship to his predecessor and relative: the prophet John. He thus initially appears in a prophetic context. Luke places no small emphasis on Jesus as a prophet, a messianic prophet at that, of which Moses spoke. This agenda can be seen in texts like Acts 2:22-24 when compared to Deuteronomy 34:10-12, but the prophetic theme is clear enough in stories such as we find in Luke 7:11-17, where Jesus is portrayed as like that other great northern prophet, Elijah (1 Kings 17:17-24), just after he is portrayed in the story of the healing of the Gentile centurion as being like Elisha (cf. Luke 7:1-10 to 2 Kings 5:1-14). Jesus tells his hometown audience in Luke 4 that he is the one through whom the Isaianic prophecies are coming true, and it is only Luke who has the saying found in Luke 13:33: "Yet today and tomorrow and the next day I must be on my way, because it is impossible for a prophet to be killed outside of Jerusalem." Jesus must go up to Jerusalem, and Luke 9:51 tells us that Jesus set his face like a flint to do so. The orientation "toward Jerusalem" in the Gospel is about Jesus in the first instance, and only after that about his disciples who must follow his lead. The difference is that Jesus received power from on high at the outset of his ministry (Luke 3:22), and the disciples will receive it after the conclusion of that ministry. Jesus then will be the one who sends prophetic inspiration and power to the disciples so they may be witnesses and prophets as he has been (see Acts 2). This stress on the prophetic role allows Jesus to be presented as in the line of prophets and so as part of ongoing salvation history.

Luke also portrays Jesus as both Savior and Lord. Yet he maintains his historical perspective. Because Luke believes that Jesus assumed the roles of Messiah/Savior/Lord at the resurrection and exaltation, he will call Jesus Lord, for example, only in the narrative framework of his Gospel (Luke 7:13) but not in the dialogue because that would be anachronistic. Lord is a role Jesus assumed after the resurrection. Furthermore, the stress on the ascension in both his volumes is a way for Luke as a historian to mark the periodization of history. There was a time after which Jesus was no longer with the disciples in the flesh. The story of Jesus is no longer a direct tangible part of the historical drama, and so in Acts Jesus makes only cameo appearances in visions (see, e.g., Acts 9). Bearing these things in mind, we can look at the development of the story in Luke's Gospel.

Luke provides what might be called a full-service Gospel, complete with birth and resurrection narratives and even a tale of Jesus as a youth, which no other Gospel has. There are all sorts of material in between the birth and resurrection stories, including all sorts of unique material. Luke is not a slave to any one source, and he provides plenty of unique material not found in either his Markan or the Q source. Luke's Gospel is a story told to the maximum length a scroll will allow, being the longest of the four canonical Gospels.

The listener to Luke-Acts will recognize from the outset that various kinds of speech not only describe but also predict and drive the drama. This is not limited to the paradigmatic speeches in Luke 4 and Acts 2, and is already the case in the birth narratives. The story of the coming into this world of John the Baptist is miraculous enough, involving angels and a priest struck dumb and a wife getting pregnant when she is too old for such surprises. Luke revels in portraying the reversal of normal human expectations. The least, last, and lost will become the first, most, and found. The lowly will be exalted, the meek will inherit, but also the high and mighty will be brought low. Thus, one needs to speak of the reversal of fortunes. It is women who often benefit the most from these reversals in a patriarchal culture, as the stories of Elizabeth, Mary, and Anna all demonstrate. No wonder that it is Mary who sings the Magnificat in Luke 1. The story of the virginal conception is told in a fashion so as to distinguish it from Greco-Roman stories of the mating of a deity with a human being. This will transpire when the Holy Spirit comes upon Mary and the power of God will overshadow and protect her in this process (1:35). Mary's response "I am the Lord's servant; may it be to me as you have said" sets the benchmark for how disciples are to respond, whether they fully understand or not. Luke is the Evangelist who stresses the role of the Holy Spirit more than any other — the Spirit fills and inspires and protects and directs, and empowers for healing and much more.

The birth of Jesus is simply told, but not as we sometimes like to think. Probably what Luke says in Luke 2:7 is: "She wrapped him in cloths and placed him in a manger because there was no room for them in the guest room." The Greek word Luke uses here is the very same word he uses for guest room in the story of finding the place for the Last Supper. The image then is not of the Savior of the world born in a barn, but rather in the back of the house where animals would be kept, because there was no room in the guest room, it being already full of relatives.

Jesus then is seen by Jews ranging from the humblest shepherds to notable temple dwellers Simeon and Anna. Good News is especially good for the lowly whose status goes up when the Savior of the least, last, and lost shows up. Luke polishes off his account by showing Jesus the miracle child becoming a young man precociously teaching in the Temple when only twelve. Luke alone among the Gospel writers has this story and as a historian he includes it to show development: "Jesus grew in wisdom and in stature and in favor with God and humankind." This is a story then that foreshadows what is to come in regard to Jesus being a remarkable teacher.

Luke not only gives John the Baptist more press at the beginning of his Gospel, he also develops his story more in Luke 3, sharing some of the content of his fiery preaching, not just the fact that he baptized Jesus. We are told already at Luke 3:19-20 that John rebuked Herod Antipas for marrying his brother's wife, and this landed him in jail. Luke prepares the audience in various ways for the further developments in the story. In the baptismal story, which in this Gospel precedes the genealogy, Luke the historian informs us that Jesus was about thirty years old when he began his ministry (3:23). The genealogy, which also appears to be a genealogy of Joseph, works its way all the way back to Adam, starting with Joseph. While Matthew wanted to show that Jesus was truly Jewish, being a son of Abraham and a son of David, Luke wants to show he is truly human, being the son of Adam, which is to say the son of man. But note the genealogy actually ends "son of Adam, son of God." Jesus' origins are then traced to the universal human figure Adam but also to the originator of the universe, God.

The Holy Spirit is the one who is said in Luke 4:1 to have led Jesus into the wilderness for the testing or tempting. The temptations turn out to be the sort only a divine Son of God could or would have faced. Turning stones into bread is not a temptation for mere mortals any more than the other two temptations are. Jesus is being tempted to act in a fashion that would obliterate his true humanity and make it impossible for him to model how a human being can faithfully follow God. So instead, Jesus resists these temptations not on the basis of his divine nature but rather on the basis of the two resources all Jesus' followers could draw on: the power of God's Word and the power of the Holy Spirit. In this Gospel it is quite clear that those are the resources Jesus draws on to perform his miracles and do other things as well.

Despite these mighty resources, however, Jesus was to experience the same sort of rejection his followers would. Luke presents the hometown sermon in Luke 4 as Jesus' first sermon. He is full of the Spirit and armed with the Word, and can even claim that the Scripture of Isaiah 61 was in the process of being fulfilled in their own day and in their midst. At first this produces the response of wonderment and positive verbiage (v. 22), but then Jesus stops preaching and starts meddling, saying that prophets are not truly accepted in their hometowns, that the people will complain about not having the same miracles done in Nazareth that were done in Capernaum, and that their true response is like the response that Elijah got. At this all in the synagogue are furious and ready to push Jesus off a cliff (v. 29), a fate which Jesus avoids by walking right through the crowd and going on his way. The quotation of Isaiah 61:1-2 has however given a blueprint for what Jesus will be doing from then on during his ministry, a fact reiterated in Jesus' remarks to the imprisoned John where the same Scripture is alluded to (Luke 7:21-23).

The story of the call of the first disciples in Luke 5 has its own nuances, as we have already seen in this study.[9] Notice how Luke emphasizes that it was a teaching moment that led to the calling of the first disciples. Luke is concerned about the historical antecedents of important events. The first four miracles of Jesus are deliberately presented so as to show the scope of Jesus' work: an exorcism comes first (4:31-37), followed by the healing of a fever in Simon's mother-in-law, followed by the healing of a man with leprosy (5:12-16), followed by the healing of a paralytic (5:17-26). All this is in turn followed by Jesus calling and then dining with Levi the tax collector and his friends (5:27-32), an event that is repeated with Zacchaeus in Luke 19:1-10. Jesus did indeed come to seek and save the lost, even cheating tax collectors who were hated turncoats, Jews who worked for the Roman overlords, bilking their fellow Jews of needed funds.

The Lukan beatitudes in Luke 6 depict a Jesus who is concerned about normal things like poverty, daily bread, human loss, and abuse, and their reverse, as the parallel woes on the rich and oppressive make clear. Yet Jesus is no vindictive savior figure repeating the mistakes of other liberators. Rather, he counsels love for enemies (6:27), a turning of the other cheek, and the like (6:29).

The theme of the universalization of the Good News receives more play in Luke than in other Gospels, and so we find Jesus encountering and

9. See pp. 80-82 above.

helping the servant of a centurion and then on top of that praising his faith (7:1-9). "I have not found such great faith in Israel" serves as a shaming word that resonates throughout the rest of the story in Luke-Acts. The compassion of Jesus for the disenfranchised widow doomed to lose her means of support when her only son dies is shown at length in Luke 7:11-17.

Luke likes to tell substitute stories. For instance, when he includes the anointing of Jesus in the house of Simon the Pharisee by a sinful woman (Luke 7:36-50), and when we see a Pharisee being less gracious or receptive and spiritually less responsive to the grace of God manifest in Jesus, we see that Luke has found a compelling story about Jesus and his effect on sinners, including sinful women, and so he does not feel compelled to tell the similar story of the anointing by Mary of Bethany that is part of the other Gospels' Passion narratives. This story also reveals Jesus' agenda to restore women's dignity, a theme that Luke pursues further in the very next passage in Luke 8:1-3, where we have the shocking tale of women who have been healed and are traveling as disciples with the Twelve in Galilee, and who even help provide for the itinerants out of their own resources. This prepares us for the famous story about Mary and Martha in Luke 10:38-42, where Jesus commends Mary for taking the position of learning at Jesus' feet instead of assuming the traditional female role of hostess of a mere physical feast.[10]

Luke does not wish to limit his story of Jesus to a story about Jesus and the Twelve, which is more nearly the case in Mark's Gospel. Thus, we have not only the sending out of the Twelve on a mission (Luke 9:1-10) but also the seventy-two (Luke 10:1-12). The Markan miracles and stories about the Twelve are set in a broader context of discipleship. Luke also does not include the harsh picture of either Jesus' family (Luke 8) or Peter being rebuked (Luke 9), which are in his Markan source. Luke's telling of the story focuses more on the positive side of the Good News.

The story of Jesus' transfiguration receives some amplification in Luke's hands (9:28-36). We are told for instance that Moses and Elijah were speaking with Jesus about his exodus, or departure (v. 31). This is quite apropos since the Old Testament says that Elijah ascended into heaven, and Jewish tradition thought it likely that Moses did as well. They then would speak to Jesus from experience about his future. In the Lukan telling of the

10. On these Lukan stories about women see my *Women and the Genesis of Christianity* (Cambridge: Cambridge University Press, 1990).

story we also are told that the disciples partook of some of the numinous atmosphere of the experience as they are said to enter the glory cloud and become afraid (v. 34). Luke also has different wording for the saying from the voice from heaven. Jesus is referred to as "my Son, the one whom I have chosen" (v. 35), and the disciples are exhorted to listen to him. Thus we have Jesus consulting and listening to Moses and Elijah, but the disciples are not to look to Moses or Elijah. They are to listen to Jesus for he is the Chosen One of God who makes the two great prophetic figures disappear into the historical background because he is the climactic figure in salvation history. Notice that it is said of him that the appearance of his face changed and his clothes shone brightly (v. 29), while the other two merely appeared in splendor. This happened while Jesus was praying. Mark does not mention praying. Jesus' glory eclipses theirs, the word about Jesus being the chosen one is spoken, and the disciples discover Jesus is alone. There could hardly be a more telling portrait of Luke's view of the singularity of Jesus and his importance. He is the Chosen One, who puts all others, whether prophets like John or Elijah or lawgivers like Moses, into the shade of his glory and makes them figures of salvation history's past.

Luke in both his volumes shows a particular concern for Samaritans and tells Jesus' story so as to show that Jesus also had such a concern. Thus, we have the story of how Jesus intended to go through Samaria and even stay there briefly on the way to Jerusalem, even though he was rebuffed (9:51-56) precisely because he was going to Jerusalem. Yet notice he rebukes his disciples for wanting to call down fire from heaven to fry the Samaritans for their rebuff. It is in the very next chapter that we find the uniquely Lukan telling of the story of the Good Samaritan (10:25-37). This should be compared to the material in Acts 8. The material in Luke 9–10 prepares the listener to hear how the universal Gospel reached Samaria.

The Lord's Prayer as part of Jesus' story is found in Luke 11:1-4. It is more simple and direct than the Matthean form of the same (Matt. 6:9-13), and, as the introduction shows, when the disciples ask Jesus to teach them how to pray in a way similar to how John the Baptist taught his disciples to pray, this is really the disciple's prayer, not the Lord's prayer. The prayer calls for addressing God in intimate terms (though not in childish talk — *Abba* means "Father dearest," not "Daddy"), hallowing God's name, asking for daily bread each day, asking for forgiveness of debts, and praying not to be put to the test. If one compares this to the scene of Jesus' temptations the similarities are evident. Jesus refused to hallow or worship anyone but

God. He refused to gratuitously produce his own daily bread out of stones. He passed the test in the wilderness, and, as we know, he also addressed God as *Abba*. Yet Jesus passed these tests as the divine Son of God relying on God's Word; his disciples must pass them through prayer to God from whom all blessing and grace flow. There is a close paralleling of the story of Jesus and the story of his followers in Luke-Acts, which becomes all the more evident in Acts when Peter, Paul, and others perform the same tasks and preach in the power of the same Spirit as Jesus had done in the Gospel.

The Jesus of Luke's Gospel also wishes to make evident that there is no one-to-one correlation between sin and disaster; we cannot deduce that a particular person is a worse sinner than others based on a disaster that happened to him (Luke 13:1-5). The Lukan Jesus addresses this theme in a way that is not dissimilar to the Johannine Jesus in John 9.

The Jesus of Luke's Gospel is a great storyteller himself whether we think of the parable of the Good Samaritan in Luke 10 or the parable of the Prodigal Son in Luke 15 or the parable of the Shrewd Manager in Luke 16 or the parable of the Rich Man and Lazarus in Luke 16, or the parable of the Persistent Widow in Luke 18, none of which occur in the other Gospels. These are all stories of surprising developments and reversals that characterize the way God's grace works with all sorts of people. These are also stories that indicate that there are eternal consequences to human choices made in this lifetime. Jesus is a sage who presents his audiences with models of behavior that are not necessarily conventional but nonetheless are characteristic of the new eschatological saving activity of God that is breaking into human history.

It is interesting that when Luke commences the story of Jesus' Passion, he decides to strike out in fresh directions in several respects. For one thing, he has the dispute between the disciples about who is the greatest as part of the tale of the Last Supper (Luke 22:24-30), and not as part of a discussion after the transfiguration. Jesus makes his last call for the disciples to follow the path of servant leadership, unlike Gentile benefactors and rulers, and promises them that they too will have a kingdom and will one day sit on thrones judging the twelve tribes of Israel (v. 30).

The Garden of Gethsemane story fills out the picture of Jesus a bit.[11] A heavenly angel appears to Jesus and strengthens him for what is to come.

---

11. There is some textual question as to whether Luke 22:43-44 is an original part of this Gospel, but probably it is.

It is written: "And being in anguish, he prayed more earnestly and his sweat was like drops of blood falling to the ground." Jesus is depicted as truly human and in great agony, praying to avoid the cross, yet submitting to God's will under great duress. The disciples themselves are also said to be asleep and exhausted from sorrow (v. 45).

Luke alone tells us in Luke 23:6-12 that Jesus appeared not only before Pilate but also before the one Jesus called "that fox" Herod Antipas who hoped to see Jesus perform a miracle. He asked many questions, but Jesus stood mute. Herod has Jesus mocked and insulted and then dresses him in royal robes as a joke and sends him back to Pilate, a joke apparently Pilate enjoyed because they became friends thereafter. This is the sort of historical anecdote — which does not really advance the story of Jesus but enlightens us about these rulers — that a historian would find useful. No other Gospel writer tells this tale. Earlier Jesus is depicted as going through a triple battery of questions from the Jewish authorities (which tale Luke abbreviates, having Jesus respond, "If I tell you, you will not believe me, and if I ask you, you would not answer. But from now on the Son of Man will be seated at the right hand of the mighty God"; 22:67-68).[12]

The Christ of Luke's Gospel is the forgiving Christ, and so even from the cross we have Christ saying about his executioners, "Father, forgive them, for they do not know what they are doing" (23:34). This fits well with the ignorance theme that comes up in Acts 2–4 in the speeches of Peter. Verse 35 calls Jesus again the Chosen One, as at the mount of transfiguration, and yet Jesus refuses to save himself. There is in addition the famous dialogue between the bandits in 23:39-43, in which Jesus famously says: "I say to you, today you will be with me in Paradise." There is some question as to whether the "today" refers to when the bandit will enter paradise or when Jesus uttered the saying, probably the former. It depends on where you put the comma. These words were a gracious response on the cross of the forgiving Jesus to the request by the bandit to be remembered when Jesus comes into his kingdom. He is the same bandit who had chided the other by saying that Jesus had done nothing wrong.

12. Notice there is nothing about the Son of Man coming on the clouds to judge the judges here. This way of putting it prepares us to find the Son of Man in the same honored and most privileged spot in Acts 7, prepared to receive Stephen. Luke is preparing for the only reference to the heavenly Son of Man in Acts.

Jesus is depicted as fully human at the last, commending his human spirit into God's hands at death (v. 46), and being commended for being a righteous man by the centurion observing the crucifixion. This is quite different than Mark's "Surely this is the Son of God," though the two pronouncements comport with one another. Luke is concerned that his Gentile audience see that Gentile officials saw Jesus as innocent, as did even one of the other persons crucified, as did even one of the executioners.

The resurrection stories in Luke do not much involve the Twelve. Instead we hear of the faithfulness of the women who were at the cross and the tomb and came on Easter morn prepared to anoint the body (Luke 23:49, 55; 24:1-11). They respond positively to the angelic vision at the empty tomb and remember Jesus' words, but their own words are rejected as old wives' tales by the male disciples (24:11). These women are depicted as more perceptive than the two going down the road to Emmaus, who are said to be slow to learn what the Scriptures said, and who do not recognize the risen Jesus until he breaks bread with them. Jesus the sage reappears in this story, giving the most glorious Bible study of all about how what happened to him had been foretold by the prophets (24:25-27). The path to glory led through suffering.

It is only at the end that Jesus appears to the Eleven in the upper room and gives tangible proof of his reality by eating and offering them a chance to touch him, which they are not said to do. The resurrection was in the body, and Jesus was alive again in the flesh. They too received the ultimate Christological Bible study from the risen sage (vv. 45-47) and are told that repentance and salvation are to be preached in his name to all nations, beginning at Jerusalem. Jesus walks with them as far as Bethany and then takes leave of them once and for all, blessing them. Finally they fall down and worship their Lord and go to the Temple, praying continually and awaiting the anointment with power. Here the ascension is depicted as a closure event, but Luke the skillful writer will use the same story to depict the ascension as the opening event of the story of the Church in Acts 1. The story of Jesus and his followers continues in volume 2, though in a different mode.

Luke has also made the story of Jesus his own, and he tells it in his own way as historian and theologian of salvation history. Jesus is the Prophet, the Savior, the Chosen One of God, the Messiah, and by resurrection he assumes the role of risen Lord to be exalted Son of Man on high. He is Teacher, Compassionate Healer, Inclusive Gatherer of disciples proclaiming a universal gospel — all persons need to be saved; God's grace is extended to all; all can be saved; but only through Jesus, as the speeches in Acts will stress.

John

The story of Jesus in the Fourth and final canonical Gospel has already been broached a bit at the beginning of our discussion of Matthew. The story is indeed told in a Wisdom kind of way. Since this has been the most influential portrait of Jesus used for evangelism, and since it is theologically most profound, we will concentrate on the Christological aspects of the story that make John's Gospel the distinctive entity it is, rather than just retelling the story.

From the outset of this Gospel the reader is alerted to the fact that he will be swimming in deep waters. The key to the story, insofar as Jesus' identity is concerned, is given in the very first chapter in the *logos* hymn or prologue: Jesus came from God and will return to God. More directly he is God the Son who preexisted. Not knowing where Jesus came from and not knowing where he is going ultimately lead to a misunderstanding of the story of Jesus. In John 1:1 we have one of the few instances in the New Testament where the one who took on flesh and took on the name Jesus is called *theos* or God. Here as in Romans 9:5 we have *theos* without the definite article, which emphasizes the generic side of things (the *logos* is of the *genus* or species called *theos*). The word order and structure in the Greek of the first verse are such that the translation "the Word was a god" is surely inappropriate. *Theos* without the article here is surely the predicate of the sentence. It emphasizes the kind of being the Word is or the Word's true nature rather than the Word's personal identity (which is indicated by either the name Jesus or by a relational term such as the Son). It also makes clear that the Word does not exhaust the Godhead. In other words, we do not have the reverse proposition here "God was the Word," or "the Word was *the* God" (i.e., all there is to God). This is also made clear by the fact that in this same verse the Word is said to be *with* God, which thereby distinguishes the Word from the one that our author usually calls *theos*, namely, the Father.

The things predicated of the Word in this Christological hymn are also predicated of Jesus Christ, the Son who has seen God and made God known and is in the bosom of the Father, as verses 17-18 state. This is why later in this Gospel the statement "before Abraham was, I am" is seen as blasphemy by outsiders, but in the Fourth Evangelist's view as a true statement about the personal existence before the incarnation of the one speaking. It is precisely because our author believes that the Son truly is and was *theos* even before the universe began, as the very first verse asserts, that what he says in the rest of the book about Jesus is assumed to be appropriate and within the bounds of the sort of Christian monotheism he affirms. The one who is the redeemer is also the one who was the creator.

Verse 14 affirms that the Word took on flesh or, as some have preferred to translate, "came on the human scene." The essence of the idea of incarnation is that a personal being who already existed added a human nature to that identity. There is nothing here to suggest that the Word turned into flesh in some sort of kenotic process where the former state is left behind and a new one taken up. Indeed, the statement "we have seen his glory, the glory of the Father's only Son full of grace and truth" surely indicates that while on earth the Word retained the divine presence and attributes that were his by nature. It is the divine preexistent Word, whose glory has been seen. This leads us to John 1:18.

Unfortunately there is a textual problem here. Does the text read "the only Begotten," or "the only begotten Son," or "the only begotten God," or simply "only begotten God"? Though the arguments are complex, it seems probable that the appropriate reading here is the last one mentioned above, with the second reading listed being the second most likely. The key term in this phrase is *monogenēs*. In texts like Tobit 3:15 it refers to an only child. More importantly in view of the Wisdom background of the Christological hymn in John 1 and indeed of this entire book, in Wisdom of Solomon 7:22 Wisdom is said to be *monogenēs*, which we may translate "alone in kind" (a translation that suits 1 Clement 25:2 as well).

What is being emphasized here is not merely the Son's personal uniqueness but his pedigree: he is the sole natural descendant of the Father. The issue here is not means or manner of birth but lineage and family connection. The term does not merely mean "beloved," as is shown by the expanded form of this phrase we find in 1 John 5:18. In short the word *monogenēs* refers to the only member of a kin or kind and, when coupled with *theos,* has the expanded sense of the only kin of God who is also God or the sole divine descendant of the Father. It is no accident that in both the Fourth Gospel and 1 John Jesus alone is called Son of God *(huios*

Theou) while believers are called children of God *(tekna Theou)*. John 1:18 reflects this distinction. The Fourth Evangelist not surprisingly reserves *theos* with the definite article for the Father, preserving some continuity with Jewish usage.

There is one further reference at John 20:28 to Christ as *theos* in this Gospel, and it comes in the climactic confession, indeed the only fully adequate confession in the Evangelist's view, in this whole Gospel.[13] It must be kept in mind that Israel had previously expressed adoration to Yahweh as the "Lord our God" (Ps. 98:8 [LXX]; 99:8 in English translation), and Revelation 4:11 indicates that the same sort of acclamation was used by Christians of the Father. There may also have been some special importance in the phrase for John's audience; for instance, when the Fourth Gospel was likely written the emperor was being extolled with the phrase "Deus et Dominus noster." As for the meaning of the phrase it recognizes not only Christ's personal Lordship over Thomas but also Christ's essential oneness with the Father, which then makes legitimate Thomas's worship of the risen One. Here both *kyrios* and *theos* are titles, not proper names, and the former probably implies the deity of the risen Jesus but the latter explicitly affirms it. Thus, what we have seen here is that this Gospel is framed by the confession that Jesus is deity, and all that comes in between is grounded in this confession. The story of Jesus in the Fourth Gospel is the story of God who took on flesh in the person of his Son.

Throughout the Fourth Gospel the identity question in regard to Jesus comes up in various forms: sometimes in the form of an acclamation, sometimes in the form of an assumption about where Jesus came from, sometimes in the form of a question, and sometimes in the form of a statement. For instance in John 3 we hear at verse 13 that Jesus, as Son of Man, is the only one who has both descended from heaven and ascended into it. We also hear in chapter 1 the acclamation of Jesus as the Lamb of God who takes away the world's sin (1:29). In John 3:2 Nicodemus admits that Jesus is a teacher "come from God," but in this irony-laden Gospel he does not realize the full significance of what he says. Knowing where Jesus has come from and where he is going is the key to understanding who he is in this Gospel.

At John 3:14 we find the first presentation of the theme that the Son

---

13. John 21 is an appendix to this Gospel added by the final editor or Fourth Evangelist.

must be lifted up on the cross in order for salvation to come. This is apparently seen as the first stage of his ascent back to be with the Father in heaven (cf. John 8:28), for the death on the cross is the moment at which Jesus is said to be glorified in this Gospel; this is his "hour" (cf. John 13:31 and 17:1). What John 3:14 shows us is that the Fourth Evangelist's theology of the Son of Man phrase is conditioned by the story of Wisdom, perhaps especially by 1 Enoch 70:2 and 71:1, where Enoch ascends and is apparently identified as the Son of Man, and by 1 Enoch 42, where Wisdom descends to earth and then returns to heaven rejected. We see this influence again at John 6:62: "What if you were to see the Son of Man ascending?" But it is also his theology of Jesus as Son of God which is affected by his sapiential way of interpreting things, for it is as Son that the *logos* was sent into the world, as John 3:16-17 reveals.

If it is true that Jesus bestrides the Johannine stage as a God, it is also true that the Fourth Evangelist goes out of his way to stress the true humanity of Jesus and his subordination to the Father, even to a degree not seen in the Synoptics. For one thing, Jesus is called a man in this Gospel far more than in the Synoptics, and it is in this Gospel that it is stressed from the outset that he is the man born to die (see John 1:29 and contrast the earliest Gospel where the Passion theme really begins half way through in Mark 8), a man who is said in John 20 to have nail-marked flesh. He is proclaimed in public at the climax of the trial in the form *ecce homo* (19:5). He is depicted, for instance in John 4, as one who experienced weariness, hunger, thirst. Yet on the other hand there is no Gethsemane agony or God-forsakenness on the cross in this Gospel. The most we have is Jesus' remark that the disciples are sorrowful about his approaching death (John 16:6), and by contrast Jesus repudiates the idea that he will ask to be saved from his "hour" (12:27). The cross scenes are suffused with glory, and even on the cross Jesus is still doing God's will and taking care of others. The Christ of glory has transfigured the image of Jesus in the entire story in the Fourth Gospel.

In John 5:19, and many times thereafter, we hear things like "the Son can do nothing on his own, but only what he sees the Father doing." This in fact is part of a Christological theme in the Fourth Gospel that is of importance. Using the Jewish language about agency, this writer portrays Jesus as God's *shaliach* or agent and apostle on earth. He has been sent to earth for a specific purpose: namely, to complete the work the Father gave him (5:36-38; 6:29). It is not just that the Son has come down from heaven, for that of course could be said of angels as well, but that he was sent down on a mission of redemption as the Father's divine emissary, fully endowed with the power and authority to carry out such a rescue operation. He has a special relationship with the Father, such that only he has seen the Father (6:46), and this equips him to reveal and speak for the Father (7:16-17).

If understanding Jesus in the Johannine way of thinking amounts to knowing where Jesus came from and is going, that is, knowing he is pursuing Wisdom's trajectory, then misunderstanding manifests itself in having a false conception of Jesus' origins or destiny. Thus, for example, in John 1:45-46 even disciples and potential disciples think they know who Jesus is by saying he comes from Nazareth and from the family of Joseph there, but they do not understand Jesus' ultimate origins. In John 7:25-27 the Jerusalemites say they know where Jesus comes from (i.e., Nazareth), but they do not know he came down from heaven. At John 7:41 it is asked, "Surely the messiah doesn't come from Galilee, does he?" (cf. v. 52). In John 8:41 it is implied that he was born out of wedlock (and thus his nature is dubious) while his opponents are true children of Abraham, to which Jesus rejoins that he preceded Abraham, which is far greater than descending from him. In John 8:48 it is asked if Jesus is from Samaria. In John 18:5ff. the opponents stress that they are searching for Jesus from Nazareth. In each case the error comes from their not knowing his ultimate origins: that he is Son of Man, Logos, Son sent from God, God's Wisdom who descends and ascends.

In John 7:35 the Jews misunderstand Jesus because they do not know where he is going. They ask if he is heading for the Diaspora to teach the Greeks. Again in John 8:21-22 when Jesus says he is going away, the Jews wrongly assume that this means he is going to kill himself. In John 14:5 even the disciples misunderstand because they do not know where Jesus is going, and so can't follow him. Likewise, even after Easter, in John 20:16-17 Mary wrongly assumes Jesus is back to stay and tries to renew merely earthly relationships with Jesus, calling him *rabbouni*. She does not understand that Jesus must ascend so she and other disciples can have a new form of relationship with Jesus. It is only when she understands the pilgrimage of Jesus as God's Wisdom that she is able to proclaim to the male disciples, "I have seen the (risen) Lord," the basic confession of the earliest Jewish Christians. All of this should be more than enough to establish that John's Christology is sapientially shaped, and that he thinks that to understand who Jesus truly is requires a knowledge of the path Wisdom, in the person of God's Son, took to and from earth. Notice how the Gospel proper ends, as far as Jesus' speaking is concerned, at John 20:29 with Jesus as Wisdom offering a Wisdom saying or beatitude to the disciples, just to reinforce the point that has been made all along about Jesus' character and nature.

Once one understands this key to the Son's true identity, then other puzzling aspects of Johannine Christology fall into place. For instance, the author's attempt to reveal the role the Son played begins with creation in John 1. He assumes the roles often predicated of Wisdom in her relationship to Israel (cf. Wisdom of Solomon 10). For instance, he is the one who came into the world enlightening God's people all along, and so Moses and the prophets were inspired by him to write about him (John 1:45; 5:46). Of Abraham it is said that he saw the Son's day (8:56). Isaiah even saw his divine glory (presumably in a vision; cf. Isaiah 6 and John 12:41). Not that anyone actually saw him before the incarnation because like the Father he was purely divine and no one was able to see him (cf. 1:18; 6:46). In other words, the Son existed before the incarnation and has had roles to play before that event as well. It is hard not to hear echoes of Wisdom of Solomon 10–11 here, where it is said that Wisdom aided Abraham (10:5), entered Moses, allowing him to perform wonders and signs (10:16), gave him and others the gift of prophecy (11:1; cf. 7:27), and was present in the wilderness and sustained Israel with manna and water from the rock (16:26; 11:4; cf. John 4 and 6). The Johannine Jesus understands himself to be the one who has aided God's people in previous generations to come through their trials.

There has been considerable debate about whether the use of *egō eimi,* "I am," by Jesus in this Gospel is in some instances (e.g., 8:24, 28, 58; 13:19) a predication of the divine name to Jesus. This question is appropriately raised not least because we are told explicitly at John 17:6, 12, and 26 that Jesus has manifested the divine name and that it is a name the Father gave to the Son (v. 12). Furthermore, in the Hebrew of Isaiah 51:12, and even more clearly in the Greek translation of this verse (which reads "I am 'I AM' who comforts you") "I am" is apparently taken to be the divine name. We may also point to the Greek translation of Isaiah 52:6, which reads, "My people shall know that 'I AM' is the one who speaks" (while the Hebrew simply says, "They shall know that it is I who speak"). We must conclude, then, that in all likelihood in some cases the use of *egō eimi* by Jesus in the Fourth Gospel is a predication of the divine name to him.

Further evidence that our author intends in various ways to say Jesus

is divine is found in John 5. Here Jesus heals a man on the Sabbath and justifies this by saying that God continues to work (even on the Sabbath), and
so must he (v. 17). This passage draws on the common belief of Jews that
despite what Genesis 2:2-3 says, God could not have ceased all activities on
the Sabbath because God had to maintain the creation in existence (cf.
Philo *Leg. All.* 1.5). Thus, the point of John 5:19-20 is to make it clear that
Jesus has God's full creative power and is undertaking the divine work that
only God can or should do. Philo puts it this way: "His creative power is
called God *(theos)* because through it he placed and made the universe
(*Mos.* 2.99).

But not only did the Son preexist and so have intimate knowledge of
what came before, he also has considerable foreknowledge of things (cf.,
e.g., John 2:24; 11:4). He thus has a sovereignty in the face of adversity that
is not emphasized in the Synoptics (cf. 8:59; 10:39; 18:36; 19:11, 30; 20:17).
Unlike the Synoptic parables and Gospel material, in general there is little
or no Christological indirectness in this Gospel. Jesus' discourses directly
reveal who he is and provoke immediate reactions of acceptance or rejection. There is a certain unearthly quality to the Johannine Jesus. If the Gospel of Mark gives us the messianic secret, the Gospel of John gives us the
unveiled face of God in the flesh. The stories are told differently in accord
with these Christological emphases.

Another Christological dimension of importance is of course the "I
am" sayings with a predicate; they characterize Jesus variously as living
bread, light of the world, the door, life, and the authentic vine (John 6:35,
51; 8:12; 10:7, 9, 11, 14; 14:6; 15:1, 5). All of these things were already said to
characterize Wisdom in the earlier Wisdom literature. In Proverbs 8:35
Wisdom says, "he who finds me finds life . . . ," and at Proverbs 3:18 Wisdom
is said to be the tree of life. In Wisdom of Solomon, Wisdom is said to be
light, indeed a reflection or effulgence of eternal light. In Sirach 24:17ff.
Wisdom is said to be a vine that buds and bears abundant fruit. In Proverbs 9:5 Wisdom beckons, "Come eat of my bread." The point of these sayings in John, as in their analogies in the Wisdom corpus, is to make it clear
that whatever one truly longs for or needs can be found in Wisdom, who in
the Fourth Gospel is identified with Jesus, the Son of God. Furthermore
the "I am" sayings are also linked to discourses that expand upon the
themes of these sayings, not unlike the Wisdom discourses in Proverbs,
Wisdom of Solomon, and Sirach.

The "I am" discourses are of course about Jesus' true identity, and they are linked with his signs, which are in various ways different from the tales of mighty works in the Synoptics. The chief reason is that John has cast these miracle stories in the form that miracle tales assume in the Wisdom corpus. Like John, the author of the Wisdom of Solomon thinks of miracles as signs from God that point to something larger beyond themselves (Wisd. of Sol. 10:16). In Wisdom of Solomon 16:6 all the wonders performed by God in Egypt and in the wilderness are seen as and called "symbols or signs of salvation" for God's people. This same text helps explain John 3:14, which speaks of Moses lifting up the serpent in the wilderness, and it is likened to the act of salvation on the cross. The connection becomes clear if one knows Wisdom of Solomon 16:6 where the lifting up of the serpent is seen as a "sign of salvation" signifying the means by which humans passed from death to life.

The use of this sort of Wisdom material is not surprising because, as in the Fourth Gospel, the author of the Wisdom of Solomon believes in and articulates a theology of eternal life and also its negative counterpart. In both of these writers' views human beings were not made for death but for everlasting life (cf. Wisd. of Sol. 2:23-24; 3:1-2; 5:15). Furthermore the discussion of the Devil's role in the Fourth Gospel is close to what we find in the Wisdom of Solomon. Death entered the world through the Devil's envy (Wisd. of Sol. 2:24); it did not come from God. This is similar to what Jesus says in John 8:44, where the Devil is seen as the father of the wicked and a murderer from the outset.

The discussion about Jesus being the way — indeed the only way — to the Father in the Fourth Gospel draws on what is said about Wisdom elsewhere. Thus, the coming of Wisdom to earth causes a division of human beings: some seek and find (cf. Prov. 8:17; Sir. 6:27; Wisd. of Sol. 6:12), while others do not seek and regret it too late (Prov. 1:28). This same language is used in John of the effect of Jesus upon human beings (John 7:34; 8:21; 13:33).

The Farewell Discourse is especially laden with language that encourages the identification of Jesus with Wisdom, especially if one already knows the Wisdom material. Sirach 4:11-13 is especially helpful at this point where we hear: (1) Wisdom teaches her children (cf. John 14–16). (2) Wisdom gives help to those who seek her (John 14:16ff.). (3) Whoever loves Wisdom loves life (John 14:15). (4) Those who seek Wisdom from early morning are filled with joy (John 15:11). (5) Whoever holds fast to Wisdom inherits glory (John 17:22). (6) The Lord loves those who love Wisdom

(John 17:26). Jesus' disciples are called little children in this discourse (13:33), just as disciples are said to be Wisdom's children in Proverbs 8:32-33 and Sirach 4:11 and 6:18.

There is a great deal more that can be said along these lines when one begins to compare John's Gospel and especially the Christological material with the Wisdom corpus. The above will suffice however to explain perhaps the major reason why John's Gospel is so different from the Synoptics: it is about Wisdom come in the flesh, and everything is spun out on the basis of the insight shared in the *logos* hymn in John 1. In fact not only this hymn but also the V-shaped plot of the career of the Son, the "I am" sayings, the conception of miracles, the use of Father language, and various other aspects of Christology are all indebted to Wisdom material, especially the late Wisdom material found in Sirach and the Wisdom of Solomon. This is not all one needs to say about the Johannine story of Christ, but it is perhaps the most important thing one can say. Jesus is the very exegesis of the Father because he is Wisdom come in the flesh, not merely one who proclaims what God is like.

Another window on Johannine Christology comes from examining the structure of the Fourth Gospel. On the simplest level we have a book with a prologue (1:1-18), an epilogue (John 21), and an account of the ministry in between in three major parts: (1) John 1:19–12:50, the so-called Book of Signs; (2) John 13:1–17:26, the Farewell Discourses; and (3) John 18:1–20:31, the Passion and resurrection narratives. What this does not in any way convey is the manner in which we have a crescendo of miracles in this Gospel climaxing with the giving of sight to the blind (John 9) and the raising of a man who had been dead for four days (John 11), and also a crescendo of confessions that become more and more insightful and adequate until John 20. Thomas's confession matches that of the prologue. Furthermore, the sign miracles are woven together with discourses, probably seven of each, indicating that in Jesus the perfect revelation or Wisdom of God has appeared on earth and that if one wants the benefits of life and light that God offers, one must accept God's agent on earth, Jesus. The overall impression left by having this large quantity of extended discourse material unlike what we find in the Synoptics is that the presentation of Jesus is much more by Word than by deed. Our author is far more interested than the Synoptic Gospels in raising and answering Christological questions, and this is shown in the way the material is arranged (a crescendo of confessions), in the repeated discussions of Jesus' origins and destiny (which one can only understand with a knowledge of the prologue and Wisdom thinking), and in the fact that the miracles are seen as signs pointing not so much to the presence of the kingdom but to the presence of the King.

In fact the crescendo of the miraculous continues into the Passion Narrative, such that the ultimate sign in this Gospel is Jesus' own death and resurrection, which the seventh sign of Lazarus's raising merely foreshadowed. By placing Lazarus's raising where he does in the Gospel, the author prepares to make a larger Christological point in the Passion material, namely, that the death and resurrection of Jesus is a sign and miracle of God, not a disaster. Like Lazarus's death, Jesus' own can be said to be for God's glory and so that the Son of God may be glorified through it (11:4). We may also note the stress in this Gospel on the way the disciples after Easter grew in understanding and awareness of who Jesus was (cf. John 2:22; 12:16), but, unlike what we find in Luke's Gospel, nothing whatsoever suggests that this Gospel is a chronicle of Jesus' own growing awareness of who he is. Notice how the baptismal scene is basically omitted, or, better said, the elements of the scene that suggest Jesus learned something about his own identity and ministry are omitted. Instead John 1:29-34 suggests that John received the revelation and then testified about who Jesus was. Also omitted is the actual act of baptizing or anything else involved with that act which might suggest Jesus' subordination to John.

Another interesting window on the story of Christ in the Fourth Gospel comes from analyzing together the sometimes neglected Son of Man sayings in the Fourth Gospel. These sayings in John, unlike what we find on the whole in the Synoptics, do not neatly fall into one of the three categories of ministry, suffering and death, or second-coming sayings. One saying in John may refer to both suffering and a future coming. This is not entirely surprising since for the Fourth Evangelist Jesus' death is already seen as a form of glorification and exaltation. In some ways, the Daniel 7 and Enoch material help us to understand some of the Johannine Son of Man sayings even more than most of the Synoptic ones. The concepts of representativeness, divine status and roles, glory, yet in a context of suffering and being in the presence of God, and perhaps corporateness, which are all present in the Son of Man material in Daniel and Enoch, are also found in the Johannine Son of Man sayings. We will look briefly at each of these sayings at this juncture. Here the concentration is not on a future Son of Man coming on the clouds, but on his first coming to earth and what he accomplished from the time of the incarnation until the time he was lifted up on the cross. Vertical eschatology about the one who comes down and will be lifted up displaces an emphasis on horizontal eschatology about the Son of Man who will one day return to judge the world.

The first of these sayings is John 1:51. This saying stresses that Jesus is like Bethel, the gate of God, the juncture between heaven and earth, between God and humankind. Notice that in this context Jesus discovers and discusses the true Israelite, just as in a sense Jacob did after wrestling with the angel. The saying reflects the notion that Jesus is the locus or center of divine activity, even in a sense holy ground, which raises the question of whether this saying prepares for what we find in John 2, where Jesus is seen as the Temple.

The second of these sayings is found at John 3:13, and here again a true Israelite is found in the context — in this case Nicodemus. Here the Son of Man is himself an ascending and descending figure, though it appears from 3:14 that the ascending has to do with Jesus being lifted up on the cross. John 3:13 probably reflects the idea that the Son of Man has both a preincarnate and a postincarnate existence, being eternal. Yet he is also human because he came to earth in human form and died.

John 5:27 reflects the judgment theme found in the Synoptic future Son of Man sayings and in Daniel. Jesus judges because he is the Son of Man and was given this role in Daniel 7. This presumably means that Jesus will judge after he has lived and himself been a defendant and a witness for others. He is able to do so because he knows in his own human nature and experience what humans are like, but he can defend precisely because he is the vindicated Son of Man.

In John 6:27 and 53 we find that the Son of Man is the provider of eternal life for God's people. It is as Son of Man that Jesus suffers and is able to provide flesh and blood (i.e., life) for the believer. Believers must be incorporated into him. This idea may go back to Daniel and imply the Son of Man's divinity since one cannot be incorporated into an ordinary mortal.

In John 6:62 ascending is mentioned again in association with the Son of Man phrase. This ascending is taken as evidence that Jesus is in fact the Son of Man and that he will be able to provide eternal life. His exaltation provides life for those who believe.

John 8:28 is a crucial saying for it indicates that recognition of the Son of Man will come only when he is crucified. The point is that only then will Jesus be seen as the representative suffering figure of Daniel 7. Then, too, knowing that Jesus is eternal ("I am") seems also to hinge on the

lifting up of the Son of Man. Notice that the "I am" here is followed immediately by a statement about Jesus' utter dependency on the Father. It is
thus not an attempt to equate the Son of Man with the Father, but perhaps
a way of indicating that, like the Father, the Son is eternal. It is interesting
how, precisely because Jesus is a dependent obedient Son, he can also be
called eternal, *theos,* Word, and the like. His correspondence with the Father's character and will is somehow related to or affected by his behavior.
It is precisely as obedient Son that he manifests that he is eternal Son.
When Jesus has been obedient even unto death, he will be revealed as all he
claimed to be, including being Son of Man (John 8:28).

John 9:35 is the only place in the Gospels where anyone is asked if he
believes in the Son of Man. Only here could the phrase be seen as a confessional title, and here the phrase seems to be almost a circumlocution for
"I." That is, Jesus is asking, "Do you believe in me?" There is certainly nothing like this in the Synoptics.

John 12:23 reflects typical Johannine language though the idea here is
not terribly different from the suffering Son of Man sayings in the Synoptics (cf. Mark 14:41). Again the debt to Daniel 7 seems likely. One must also
consider John 12:34, where the phrase is found on the lips of the crowd
who fail to even understand who the Son of Man is. The connection of Son
of Man with being lifted up, which entails suffering and yet glory, shows
the correlation of this saying with others in John and also with the background in Daniel and Enoch.

John 13:31 is the tenth and last of these sayings, and once again Passion and glory are associated, plus the Son of Man's relationship to the Father is expressed. The Son of Man's glory also belongs to the Father.

Notice that all these sayings appear in the first half of this Gospel,
with the exception of the last one. All of the sayings are relatively uniform
in their meaning or range of meaning, and it seems clear that all are better
understood when read in light of the background of Daniel 7 and the
Enoch material. It is clear enough that our author wants to reveal the
ascending-descending divine one in these sayings — in other words, the
one who fleshes out the roles predicated of Wisdom in Jewish Wisdom literature. The phrases are used to help focus on the idea that Jesus is the
juncture of the divine and human, of heaven and earth, and so they focus
not just on his roles but on his identity. Indeed at one point the question is
even raised as to who this Son of Man is so that he can be believed in, not
merely identified. In these sayings we have allusions to the full scope of

Christ's work as it is envisioned by the Fourth Evangelist: he has a preincarnate existence, he becomes incarnate, he dies, he is exalted, and he will serve a judging function.

The Son of Man is thus a heavenly and earthly figure, but also an eschatological figure who is human and dies, yet has divine authority. In these sayings John intends to present the full cosmic and historical scope of the work of Christ. There is exaltation even in death; there is present suffering but then vindication; there is salvation and yet also judgment; there is representativeness but also corporate personality. In short the Son of Man sayings are just another expression of the familiar Johannine high Christology. All such titles tend toward the revelation that the Son is in the Father and vice versa, which is to say they are preoccupied with making it clear who Jesus is in relation to both the Father and to human beings, especially his followers.

If we turn to the specific use of Son or Son of God language in the Fourth Gospel, there is no question but that this language is more prominent here than in the Synoptics. Already we find the term Son in the prologue, and it is present with some frequency in John 3, where it is made clear that the Son was sent by the Father (hence the Son preexisted, as the prologue stated), and sent for the purpose of saving the world. The Son is not only the one sent but also the sole descendant of the Father (cf. above on *monogenēs*) and the one in whose hands God has placed all things, like an heir to the Father's fortune.

The first major discussion of Jesus' Sonship does not really transpire until John 5:19-20. This may be seen as something of a parable and could be called the parable of the Apprentice. Jesus as Son does only what he sees the Father doing. He can do nothing on his own. He is a man under authority and under orders. Of course in relationship to all other human beings he is a man in authority and can give commandments or orders. The preexistence and divinity of the Son come out in these Sonship sayings in a way that is seldom the case in the Synoptics, but other aspects of these sayings are not without parallel in the Synoptics.

In any detailed discussion of Sonship language, besides the texts already mentioned one would also have to examine John 7:29; 8:28; 10:15, 37; 12:49; 13:3; 14:10, and 17:5, 25. Furthermore, since the Gospel begins in John 1 and ends in John 20 with Sonship language (see especially the purpose statement in 20:31), there is something to be said for the conclusion that this is a very key term or category for the Fourth Evangelist. It is to be noticed that the term Son or Son of God almost always comes up in contexts where the Father is also mentioned. In short, it is relational language. The term or phrase sometimes comes up in the same context as the Son of Man phrase, but the terms do not seem to be interchangeable.

We have seen in this survey the great importance to the Fourth Evangelist of using three sorts of language to tell the story of Christ: (1) the Wisdom language which explains the most about this Gospel; (2) the Son of Man language which helps bridge the human and divine sides of the Son; and (3) Sonship language which like both these other two sorts of terminology can be used to express the full gamut of the career of the Incarnate One. There are of course other titles which are sometimes used, such as Shepherd, or the Lamb of God, or the Holy One of God (John 6:69), or Teacher and Master (John 13:13-14), or the King of Israel (John 1:49), or in the Passion account King of the Jews (John 18–19), but they play minor roles compared to these three categories we have discussed. John of course uses the term Christ with some frequency and knows for instance that Christ is not just a name but rather first a title (John 4:25-29), and one especially appropriate for a Jew to confess of Jesus (John 1:41; 7:26-31; 11:27). Indeed he thinks it is something Christians must believe and confess (John 20:31). But John wishes to go beyond more limited Jewish categories in order to say something about a universal savior, not unlike what Luke did, and furthermore the verses where the term Christ appears do not really add much to what we have already noted from these other categories. Notably, Christ is almost never a term that Jesus uses to speak of himself in this Gospel (but cf. 17:3, where it is a name).

Finally we should recognize that the Jesus of this Gospel tells no parables, exorcises no demons, and basically does not call disciples. All sorts of people are attracted to him by some sort of spiritual gravity. This is the seeker Gospel that so focuses on the central character of the Christ that even the disciples do not get the full attention we find in other Gospels. In John, "the things of earth will grow strangely dim in the light of his glory and grace," to borrow a phrase from an old hymn. The story then reaches from before all time, to prime time when Jesus' hour transpires and he is lifted up on the cross, up from the dead, up into glory. The resurrection stories are told in full in John 20 and 21 to punctuate and make clear why Christ's glory radiates from every page of this Gospel. The claim of the Beloved Disciple is not merely "we have heard his teaching and seen his miracles" but rather "we have seen his glory, the glory of the Only Begotten Son who came from the Father full of grace and truth. . . . No one has ever seen God, but the Only Begotten God who is at the Father's side has made him known" (John 1:14, 18).

Conclusions

Four Gospels but, recognizably, one and the same Jesus. The stories, however, are told quite differently, as we have seen. The reason for this is in part that the story of Christ is complex, and also because Jesus himself was a towering historical figure who fits no one formula or telling. The Church was right to reject the *Diatesseron*, which was a blended version of the four Gospels and for a time was quite popular in the Early Church. Four Gospels cover more territory, tell more stories, give us more portraits, and provide us with more insight into the singular Christ. They provide both the core of the story and the outer limits of the story, showing how differences as well as similarities in the accounts can be fruitful in shedding more light on the meaning of the story of Jesus.

The stories of Jesus focus necessarily on the crucial last week of his life. Here the stories converge more because we have reached prime time and even the details are magnified and matter more. Jesus' hour is at the same time the hour of decision for the world, as the Evangelists see it. The stories of Jesus and the cross and the resurrection suggest that their outcome determines whether there is salvation for the world or not. There was a lot hanging in the balance in telling the end of this story.

More than information or revelation there was the issue of transformation. More than Good News there was the issue of saving tidings. Was Jesus indeed the one to redeem the world or not? Could God overcome death through the death and resurrection of Jesus? Could God overcome sin through the atoning sacrifice of Jesus? Could God rescue through Jesus a floundering world caught in the clutches of the powers of darkness? These were the sort of questions the Evangelists hoped to answer in their tellings of the stories of Jesus, which means that they believed that the story was inherently about both theology and history, about both God's activity and human response, about both Israel and the nations, about both the past and the future, about both heaven and earth.

This was an all-encompassing story about a universal Gospel and a universal Savior dealing with a universal human dilemma. One could say that even four Gospels were not enough to fully tell this tale. The Fourth Evangelist was right when he said at the end of his Gospel, "Jesus did many other things as well. If every one were written down, I suppose that even the whole world would not have room for the books that would be written" (21:25).

In the end, the reason the other twenty-three New Testament books were written is that they too had something to say about the story of Jesus, they too wanted their opportunity to retell the tale in some form or fashion, or at least to tease out the implications of the story for day to day Christian living. The story of the New Testament and the stories in the New Testament converge in the end, for they are both stories about the divine-human encounter and about the one person whom Christians believed embodied that encounter from both sides. As John Donne once said, "'Twas much that man was made like God, long before; But that God should be made like man, much more."

Were these various writers here today they might well add: More than salvation history there was the Savior. More than new prophecy offered there was the One who fulfilled the prophecies. More than a miracle worker there was the Man who was the Miracle. More than a sacrificial lamb there was atonement for sin, a remedy for human fallenness, a transcending of death. Beyond a horrendous death, there was a triumphant risen Lord. The New Testament writers fervently believed these things were true and would have all affirmed what the Evangelist said: "These things were written that you might believe that Jesus is the Christ, the Son of God, and that by believing you may have life in his name" (John 20:31). The question is, Will we see our stories in the light of this Story, such that Christ's history is not just his story, but ours as well? It is a question each individual must answer for oneself.

....

Exercises and Questions for Study and Reflection

→ Write a letter to someone who is confused by the different presentations in the four Gospels. Explain in a layperson's terms the nature of the differences and similarities between the four Gospels. Include in your letter an explanation of at least three to four puzzling texts, such as the two birth narratives. Explain why they are so different, and yet still have some key components in common.

→ List several of the revelatory moments in the Gospel of Mark. How do they function in terms of revealing Jesus' identity? To whom are these revelations addressed?

→ Examine two of Matthew's major blocks of teaching material. What sort of early Christian do you suppose would need this advice? Does it mainly address new Christians or more mature ones? Take the two versions of the Beatitudes and the Lord's Prayer in Matthew and Luke and compare and contrast them. Which version seems likely to be closer to its Jewish point of origins?

→ Luke writes as an ancient historian. What are the telltale signs that he is not trying to present this material in the same way that the other Gospel writers are?

→ Since the Gospel of John does not include parables or exorcisms, what sort of image is the dominant image of Jesus in the Gospel of John? What sort of teacher is he presented as?

→ What difference does knowing where he came from and where he is going make toward understanding his identity in this Gospel?

The Word's Worth

Spoken into being,
The world from the Word,
Silence starts nothing,
The void absurd.

His Word was action
Not null or annulled;
The darkness divided,
His light not dulled.

The Word became story,
Symbol and sign,
Metaphor and meaning,
Salvific design.

But the story was tragic,
The plot past belief,
The Creator rejected,
His Word came to grief.

The Word seemed to falter,
Its Laws disobeyed,
Its prophecies left dangling,
Its promises mislaid.

But the Word became flesh,
His Word was his bond,
He fulfilled it Himself,
He came and was gone.

He disciplined disciples,
He crucified sin,
He passed on the story,
The Word arose once again.

Alpha, Omega,
From first Word to last
The Living Word creates
Future from past,

Light from the darkness,
Life from the grave;
The New Testament story
Continues to save.

BWIII
July 5, 2003

Appendix 1:
Basic Acts Time Line

A.D. 30 — Jesus is crucified under Pontius Pilate. Resurrection appearances, Pentecost, initial growth of the church in and around Jerusalem.

A.D. 31-33 — The events of Acts 3–7 transpire with mounting concern on the part of Jews and especially the Jewish authorities in Jerusalem. The rising tension results in vigilante action taken against Stephen, and then an authorized effort under Saul to disrupt and even destroy this new messianic sect, involving persecution and even the death of some Christians (cf. Acts 8:1-3 to Gal. 1:13). The persecution led various Christians such as Philip to go elsewhere, such as Samaria, and bear witness (Acts 8:4-40). THE FIRST EIGHT CHAPTERS OF ACTS COVER ONLY THE PERIOD FROM ABOUT 30 TO 33.

A.D. 33 or 34 — Saul is converted on the road to Damascus during his period of persecuting the church (Acts 9; Galatians 1).

A.D. 34-37 or 38 — Saul is in Damascus and Arabia; he returns to Jerusalem for the first time as a Christian in 37.

A.D. 37-46 — Saul sent off to Tarsus and his home region. In the meantime, Peter has a notable ministry up and down the Mediterranean coast between Lydda, Joppa, and Caesarea, involving at least one notable Gentile and his family. This, in turn, leads to a report to the Jerusalem church (Acts 11). The precise timing is unknown.

A.D. 43 — James (brother of John) is killed, and Peter is imprisoned.

A.D. 44 — Agabus's prophecy in Antioch; Herod Agrippa dies.

NOTE THAT LUKE'S DATA FOR THE PERIOD A.D. 37-46 ARE CLEARLY SKETCHY. HE IS BETTER INFORMED ABOUT THE PERIOD AFTER

273

THE JERUSALEM COUNCIL (49), IN PARTICULAR ABOUT THE PAULINE PART OF THE STORY.

A.D. 46-48 — famine in Judea.

A.D. 48 — Second visit by Paul to Jerusalem (with Barnabas, cf. Galatians 2) for famine relief to Jerusalem (Acts 11:29-30).

A.D. 49 — Claudius expels Jews from Rome; Priscilla and Aquila go to Corinth; Jerusalem council (Acts 15).

A.D. 50-52 — Paul's second missionary journey (Acts 15:36–18:23).

A.D. 51 or 52 — The Gallio incident in Corinth (Acts 18).

A.D. 53-57 — Paul's third missionary journey (Acts 18:23–21:26).

A.D. 57-59 — Paul in custody under Felix, and then briefly under Festus.

A.D. 59-60 — Paul goes to Rome (for a fuller discussion of the Pauline material for the period from 48 to 50, see below).

A.D. 60-62 — Paul under house arrest in Rome.

Appendix 2:
Chronology of Paul's Life and Letters

Phase One — Pre-Christian Saul

A.D. 5-10 — Saul is born in Tarsus in Cilicia of orthodox Pharisaic Jews who are Roman citizens.

A.D. 10 + — Saul's family moves to Jerusalem while he is still quite young (Acts 26:4).

A.D. 15-20 — Saul begins his studies in Jerusalem with Rabbi Gamaliel, grandson of Rabbi Gamaliel the elder.

A.D. 30 (or 33) — Jesus is crucified by Pontius Pilate.

A.D. 31?-34 — Saul persecutes the church in Jerusalem/Judea, Samaria; Stephen is stoned (Acts 6–7, ca. 32-33).

Phase Two — Conversion and "Hidden Years"

A.D. 33 (or 34) — Saul is converted on the Damascus road and then travels on to Damascus (Ananias episode).

A.D. 34-37 — Saul in Arabia, the Nabatean region of Syria east of Damascus and in the Transjordan (cf. Gal. 1.17). Saul returns to Damascus and narrowly escapes the authorities under King Aretas IV, who may have controlled the city beginning in 37 once Gaius Caligula became Emperor (cf. 2 Cor. 11:32/ Acts 9:23-25).

A.D. 37 — Saul's first visit to Jerusalem, a private meeting with Peter and James (Gal. 1:18-20). Saul preaches to the Hellenists, and escapes to his home region of Syria and Cilicia by way of boat from Caesarea Maritima (Acts 9:29-30).

A.D. 37-46 — Saul preaches in his home region; results unknown or inconsequential (possible great persecutions, cf. 2 Cor. 11:23-29).

A.D. 41-42 — Saul has a visionary experience; receives "thorn in the flesh" (2 Cor. 12:1-10), a physical malady possibly involving his eyes (Gal. 4:13-16).

A.D. 47 — Saul is found by Barnabas in Tarsus and brought to Antioch; preaches there for a year (Acts 11:25-26).

A.D. 48 — Second visit to Jerusalem (the famine visit) with Barnabas and Titus (Acts 11:27-30/Gal. 2:1-10). Private agreement between Saul and the church leaders that he and Barnabas would go to Gentiles, Peter and others to Jews, and circumcision not be imposed. Issues of food and fellowship between Jewish and Gentile Christians unresolved (cf. Gal. 2:11-14).

Phase Three — Paul Begins His Endorsed Missionary Travels and Efforts

A.D. 48 — First missionary journey with Barnabas and Mark; commissioned by Antioch church after basic endorsement from Jerusalem (Acts 13–14). Saul uses his Greco-Roman name Paul (Paulos).

A.D. 48 — Return to Antioch. Antioch incident with Peter and Barnabas withdrawing from fellowship meals with Gentiles due to pressure from Judaizers from Jerusalem (Pharisaic Jewish Christians, Gal. 2:11-14).

A.D. 49 (early) — Paul discovers the Judaizers had moved on to Asia Minor and were upsetting some of his converts made during the first missionary journey in south Galatia (Pisidian Antioch, Iconium, etc.). He writes his letter to the Galatians shortly before going up to Jerusalem for the third time.

A.D. 49 (later) — Apostolic council in Jerusalem. Public agreement that Gentiles not be required to become Jews in order to become Christians. Apostolic decree mandates that Gentiles must forsake idolatry and immorality, in particular, dining in pagan temples where such things transpire (i.e., no eating of meat offered to and partaken of in the presence of idols, Acts 15).

A.D. 50-52 — Second missionary journey of Paul with Silas (Silvanus) instead of Barnabas and Mark. This is important, for Silas is the apostolic delegate who was to explain the decree to the churches, and he had independent authority from Jerusalem, not from Paul (Acts 15:22). Paul travels to Philippi and Thessalonica, and eventually he stays a considerable time in Corinth before going to Ephesus and then Jerusalem, returning afterward to Antioch (Acts 15:40–18:23). On this journey he picks up Timothy in Lystra (Acts 16:1) and Luke in Troas (16:10ff.).

A.D. 51-52 — During his stay in Corinth, Paul writes 1 and 2 Thessalonians, with the help of Silvanus.

A.D. 51 or 52 — The Gallio incident (Acts 18:12-18) and increasing troubles from

Jews in Corinth eventually precipitate Paul's leaving Corinth after staying between eighteen and twenty-four months.

A.D. 52 — Second missionary period concludes apparently with a report to the Jerusalem church (Acts 18:22) and a return to Antioch.

Later Pauline Chronology

A.D. 53-57(58) — Third missionary journey. After an eighteen-month stay in Corinth (Acts 18:11), Paul sails for Syria, probably in the spring of 52, stopping briefly in the port of Ephesus and leaving Aquila and Priscilla to lay the groundwork for future missionary work (cf. below). After preaching once in the synagogue and promising to return (18:19), he goes to Caesarea Maritima, visits briefly in Jerusalem, and returns to Syrian Antioch. After a stay there, Paul sets out on his last major missionary period as a free man, passing through the Galatian region and strengthening the congregation there, but pressing on to Ephesus where he stays for at least two and perhaps three years.

A.D. 54 (55) — Paul writes 1 Corinthians from Ephesus. Not the first letter he had written them, but the first one still extant (cf. 1 Cor. 5:9-10). This letter addresses the many questions and problems raised by the Corinthians both orally and in writing in their communication with Paul since he had left there. First Corinthians failed to solve the problems in Corinth, however, as 2 Corinthians makes evident. News, perhaps from Timothy, comes to Paul of real trouble in Corinth after writing 1 Corinthians.

A.D. 55 — The painful visit to Corinth (2 Cor. 2:1, not mentioned in Acts). This visit is a disaster, as opposition comes to a head. Paul's authority is questioned and he leaves, feeling humiliated. As a result, Paul writes a stinging, forceful letter (the so-called severe letter), a fragment of which may be found in 2 Corinthians 10–13. Titus is the bearer of this severe letter. Paul begins to regret this letter, and after some missionary work in Troas he crosses over into Macedonia anxious to hear Titus's report on the results of the severe letter (this journey corresponds to the journey from Troas to Macedonia found in Acts 20:1-16).

Fall A.D. 55 or 56 — After hearing some good news from Titus, Paul writes 2 Corinthians (at least chaps. 1–9) with some relief, though he realizes there are still problems to be overcome. Shortly after, he journeys to Corinth, where he stays for three months, then returns to Philippi in Macedonia at Passover.

Late A.D. 56 or early 57 — Paul writes Romans from Corinth (cf. Rom. 16:1), shortly before setting out for Jerusalem for the last time (Rom. 15:25).

A.D. 57 — Paul travels by way of boat from Philippi to Troas (where the famous Eutychus incident happens, Acts 20:7-12), and then to Miletus, where he makes his famous farewell speech (Acts 20:18ff.), and finally hastens on to be in Jerusalem in time for Pentecost in May 57. Landing at Tyre, he strengthens Christians there and is warned not to go to Jerusalem, but he continues southward, stopping at Caesarea Maritima to visit with Philip the evangelist and his prophesying daughters (Acts 21:8-9). Here he encounters Agabus, who prophesies his being taken captive and handed over to the Gentiles (NOTE THAT LUKE WAS WITH PAUL ON THIS JOURNEY AND LATER CHRONICLED THESE EVENTS).

A.D. 57-59 — After an incident in the temple courts which leads to Paul's being taken into custody by a Roman tribune, Paul asks to speak to his people and recount his conversion and mission (Acts 22, in Aramaic). A near riot breaks out, and Paul is taken to the Roman ruler's Palestinian headquarters in Caesarea Maritima so that Governor Felix can deal with Paul. He is allowed to languish in some kind of prison or house arrest situation for two years until Festus becomes governor (probably in 59 or, at the latest, 60). Some scholars believe Paul wrote the Captivity Epistles (Philemon, Philippians, Colossians, and Ephesians) from Caesarea before departure for Rome by boat.

A.D. 59-60 — Seasonal data suggest the journey to Rome took place in late 59, during the risky time for sea travel, and that Paul probably arrived in Rome at least by February of 60 (cf. Acts 27–28).

A.D. 60-62 — Paul is under house arrest in Rome, during which time he is traditionally thought to have written the Captivity Epistles, with Philippians probably being the last of these (in 62, shortly before the resolution of Paul's trial).

NOTE THAT ALL DATA BEYOND THIS POINT ARE LARGELY INFERENTIAL AND CONJECTURAL SINCE ACTS ENDS WITH PAUL IN ROME, AND SINCE EVEN IF THE PASTORAL EPISTLES ARE BY PAUL, THEY DO NOT TELL US A GREAT DEAL ABOUT PAUL'S MOVEMENTS.

A.D. 62 — The conclusion of Acts shows that Luke knows that Paul was under house arrest for only two years, and it is to be pointed out that at no point in his many interviews or trials is Paul ever found guilty of any crime at the hands of the Romans (cf. especially Acts 24–26). Furthermore, if Paul's case was resolved in 62, this was before the time of the fire in Rome (July 64), which also means it was before the time Nero descended into tyranny and was looking for scapegoats, and before Christianity really had come under close imperial scrutiny. Note, too, that the Pastorals do not suggest a situation of house arrest but rather imprisonment by Roman authorities; in other words, a situation that Paul was not in during the period from 60 to 62, so far as we know. The following scenario is possible if Paul was released in 62.

A.D. 62-64 or later — Paul travels back east in response to problems. This includes a possible summer in Asia Minor (Ephesus?) and a summer and winter in Crete and Greece.

Sometime after July 64, Paul is arrested in Asia Minor and taken overland to Rome.

A.D. 64 (late) to 68 — The years of the Neronian tyranny and paranoia. If the Pastorals are by Paul, then they were likely written during this time when Paul appears to have been in Mamertine prison, or a similar facility in Rome. Under such circumstances, it is likely that Paul would have had to rely heavily on a trusted amanuensis (secretary) to write the Pastoral Epistles for him. The most likely conjecture is that Luke provided this service, which explains why these letters often reflect Lukan style, diction, and even some ideas.

A.D. 65-68. Paul is executed as a Roman citizen by beheading.

Units of Weight and Measure with approximate metric and English equivalents

Biblical Name[1]	Biblical Weight or Measure	Metric Weight or Measure	English Equivalent
WEIGHT			
Old Testament:			
gerah	—	0.57 g.	0.02 oz.
beka	10 gerahs	5.7 g.	0.2 oz.
pim	1.33 bekas	7.8 g.	0.27 oz.
shekel	2 bekas	11.4 g.	0.4 oz.
New Testament:			
mina	50 shekels	571.2 g.	1.26 lb.
talent	60 minas	34.27 kg.	75.6 lb.
pound[2]	—	340 g.	12 oz.
LINEAR			
Old Testament:			
finger	—	1.85 cm.	0.73 in.
handbreath	4 fingers	7.4 cm.	2.92 in.
span	3 handbreaths	22.2 cm.	8.75 in.
cubit	2 spans	44.5 cm.	17.5 in.
long cubit	7 handbreaths	51.9 cm.	20.4 in.
reed	6 cubits	2.7 m.	8.75 ft.
New Testament:[3]			
cubit	—	42-48 cm.	17-19 in.
fathom	4 cubits	1.8 m.	6 ft.
stadion	400 cubits	183 m.	200 yds.
mile	8 stadia	1480 m.	1618 yds.
CAPACITY (Dry and Liquid)			
Old Testament:			
kab	4 logs	1.2 l.	1.3 qt.
omer	0.1 ephah	2.2 l.	2.3 qt.
seah[4]	2 hins	7.3 l.	2 gal.
ephah	3 seahs	22 l.	5.8 gal.
lethech	5 ephahs	110 l.	29 gal.
cor/homer	10 ephahs	220 l.	6.25 U.S. bu.
New Testament:			
modios	—	7.4 l.	.5 U.S. bu.
Old Testament:			
log	—	0.3 l.	0.63 pt.[5]
hin	12 logs	3.6 l.	1 gal.
bath	3 seahs	22 l.	5.8 gal.
homer	10 baths	220 l.	58 gal.
New Testament:			
choinix	—	.95 l.	1 qt.
modios[6]	—	38-115 l.	10-30 gal.

[1] NRSV terminology except where NRSV transposes into modern units.
[2] Gk. *lítra* also represents a unit of capacity equivalent to ca. 0.5 l. (1.13 gal.).
[3] NT linear measures differ according to whether Roman, Greek, or Palestinian units are used.
[4] Also referred to as a "tenth" (i.e., of an ephah).
[5] English units of capacity are U.S. liquid units.
[6] NRSV transposes into gallons.

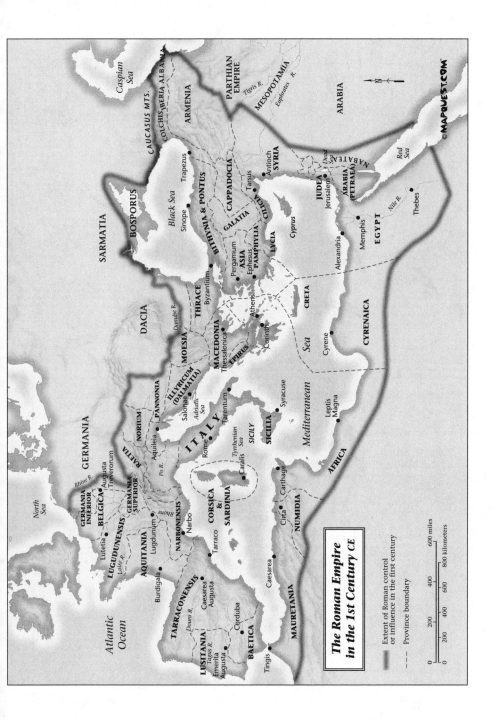

The Roman Empire
in the 1st Century CE

Extent of Roman control
or influence in the first century

– – – Province boundary

| 0 | 200 | 400 | 600 miles |
| 0 | 200 | 400 | 600 | 800 kilometers |

©MAPQUEST.COM

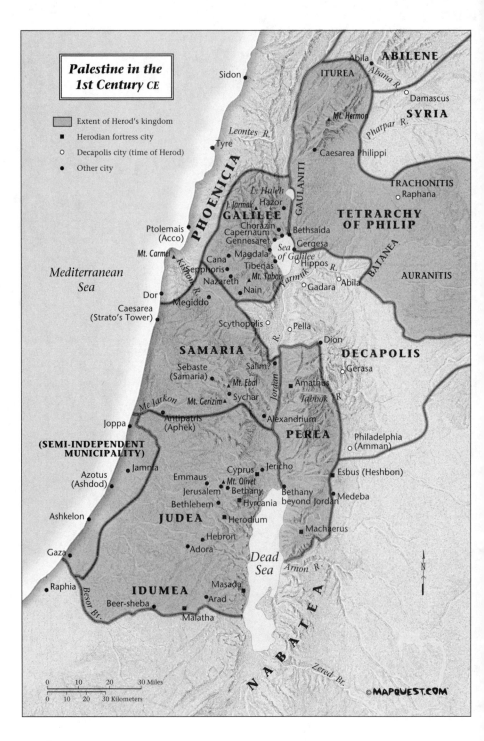

Palestine in the
1st Century CE

Extent of Herod's kingdom
Herodian fortress city
Decapolis city (time of Herod)
Other city

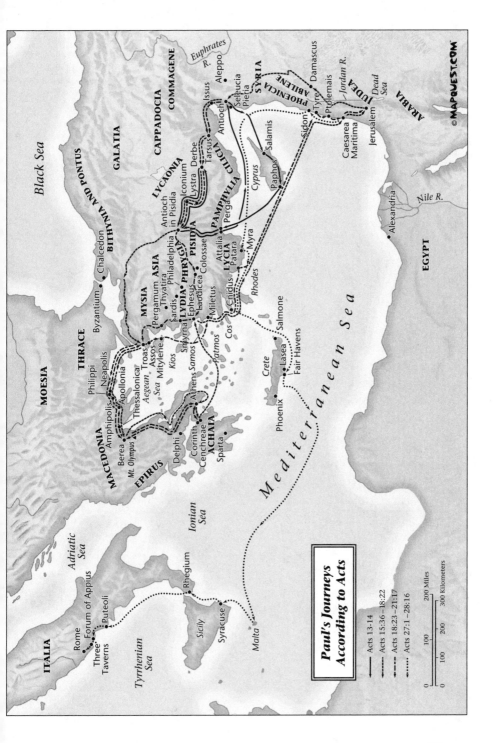

Paul's Journeys
According to Acts

Acts 13-14
Acts 15:36 – 18:22
Acts 18:23 – 21:17
Acts 27:1 – 28:16

0   100   200 Miles
0   100   200   300 Kilometers